HARM to OTHERS

The Assessment and Treatment of Dangerousness

AMERICAN COUNSELING
ASSOCIATION

5999 Stevenson Avenue | Alexandria, VA 22304 | www.counseling.org

HARM to OTHERS

The Assessment and Treatment of Dangerousness

10   9   8   7   6   5   4   3   2   1

American Counseling Association

5999 Stevenson Avenue | Alexandria, VA 22304

Associate Publisher | Carolyn C. Baker

Digital and Print Development Editor | Nancy Driver

Production Manager | Bonny E. Gaston

Copy Editor | Ida Audeh

Cover and text design by Bonny E. Gaston.

Library of Congress Cataloging-in-Publication Data

Van Brunt, Brian.
Harm to others: the assessment and treatment of dangerousness/ by Brian Van Brunt, EdD.
    pages cm
  Includes bibliographical references and index.
  ISBN 978-1-55620-342-8 (pbk. : alk. paper)
1. Violence—Evaluation. 2. Violence—Treatment. 3. Violence in the workplace. 4. Violence in the workplace—Prevention. 5. School violence. 6. School violence—Prevention. 7. Violence—Case studies. I. Title.
HM1116.V36 2015
303.6—dc23   2014016245

"**You see us as you want to see us** . . .
In the simplest terms, in the most convenient
definitions. But what we found out is that each
one of us is a brain . . . and an athlete . . . and a
basket case . . . a princess . . . and a criminal.
Does that answer your question?"

—*The Breakfast Club*

"**Passion . . . it lies in all of us.** Sleeping, waiting,
and though unwanted, unbidden, it will stir, open
its jaws, and howl. It speaks to us, guides us . . .
passion rules us all. And we obey. What other
choice do we have? Passion is the source of our
finest moments; the joy of love, the clarity of
hatred, and the ecstasy of grief. It hurts sometimes more than we can bear. If we could live
without passion, maybe we'd know some kind of
peace. But we would be hollow. Empty rooms,
shuttered and dank . . . without passion, we'd be
truly dead."

—Angelus, *Buffy the Vampire Slayer*

Dedication

To Bethany,
"There's something you'd better understand about
me 'cause it's important, and one day your life
may depend on it: I am definitely a mad man with
a box!"

—*Dr. Who*

Kat is a guppy.

—*Dad*

Table of CONTENTS

PREFACE

Over the years, I have had the opportunity to offer trainings to thousands of clinicians, administrators, and law enforcement officers interested in reducing the likelihood of violence in educational settings and in the workplace. Through the process of writing this book, I've had a chance to smooth out some of the concepts I want to share, and I've had the opportunity to receive feedback from individuals I've taught about the effectiveness of how I share the concepts. It's my hope that this book provides the very best summary of my thoughts, clinical expertise, and experience in the area of assessing and treating violent individuals. I make use of frequent case examples and try to keep my language grounded and conversational—to make this book the kind of book I like to read when it comes to learning new tasks and looking at innovative ways to work with clients. I hope the style is one that sits well with you.

The central theme of this book is this: The most effective solution to rampage violence is early, easy, and frequent access to care for potential perpetrators. This care involves (a) assessment to identify the individuals who are at risk and (b) treatment to move those individuals off the pathway to violence.

The first part of this book, which covers Chapters 1–7, is centered on the assessment of violence. Using my clinical experience and the threat assessment literature, I outline what counselors need to be aware of and vigilant for when working with threat assessments. Part II, Chapters 8–13, explores a variety of treatment options available for longer term treatment of potentially violent clients.

Counselors, psychologists, social workers, couples therapists, and pastoral counselors are likely to be familiar with the phrase "danger to self or others." There are hundreds of books, trainings, journal articles, and graduate school classes dedicated to assessing suicidality and treating clients who are at risk for killing themselves. Organizations that focus on this population include the Jed Foundation (http://www.jedfoundation.org), Suicide Prevention Resource Center (http://www.sprc.org), and American Association of Suicidality (http://www.suicidology.org/home).

Clinical staff typically are asked to assess individuals with mental health disorders who pose a potential for risk to others. Examples include the individual experiencing a manic phase in his or her bipolar disorder or a patient who has a psychotic break and begins to act the commands issued by hallucinatory voices. "Harm to others," in other words, is focused more on mental health motivating causes that drive individuals to violence. However, the problem lately has been that many of the individuals being dropped off at the counselor's office (particularly in K-12 and higher education settings) are making threats or posing a threat to others but have no indication of mental health problems. A student, upset at a friend, posts on Facebook that she is "coming over to your house with a knife to kill you." Another student threatens a college professor as a result of a poor grade on an assignment. Still another uses social media and tweets: "I'm going to bring a bomb to school tomorrow."

Although mental illness may be an important contributing factor in any of these three examples, the core of any assessment must be based on threat assessment principles, not clinical pathology. An entire community of law enforcement, human resources, and federal agencies (Naval Criminal Investigative Service, Central Intelligence Agency, Federal Bureau of Investigation, Homeland Security) is exploring the assessment of threat and dangerousness. This is the information I want to bring to the counseling community in the first half of this book. One quick summary of the approach is offered by Mohandie (2014): "Four categories of information inform threat assessment: (1) warning signs or leakage, (2) risk factors, (3) stabilizing factors, and (4) precipitating events" (p. 129).

It's my hope to reach out to counselors, psychologists, social workers, and other clinicians who are required to assess violence in schools (K-12), in higher education settings (residential and community colleges), and within the community in order to provide them with a better understanding of threat assessment principles as they apply to the assessment of dangerousness.

Chapter 1 introduces several key concepts (e.g., leakage, direct communicated threats, and the importance of attending to writing and social media) that are useful in understanding the literature and history of assessing dangerousness. Chapter 2 describes what should be included in an informed consent document, the difference between assessment and treatment, and the importance of gathering information from various sources. Concepts such as establishing rapport, building connections, and lowering client defensiveness are reviewed.

Chapter 3 introduces the two case studies, Stacie and Dustin, that are used throughout the book to illustrate key points related to assessment. The cases of Stacie and Dustin are teaching demonstrations that draw on past threat assessment cases with identifying details heavily disguised to protect anonymity. Full transcripts of each case are provided to give the reader a more in-depth view of the clinician's exploration of risk factors for future violence. Each case study ends with a hypothetical threat assessment that explains the client's risk profile and offers suggestions for follow-up and treatment.

Chapter 4 reviews six core issues related to threat assessment. Chapter 5 highlights a secondary set of core issues useful in assessing violence, such as weapon and bomb access and knowledge, attitudes toward authority, availability of support, and mental health issues. Chapter 6 reviews additional risk factors that are supported by literature and agencies that have been tasked with preventing violence, such as the U.S. Post Office and Federal Bureau of Investigation. These risk factors should be explored by clinicians during threat assessment interviews.

Chapter 7 introduces an approach to threat assessment and management, structured professional judgment, that provides the clinician with a framework to better conceptualize the motivations (disinhibitors and destabilizers) useful to develop a good formulation of risk. Concepts such as scenario planning and case management are introduced as the discussion shifts into treatment and management of risk.

The second half of the book is drawn more from my clinical experience working as a child and family therapist, college counselor, and director of two college counseling centers and focuses on treatment. My treatment suggestions in the second half of the book are drawn from my clinical insights and an eclectic mix of treatment theories drawing from such authorities as Carl Rogers's (1961, 1980) humanistic person-centered approach, Irvin Yalom's (1980) existential therapy, Michael White's narrative therapy, Albert Ellis's (2007) rational emotive behavior therapy, and Stephen Rollnick's motivational interviewing. This is not a graduate course in these therapeutic approaches but instead a seasoned clinician's insights on how each of these clinical treatment approaches has been useful to me when working with clients who presented a risk to others. Obviously, simply reading a book on a topic doesn't make anyone an expert in threat assessment any more than watching a video about car tune-ups makes a person a mechanic.

Chapter 8 introduces a case study with an individual who is angry and alone in order to illustrate the importance of developing active listening skills, forming connections to others, creating shared communication, and avoiding objectification. These are the concepts and theories central to Rogers's work and the humanistic approach to treatment.

Chapter 9 explores the concepts of narrative therapy through a case study with an individual who has been abused and broken. Concepts such as learning, externalizing, and mapping the client's story are discussed. The importance of attending to metaphors with clients and how to use metaphors in treatment are highlighted.

Chapter 10 uses a case study of a paranoid and anxious client to demonstrate the cognitive–behavioral approach to treatment with an at-risk individual. Specific techniques, such as identifying and managing triggers as well as catching irrational thoughts, are explored in this chapter; so too are plan development and managing anger.

Chapter 11 looks at an impulsive and violent client and explores the techniques of motivational interviewing and transtheoretical change theory to address the client's reluctance to change, effective methods to avoid escalation of negative emotion and build trust and understanding treatment approaches. Larger concepts of how to teach patience and redefining perceived failure are also discussed.

Chapter 12 explores the use of existential therapy with a client who is isolated and distant from others. Concepts such as wrestling with freedom, death, isolation, and meaningless can be used to empower the client and encourage further exploration of the factors that may be contributing to a violent outlook.

Chapter 13 examines treatment that might be useful for Stacie and Dustin, the cases introduced in Chapter 3. Although these case histories were primarily offered to illustrate assessment techniques, it is useful to explore the treatments that might be beneficial following the initial assessment.

Clinical staff across the country are increasingly being asked to participate in threat assessment teams and behavioral intervention teams and conduct these kinds of assessments. I hope that sharing what I have learned over the years helps clinical staff conduct substantive assessment.

About the
AUTHOR

Brian Van Brunt, EdD, LPC, joined The National Center for Higher Education Risk Management (NCHERM) Group as Senior Vice President for Professional Program Development in January 2013. He is past-president of the American College Counseling Association, president of the National Behavioral Intervention Team Association, and managing editor for *Student Affairs eNews* and the *Journal of Campus Behavioral Intervention* (J-BIT). He has a doctoral degree in counseling supervision and education from the University of Sarasota/Argosy and a master's degree in counseling and psychological services from Salem State University.

Brian is a regular speaker at academic conferences around the world. He has presented dozens of workshops with the American College Counseling Association, Association of Student Conduct Administrators, National Association of Forensic Counselors, American College Personnel Association, Association of University College Counseling Center Directors, Student Affairs Administrators in Higher Education, Association of Threat Assessment Professionals, and European Congress on Violence in Clinical Psychiatry.

Brian has presented hundreds of online training seminars and classes. These trainings have reached well over 150,000 individual staff and faculty at colleges and universities across the country. He has developed remote, asynchronous training modules on violence, mental health, and suicide prevention for resident advisors through Magna Publications and created a behind-closed-doors-style card game for resident advisors called RACE! He developed a mental health crisis guide for study abroad advisors for the American Councils and has written textbook test banks and instructor guides for Pearson Education.

Early in his career, Brian provided case management services through the Massachusetts Department of Mental Health, coordinated involuntary psychiatric commitments for law enforcement and hospital emergency departments, offered medical care as an Emergency Medical Technician and Ski Patrol member, and was a registered white water rafting guide in the state of Maine. Brian is certified in Brief Alcohol Screening and Intervention of College Students (BASICS) and the Question/Persuade/Refer (QRP) suicide prevention gatekeeper trainer programs.

Brian has taught at a number of universities and colleges. He has offered classes in counseling theory, ethics, program evaluation, statistics, and sociology for both graduate and undergraduate students. Brian has served as the director of counseling at New England College and Western Kentucky University. He is the author and coauthor of several books, including *Ending Campus Violence: New Approaches in Prevention* (2012), *A Faculty Guide to Addressing Disruptive and Dangerous Behavior* (with W. Scott Lewis, 2013) and *The Prevention and Management of Mental Health Emergencies* (with David Denino, Mary-Jeanne Raleigh, and Michelle Issadore, 2015). Brian is an expert on campus violence and has been interviewed by the *New York Times*, National Public Radio, *Los Angeles Times*, and *USA Today* and has appeared on *Headline News* and *Anderson Cooper 360*. He frequently is an invited keynote speaker and has offered training to law enforcement, homeland security, the Federal Bureau of Investigation, college faculty, and staff.

PART 1
Assessment
of Violence

Introduction

The first half of this book focuses on assessing violence. Meloy described assessment this way: "Assessment is, most generally, the process of gathering information for the use in making decisions" (Meloy, Hart, & Hoffmann, 2014, p. 4). Information is gathered from the individual and understood in the context of analytical process (such as structured professional judgment, highlighted in Chapter 7), and the clinician assesses the information and writes an opinion for the referral source.

Threat or violence risk assessment techniques are used to determine individuals' risk to the greater community through asking contextual questions about the nature of the threat and risk and assessing risk factors that can help determine potential dangerousness (Meloy & Hoffmann, 2014). Threat assessments generally take place after a communicated threat has been made. There may or may not be a history of violence. Threat assessments become forensic in nature when they are in response to legal issues (such as competency to stand trial), criminality (breaking laws such as terroristic threatening), or mental health commitment.

Violence risk assessments, on the other hand, typically focus more on past behavior and a more subjective concern expressed by the referral source. They often occur with individuals who are in a secure location, such as an inpatient unit, prison, or hospital, and there has been a past history of violence.

Meloy, Hoffmann, Guldimann, and James (2011) described the difference between threat and violence risk assessment in this way:

> Threat assessment and risk assessment have developed as somewhat overlapping fields. Violence risk assessment has an older provenance, and is a method by which the probability of generally violent behavior is estimated for an individual based upon his membership in a particular at-risk group. Threat assessment is concerned almost wholly with the risk of targeted violence by a subject of concern, and has a behavioral and observational policing focus. Risk assessment may address different domains of risk than threat assessment, and typically relies on more historical and dispositional (status) variables. (p. 257)

The American Society of Mechanical Engineers Innovative Technologies Institute (2010) recommends the following statement in terms of resolving risk:

> Evaluating options for reducing risk (usually by considering benefit/cost) and selecting, implementing and managing those that are selected. Risk resolution also includes systematic implementation of the selected options, monitoring and evaluating the options for effectiveness, carrying out corrective actions when needed, and repeating this cycle. Risk resolution in institutes of higher education generally considers a more comprehensive set of variables including business continuity, academic continuity, and maintaining the core missions of the institute. (p. 16)

Threat and violence risk assessments have the added focus on answering the central question of "Does this individual pose a risk of violence to the community?" The recent American Society of Mechanical Engineers Innovative Technologies Institute (2010) American National Standard Institute defines *risk analysis* as follows:

> The process of estimating the components of risk and combining them into the estimate of risk. Risk analysis provides the processes for identifying threats, hazards or hazard scenarios, event-probability estimation, vulnerability assessment and consequence estimation. The risk analysis process answers four basic questions: (1) What can go wrong?; (2) How can it happen?; (3) What is the probability that it will go wrong? and (4) What are the consequences if it does go wrong? (p. 14)

The evaluator brings skills and training to bear on the what, when, how, why, and where of potential dangerousness. Reports and recommendations typically focus on mitigating risk factors to thwart an attack.

It is generally agreed that violence is either affective or predatory.

> Affective violence, sometimes referred to as reactive, impulsive, or emotional violence, is preceded by autonomic arousal, caused by a reaction to a perceived threat, and accompanied by intense feelings of anger and/or fear. It is a defensive violence, and its evolutionary basis is self-protection to live another day. . . . Predatory violence, sometimes referred to as instrumental or premeditated violence, is characterized by the absence of autonomic arousal and emotion, the absence of an imminent threat, and planning and preparation beforehand. It is offensive violence, and its evolutionary basis is hunting for food to live another day. (Meloy, Hart, et al., 2014, p. 5; see also Meloy, 1997, 1998, 2006, 2012)

The tendency toward violence is a genetically predisposed quality that has been useful for the survival of our species.

> None of us would be here if our ancestors had not excelled at both affective and predatory violence; hence the theory that we have the biological capacity for both modes of violence and the accumulating empirical evidence that this is correct. (Meloy, Hart, et al., 2014, p. 5; see also Gregg & Siegal, 2001; McEllistrem, 2004; Raine et al., 1998; Viding & Firth, 2006)

Yet the innate capacity for violence must be tempered with a judicious process of control in our modern society. Irrespective of the type of violence and whether it is influenced by hard-wired biology or environmental factors, it presents an assessment and management challenge.

As we begin to look more closely at the concept of threat assessment, it is important to ensure that the clinician performing the evaluation has the education and experience and information necessary to develop an accurate picture of the potential threat. Van der Meer and Diekhuis (2014) described it this way:

> Four elements can be identified as important to guarantee a good-quality threat assessment: (1) education, experience and subject matter expertise; (2) access to sufficient information to perform the assessment; (3) a level of certainty that the received information is indeed reliable; and (4) a professional objective assessment of the available material. (p. 54)

When a threat assessment goes poorly, it is often because of one of these four factors identified in the preceding extract. A clinician is put in the position of assessing the threat without sufficient training or expertise. There is not enough information available to make an accurate review of the potential for violence. The information is reliable, but the accuracy of the information is called into question because of bias or contamination. The objectivity of the professional conducting the assessment is called into question. All present a challenge for those looking to conduct forensic threat or violence risk assessments.

It is my hope that this book helps reduce the risk of these factors interfering with the process and that the clinician conducting the assessment may be better prepared to accomplish the task. S. White (2014) starts our journey together with these words of wisdom:

> The central task of a workplace threat assessment protocol is to (1) sort out the large majority of cases that present a very low level of concern for violence and do not need intensive case management; (2) identify the few cases that credibly suggest a high or imminent level of concern about serious violence and therefore justify the necessary, costly, and potentially disruptive measures to protect safety; (3) for the midlevel cases, find appropriate and reasonable strategies for ongoing assessment and monitoring until the pathway toward or away from violence is clear. (p. 91)

Chapter 1

Understanding
VIOLENCE

Chapter Highlights

1. This chapter explores the concepts of violence and harm to others, forensic threat assessment, and violence risk assessment.
2. *Leakage* is communication by an individual planning the attack to a third party. This chapter explores various forms of leakage (e.g., writing, social media posts) and how they should factor into the threat assessment.
3. *Directly communicated threats* are threats that are made to the target. These threats can be direct, veiled, or contingent on future action. Disruptive behavior as a potential nonverbal threat is also described. Warren, Mullen, and McEwan's (2014) typology of *screamers, shockers, shielders, schemers,* and *signalers* is discussed.
4. G. Deisinger, Randazzo, O'Neill, and Savage's (2008) *pathway to violence* is described as a four-step model involving ideation, planning, acquisition, and implementation.
5. O'Toole and Bowman's (2011) book *Dangerous Instincts* provides insight into potential blind spots for clinicians, such as *normalizing, rationalizing, explaining it away, ignoring,* and *icon intimidation.*

My research methods professor in graduate school emphasized the importance of operationalizing definitions. She gave the example of a student in fourth grade being observed for an individualized education plan assessment. The student in question had attention-deficit/hyperactivity disorder and struggled with focus in the classroom. The example of a bad assessment measure was the frequency of student disruption in the classroom. A better assessment goal was the frequency of the student's out-of-seat behavior. When trying to wrestle with assessing something or measuring behavior, it is good practice to have a clear understanding, or definition, of the concept that is being assessed.

This brings us to *danger to others*. Defining this term is no easy task because the concept of violence means different things to different people. Are we assessing in a formal, structured capacity a student like Adam Lanza (Sandoval & Siemaszko, 2013), who shot 20 children and six adults at Sandy Hook Elementary School in December 2012, to determine whether he posed a risk of rampage shooting violence? Are we evaluating the 11-year-old fifth grader Brandon Rogers, who brought a knife to school because he was teased by bullies (Li, 2012)? Are we assessing the University of Central Arkansas student Ching-Han Hu, who posted on Facebook: "My current wish is to take gun and shoot all my classmates, enjoying their blood and scary" (Ford, 2011, p. 1)? Are we assessing a student like George Huguely, who had an angry and violent obsession with his ex-girlfriend, Yeardley Love, the University of Virginia senior he killed (Smolowe, 2010)?

The answer is: Yes. I'm using *violence* in a broad sense. Meloy, Hart, et al. (2014) defined it this way:

> By violence we mean any actual, attempted, or planned injury of other people, as well as any communication or behavior that causes other people to reasonably fear for their health or safety; it is intentional, non-consenting, and without lawful authority. (p. 3)

For the purposes of this book, the violence being planned could target one person or a movie theatre full of people, as with the James Holmes case in Aurora, Colorado (Elliot, 2013). In each instance, I believe there are core concepts in threat assessment that can help the clinician assess the risk of violence. Table 1.1 explains some of the similarities and differences among psychological, threat, and risk assessments as referenced in Meloy, Hart, & Hoffman (2014).

In Chapter 7, I discuss in more detail the process of structured professional judgment and the groundbreaking work of Stephen Hart in this area (Hart & Logan, 2011; Hart, Sturmey, Logan, & McMuran, 2011). This process is the foundation for every threat assessment I conduct. The process focuses on the potential scenarios for violence and ways to reduce the risk of violence. Similarly, it explores the positive scaffolding that could be put in place to help move the individual further from the "path toward violence" (O'Toole, 2000, p. 7) and more toward social integration with the larger community. (This movement is a focus of the second half of this book.)

I've introduced a few examples of violence; now I highlight some ways that violence is foreshadowed in order to illustrate the variety of concerns that clinicians face: leakage, direct threat, disruptive be-

Table 1.1 | **Comparison Among Psychological, Threat, and Violence Risk Assessments**

Variable	Psychological Assessment	Threat Assessment	Violence Risk Assessment
Evaluator	Licensed mental health counselor, psychologist, social worker	Law enforcement, student conduct officers, security professionals, clinical counselors, psychologists, social workers	Medical or mental health clinical staff, human resources, social service professionals
Objective	May be broadly defined around psychological disruption and odd behavior, determining suicide risk or harm to others	Evaluates the risk from an identified threat to the community; provides decision makers with an estimation of dangerousness and potential lethality	Assists with decision making regarding future violence risk with a focus on both reducing negative thoughts/behaviors and increasing positive thoughts/behaviors
Techniques	Personality tests (PAI/MMPI-2), objective symptoms-based assessments (BDI/BHS/BSS), structured clinical interview, review of past records and information gathering from incident reports	Structured interviews, information gathering from multiple sources (work, family, peers, criminal history); use of measures such as HCR-20, WAVR-21, SIVRA-35, MOSAIC, RAGE-V, FactorOne, FAVT	Structured Professional Judgment (SPJ) models, interviews, chart and case review. Use of measures such as the HCR-20
Outcome	Formalized report, testing summary letter; goal to improve decision making and developing treatment goals	Summary of violence of violence risk factors; suggestions for mitigation steps to address violence	Summary of dangerousness with a discussion of risk factors and supportive factors; focus toward ongoing case management and adjusting the plan to mitigate risk over time

Note. PAI = Personality Assessment Inventory; MMPI-2 = Minnesota Multiphasic Personality Inventory–2; BDI = Beck Depression Inventory; BHS = Beck Hopelessness Scale; BSS = Beck Suicide Scale; HCR-20 = Historical Clinical Risk-20; WAVR-21 = Workplace Assessment of Violence Risk; SIVRA-35 = Structured Interview for Violence Risk Assessment; MOSAIC = computer assisted comprehensive assessment; RAGE-V = Risk Assessment Guideline Elements for Violence; Factor One = Factor One Cawood Risk Rubric; FAVT = Firestone Assessment of Violent Thoughts.

haviors and indirect threat, and social media. Assessing the pathway to violence and identifying potential blind spots by the clinician are two additional areas that are covered in this chapter. By understanding the progression from ideation, planning, acquisition, and implementation, the clinician is in a more advantageous position to identify potential warning behaviors (Meloy et al., 2011) and leakage that occur prior to an attack.

Additionally, by understanding some common blind spots, such as normalization, rationalization, and icon intimidation, the clinician increases his or her chances of more accurately assessing the violent individual. Following this section, I share some insights from the O'Toole and Bowman book *Dangerous Instincts* (2011), which addresses potential blind spots that clinicians might encounter.

The chapter ends with a discussion of the importance of attending to writing and social media posts. Several cases are reviewed to demonstrate the potential leakage that can occur from the potentially violent individual in this format.

Leakage

Leakage is the communication to a third party of intent to do harm (Meloy & O'Toole, 2011). Therapists have opportunities to detect a potential attack during a structured assessment and during ongoing treatment (less structured). An example of leakage occurred in January 2011 at California State Northridge when David Everson told a therapist in the counseling center his thoughts about killing others (Dobuzinskis, 2011). The counselor shared this information with police, who found bomb-making materials and a shotgun in the student's dorm room. In this book, I reference dozens of examples where leakage preceded an attack (Van Brunt, 2012).

For clinical staff, the challenge with leakage is understanding when and how to share the information with others in order to reduce the risk of violence. During a structured, formal threat assessment, clinicians have a wide range of permission to share their concerns with the referral source. Clinicians offering ongoing treatment to clients have permission, and in some cases a duty, to share clients' risk to harm themselves or others. These permissions and responsibilities are defined by counselor and psychologist state licensure regulations and by the ethical guidelines outlined by the American Counseling Association (2014) and the American Psychological Association (2010).

In the context of violence risk assessments, the person conducting the assessment should always remember that violence is rarely spontaneous. Those who act violently take time to rehearse and fantasize about violent acts. This presents an opportunity for others to overhear or observe potential leakage that could then be used to prevent an attack. For example, Jared Cano planned an attack that was stopped after an anonymous tipster notified the police in August 2011 that Cano shared he planned to plant pipe bombs in the school the following week (Teicher-Khadaroo, 2011). Police found quantities of fuel, shrapnel, plastic tubing, timing and fusing devices for making pipe bombs, along with marijuana and marijuana cultivation equipment. Cano had been expelled from Freedom High School in North Tampa in 2009; in planning his attack, he recorded a 60-second video on his cell phone in which he described his plans:

> For those of you retards who don't know who I am, I'm the Freedom High School shooter in Tampa, Florida. Well, I will be in a couple months. I thought I would run over my game plan with ya'll. The cafeteria at Freedom. My plan is to set a bomb here at point A, here at point B,

point C and point D. Then I got to get to the side entrance of the school by 7:24. The bombs blow at 7:26. I'm going to come in and advance on the courtyard where there'll probably be at least sixty people. (I'll) come through the door then shoot everybody at the front desk. Mr. Costanzo's office is right here, I've got to kill him. Mrs. Carmody is here I've got to kill her. Mr. Pears is here, I've got to make sure he doesn't die, because I like him. There's nothing I can do about it, there's nothing anybody can do about it other than wait for it to unleash. If you don't like it just find a way to find people like me and just line us up and shoot us. (Pow, 2012)

The presence of this kind of leakage prior to an attack gives evidence to support the idea that those who plan this kind of mass casualty violence often plan, fantasize, and talk about the event prior to an attack. This offers an opportunity to discover this leakage and thwart the potential assault. Campus behavioral intervention teams are set up on this principle of detecting potential leakage that may occur in the community. These teams encourage training of community members to attend to this potential leakage and report concerns to the teams (Sokolow et al., 2011).

Directly Communicated Threats

Directly communicated threats are threats that are expressed verbally or in a written format to the target person. For third parties, the challenge with directly communicated threats is determining whether they represent potential leakage (behaviors or actions that are communicated prior to an attack that are made to a third party) or simply an impulsive expression of frustration. Meloy (2001) wrote: ". . . for directly communicated threats and subsequent violence: most individuals who directly communicate a threat are not subsequently violent and most individuals who do not directly communicate a threat are not subsequently violent" (p. 1213). Direct threats identifying the target of violence rarely result in an attack (Scalora, Simons, & Vansly, 2010; Turner & Gelles, 2003) and Fein, Vossekuil, and Holden (1995) made the clear distinction between posing a threat and making a threat.

Calhoun and Weston (2009) wrote a seminal book on threat assessment called *Threat Assessment and Management Strategies: Identifying the Howlers and Hunters*. Their central premise is that those who plan to attack rarely communicate this in advance.

Threat management involves managing two very different types of individuals. One group consists of hunters. They truly intend to use lethal violence to aggrieve some perceived injustice. Hunters develop a reason for committing violence, come up with the idea to do so, research and plan their attack, prepare for it, then breach their target's security and actually attack. Whatever their reason, those who intend to act violently go through the process of intended violence. (p. 7)

Threats take on various qualities and definitions in the threat assessment literature. Direct threats are expressed in nonconditional language and leave very little to the imagination. An example might be, "I am going to come back to work and shoot my supervisor in the head." Indirect and veiled threats often contain if/then language and options, such as, "If things don't change around here, I'm going to take matters into my own hands and change them for you."

Warren et al. (2014) identified five types of threateners:

Screamers, whose threats are responses to provocations in the form of expressions of emotion that are cathartic. The threats take the form of an expletive, usually in response to an exciting situation. These are the commonest type of threat uttered in the community. Members of this group rarely find themselves in court or in a consulting room on account of their threats. Screamers usually make threats in a context and a manner where their target(s) understand that no harm is intended or contemplated. The context and nature of the threats usually make clear that they are expressions of emotion rather than commitments to act. . . . Those rare instances where there may be some commitment involve angry and resentful individuals who typically threaten repeatedly in response to a wide range of provocations and direct their threats to more than one victim.

Shockers, whose threats are calculated to induce fear and produce an immediate impact in terms of increased anxiety in the target. Typically this is primarily a way of striking out and harming the targets or of establishing dominance over them. Occasionally such threats are intended to bring attention to the threatener. They take the form of stating an intention to engage in behavior that will have terrible consequences. The commitment is to produce an immediate reaction in the target rather than to any subsequent action. Only if pushed to prove it are they likely to progress to enactment.

Shielders, whose threats are self-protective in that they are intended to ward off potential aggression or incursions by others. Threats from shielders take the form "I am more dangerous than you think, do not interfere with me." The commitment is to self-protection.

Schemers, whose threats are instrumental and motivated by the desire to influence or coerce others into complying with their wishes. These threats are usually premeditated and take the form of promising to engage in behavior harmful to the person or persons targeted unless they comply with the threatener's demands. The commitment is to further the shielder's interests, which, when the threat is insufficient and commitment sufficiently strong, may be followed by enactment.

Signalers, whose threats are warnings that promise future harm to the target. Such threats take the form of stating an intention to engage in retaliation against the target for actual or perceived harm caused to the threatener. There is a commitment to enactment inherent in such threats.

Whether the commitment will lead to action depends on both the target's responses and the threatener's personality, defined by such variables as prudence, social conformity, and impulsivity. (pp. 20–21)

Although there is evidence that most direct communicated threats do not lead to violence, it is important to explore the contextual risk factors related to the specific case at hand (see also Chapter 3). Calhoun and Weston (2009) summed it up: "Writing letters is easy; shooting someone or setting him on fire presents a considerably more difficult challenge" (p. 29). It is challenging to determine whether a violent or threatening behavior (arguably, even "developmentally" appropriate in some instances) is simply a bad decision on the part of the individual, or if the threat or violence is the proverbial "tip of the iceberg" exposing deeper trauma, psychosis, or psychopathic tendencies that portends a more dangerous event to occur in the future. In most extreme events of campus violence, it is the behavior of the student, and not a directly communicated threat of violence, that provides a clue. Scalora et al. (2010) wrote:

Unlike disruptive and other forms of aggressive behavior, violent or directly communicated threat always requires immediate investigation and evaluation . . . While most communicated direct threats do not end in violence, this can only be determined after directly questioning and assessing the student in question. (p. 5)

Take the University of Central Arkansas (UCA) student Ching-Han Hu, who posted on Facebook: "My current wish is to take gun and shoot all my classmates, enjoying their blood and scary" (Ford, 2011, p. 1). This is an example of a direct communicated threat. The details of this case involve her getting into an argument with a fellow student in an orchestra class and then returning to her room to make this post in her native language (Chinese):

Hu's Facebook post, written in Chinese, was discovered by Walla who, along with other UCA students, contacted police. Police asked Walla to show them Hu's post. The police got a translator to interpret Hu's Mandarin and then pulled Hu from class for an interview. In the interview, police said that Hu giggled when asked about her Facebook post. Hu, with help of an interpreter, said that it is "very difficult to get a gun in China and it would be impossible for this to happen." Hu said that in China "you can say these things people know that she would never follow through with the comment." She also said that she was "just mad but does not want to kill anyone." (p. 1)

The University suspended Ching-Han Hu, and she was sent back to Taiwan. The details of this case are not available for review, but it is an important example of assessing violence and dangerousness beyond the simple directly communicated threat. A clear directly communicated threat should be seen as a starting place for further assessment, not as the culmination of the process.

For the clinician conducting a threat assessment, it is essential to avoid making assumptions. The threat itself should be explored for its validity, lethality, and likelihood of the attack taking place. Directly communicated threats should never be assumed to be of no real concern because the student was joking or had made similar threats that had not preceded a violent act. Each communicated threat should be explored with attention to the principles explored in Chapter 4.

An example of a direct threat occurred at a previous institution where I worked. A student who had Asperger's syndrome stood up in a history class and told the professor, "I'm going to cut off your head with a guillotine." During the threat assessment, I determined that understanding Asperger's syndrome (now part of autism spectrum disorder; American Psychiatric Association, 2013) was important to assessing the significance of the threat. The threat was an impulsive action by the student, and the likelihood of him assembling a guillotine on campus and enticing the professor to lay his head in the slot for decapitation was pretty low. However, the impulsive statement caused a significant disruption in the classroom and raised the question about what the student might be capable of in light of his poor insight and judgment. The student's impulsivity and frustration became important indicators of the need for further exploration and potential observation.

Calhoun and Weston (2009) offered some advice to help understand those who issue direct threats (howlers) and those who carry out the violence (hunters):

> The key to understanding hunters versus howlers lies in the difference between acting and talking. Threatening someone is a behavior, but alone is not a behavior that lends itself to carrying out the threat. Threats are actually promises of some future action. Many are conditioned on the target's doing or not doing something, others are deferred in time, some are veiled (sometimes to the point of obtuseness) . . . Other threats warn of terrible threats perpetrated by someone else, sometimes a vague deity, superior being or alien. Despite their variety, threats are only one form of behavior. Carrying them out requires a whole different set of actions. (p. 29)

Disruptive Behaviors and Indirect Threat

An individual's threatening behaviors might not be communicated through a direct threat yet remain cause for concern. Third parties such as teachers, professors, administrators, and front office staff often come across concerning behaviors or language from individuals that are not a directly communicated threat. Many highly publicized shooters, such as Seung-Hui Cho at Virginia Tech, Jared Lee Loughner from Pima College, Major Nidal Malik Hasan at Fort Hood, and

Pekka-Eric Auvinen in Jokela, Finland, had worried peers, faculty, and staff prior to their shooting events (Van Brunt, 2012).

At what point does a person's threatening, odd, or violent behavior indicate the potential for actual violence? The only way we can understand and assess the potential threat is to understand the context of the behavior. This happens through talking with the potentially violent individual to further assess the context, motivators, disinhibitors, and destabilizers that influence the likelihood of violence. (These concepts are covered in more detail in Chapter 5.)

Indirect, passive, or conditional threats can be verbal or behavioral in nature. A student may be frustrated with an instructor and harbor a desire to harm that person at a future date. The only clue we might have is the student's muttering or glaring at a staff member at the school. Loughner's verbal and behavioral outbursts at Pima College were well documented the fall prior to the shooting (Van Brunt, 2012). Loughner frequently got into arguments with his professors around his perceived right to be able to say whatever he wanted to in class. When given a B in his Pilates class, he became so tense that his professor feared for her safety. He would often rant about his rights and "freedom of thought" and was unwilling to see that others might have different perspectives on his behavior (Johnson, Kovaleski, Frosch, & Lipton, 2011). In June 2011, he had disrupted a math class, arguing that the number 6 was really the number 18, and went on to talk about being persecuted and scammed by the school. No direct threat was made, but, in retrospect, these incidents offer some insight into Loughner's decompensating thinking. Reviewing his disruptive behavior provides an opportunity for further exploration and potential observation for additional leakage or thoughts around future violence.

Assessing the Pathway to Violence

G. Deisinger et al. (2008) described a four-step pathway to violence: ideation, planning, acquisition, and implementation. Individuals on a pathway to violence provide clues in their escalation.

Imagine a student who becomes obsessed with another classmate in high school and begins to see a relationship with her as the ultimate experience of his entire life. He spends his days fantasizing about a relationship, placing her on a pedestal, and objectifying her as a manifestation of a perfect woman. He finally works up the nerve to talk to her and it does not go well. He stutters, his advances confuse her, and she laughs, thinking it is some kind of joke. Others watch the failed attempt at flirtation and begin to tease him. The student becomes more disillusioned by his failure and draws his attention to those who tease him and the girl who rejected him. He might make a direct threat (e.g., "If you keep teasing me, I'm going to make you pay!"), or he might become more withdrawn, socially isolated, depressed, tearful, and hopeless about his chances at finding love. If he were to plan to harm those around him, it might be that he begins by thinking (ideating) and fantasizing about hurting those who teased him or the girl who spurned his advances. He may then escalate this by planning what he would do to seek his revenge. He could draw his plans out in a notebook or as a thinly veiled revenge story in his English class. These plans might become real if he started to acquire the weapons, schematics, explosives, or other elements needed to carry out the attack. The moment of implementation comes when he acts on his plan.

Calhoun and Weston (2009) offered some additional insight into how an attacker might move toward violence:

> Attack-related behaviors are best conceptualized as steps hunters must take to carry out acts of premeditated violence. We call this concept the path to intended violence. Essentially, the stepping-stones consist of:
>
> - Grievance, which is the motive or reason compelling the hunter to act.
> - Ideation, which requires actually settling upon the idea that violence is justified and necessary.
> - Research and planning, which means going beyond the idea to actually figuring out how to consummate the violence.
> - Preparation, which involves obtaining the necessary equipment, such as weapon of choice, and taking other actions required to initiate the plan.
> - Breach, which entails initiating the plan by circumventing the target's security (however primitive or sophisticated that may be) to launch the attack.
> - Attack, which is the actual physical assault. (p. 43)

This consistent, hierarchical progression suggested by Deisinger, Calhoun, and Weston provide a conceptual basis for clinical staff to better understand how those planning an attack approach their planning.

Dangerous Instincts

O'Toole (2000) observed:

> In general, people do not switch instantly from nonviolence to violence. Nonviolent people do not "snap" or decide on the spur of the moment to meet a problem by using violence. Instead, the path toward violence is an evolutionary one, with signposts along the way. (p. 7)

These signposts prior to the implementation of a plan often consist of behavioral and emotional escalations that are available for exploration by a threat assessor who is willing to attend to the more subtle passive indicators of violence.

One popular approach to threat assessment is found in "looking for the silence" or the times when a previously concerning student has "dropped off the radar." Although the optimistic might conclude that the student spontaneously got better and improved, a more realistic assessment is that the student has fallen further away from those relationships that may have been stabilizing factors and is now without much support.

Quiet periods for the predatory aggressor (Meloy, 2000, 2006) might be the time when he is developing a plan of attack, acquiring weapons, learning the schedule and habits of his target, and moving closer and closer to implementation. Jared Loughner was quiet for close to 4 months between his October 4 voluntary withdrawal from Pima College and his January 8 attack. Seung-Hui Cho had no reports of any concerning behaviors in the spring of 2007 prior to his April 16 assault. He calmly and methodically obtained weapons, rented a van, recorded a manifesto, practiced his shooting, locked the doors with chains, and planned the other details of his deadly assault. All of these behaviors provided potential clues and information useful to thwarting the attack, yet very few of Cho's behaviors prior to the attack could be described as directly communicated threats.

With the more extreme predatory, aggressive individuals, the best hope of thwarting their plan requires an attention to patterns and behaviors that, when viewed together as part of a larger picture, may help illuminate the individual's path to violence. A clinician performing the assessment is in an ideal position to build trust and rapport while looking carefully for signs of escalating violence.

Mary Ellen O'Toole, a former Federal Bureau of Investigation profiler, stressed the importance of developing awareness for blind spots and the dangers of misinterpreting details. When assessing dangerous behaviors, it is necessary to avoid the common problems of "normalizing, rationalizing, explaining it away, ignoring and icon intimidation" (O'Toole & Bowman, 2011, p. 95).

- *Normalizing.* Here the clinician may become lost by accepting an average explanation for a piece of data that might otherwise be cause for concern. An elementary student's social isolation and idiosyncratic behaviors are explained by autism spectrum disorder and dismissed as potential for risk or violence. Two students often are engaged in heated arguments over their relationship. Because this has been going on for some time, the guidance counselors and school administrations dismiss the behavior as "normal teenage dating hysteria." One of the greatest challenges for clinicians engaged in threat assessment is always keeping an awareness of a potentially plausible rival hypothesis. We must stay diligent and always ask ourselves, "What else might be going on here?"

- *Rationalizing.* The clinician accepts another explanation for the student's behavior because he or she lacks confidence in further exploring the context of the issue at hand. A student may be distracted and impulsive in class, failing to follow instructions and getting into frequent arguments with the professor and with group members on team projects. The clinician may see this as related to focus and attention problems well documented in the student's chart as attention-deficit/hyperactivity disorder. The clinician refers the student to his or her psychiatrist for a medication adjustment and assumes the behavior will stop. The clinician assumes that the child's behavior is the product of too much TV and too much stimulation, effectively closing off other ways of seeing and responding to this behavior.

- *Explaining it away.* This is the process of finding some other explanation for the concerning detail. Perhaps the individual is guarded, provides short answers, and comes across as unwilling to share very much with the counselor during the interview. The counselor may dismiss his or her concerns, explaining them away with "the student is probably just nervous. That's a very common reaction to this kind of situation." If a student is threatening, is pushy, has a past history of alcohol and drug use on campus, but continues to do well academically and has several "advocates" around campus, future behavior may be ignored. If the student is close to graduating, the clinician might decide to just wait it out.

- *Ignoring.* Clinicians may be tempted to just ignore behavior or issues that they don't have time or a desire to address. A well-meaning clinician may ignore problem behavior if the student is doing well academically and is close to graduation, hoping that by waiting it out, the student will no longer be the institution's problem.

- *Icon intimidation.* An individual's status, fame, or power may influence how his or her actions are seen. The person being evaluated may have some kind of standing in the community as an athlete or scholar or may hold a place of prominence in the community because of family connections. The threat assessment process can also be derailed if the individual being evaluated is so threatening or charismatic during the interview that these qualities influence the clinician's judgment and begin to unfairly weight observations and conclusions about risk.

The behaviors from which these concepts are derived alert clinicians to the potential minefield of missteps and blind spots they must attend to during the threat assessment process.

Writing and Social Media

Social media posts and disturbing writing are areas that require attention in the threat assessment process. In numerous cases, individuals who planned mass casualty violence provided written clues about their intentions.

Seung-Hui Cho, who killed 32 and wounded 17 during the April 16, 2007, Virginia Polytechnic Institute shootings, wrote several violent plays that caused his English teacher concern (Virginia Tech Review Panel, 2007). "Richard McBeef" describes violent arguments between a boy and his stepfather that involve accusations of rape and a mother wielding a chainsaw; the stepfather finally kills the 13-year-old protagonist. "Mr. Brownstone," another play by Cho, explored three teenagers' hatred for their math teacher. They describe him as an "ass-raper" and talk about wanting to "watch him bleed like the way he made us kids bleed" (Van Brunt, 2012, p. 42). While gambling at a casino illegally, the teens run into Mr. Brownstone, who proceeds to report them to security and steals their jackpot on the slot machine.

Amy Bishop, the professor who shot six and killed three during her 2010 attack at Huntsville, Alabama (T. Smith, 2010), wrote a novel called *Amazon Fever*, whose protagonist, Olivia, is a professor worried about being denied tenure while fighting against a worldwide pandemic. The plot parallels Bishop's life as she writes about Olivia's depression and her fear of losing a faculty position at a university. Another of Bishop's unpublished books, *Easter in Boston*, described a protagonist (Beth):

> The empty clip slid into the 9 mm easily. Beth sat on her bed, the gun and its paraphernalia, strewn about, while she worked on it . . . [She] sat back down with the dictionary. She mulled over words like love, loneliness, hopelessness, despair. She looked at words like suicide and murder. (Van Brunt, 2012, p. 42)

Kimveer Singh Gill, the shooter at Dawson College who killed one and injured 19 others on September 13, 2006, writes extensively online on www.vampirefreaks.com about his avatar killing others:

> The disgusting human creatures scream in panic and run in all directions, taking with them the lies and deceptions. The Death Knight gazes at the humans with an empty stare, as they knock each other down in a mad dash to safety. He wishes to slaughter them as they flee. (Van Brunt, 2012, p. 253)

Does Cho's fiction foreshadow a desire to kill, or is he simply the next Quentin Tarantino or Stephen King? Is Bishop's fiction a magnifying glass into her dark desires? Should Gill's writing have triggered some kind of further evaluation of his potential threat and mental state? The answer across the board is "maybe." Violent writings, particularly those involving a direct threat, should be explored and assessed for their level of potential violence.

Threat Triage, a text analysis company, uses a set of risk factors created by S. Smith (2007) to review threatening written communications.

S. Smith, Woyach, and O'Toole (2014) provided a summary of these risk factors (see Exhibit 1.1).

There are times when an attacker might leak or share clues about attacks with others, and these clues must be explored and investigated. Matti Juhani Saari wrote of his hatred for mankind and posted several threatening YouTube clips prior to his 2008 Finland shootings. Jared Loughner posted similarly odd YouTube videos about Pima College prior to his shooting in Tucson (Van Brunt, 2012).

When violent writing or other content is discovered, it should be explored. This is one of the central recommendations in a 2008 report to the Massachusetts Department of Higher Education by O'Neill, Fox, Depue, and Englander: "Writings, drawings, and other forms of individual expression reflecting violent fantasy and causing a faculty member to be fearful or concerned about safety, should be evaluated contextually for any potential threat" (pp. 32–33).

Students are entitled to express themselves; self-expression is one of the main developmental tasks for students at a college or university. It is important in the process of development to express divergent opinions, share creative expressions, and emotionally connect with others. Students should not, however, threaten others with graphic or concerning artwork, photographs, cartoon drawings on tests, or quotes from

Exhibit 1.1 | Threat Triage Risk Factors and Their Definitions

Conceptual complexity: A scalar measure; the higher the score for conceptual complexity, the more likely it is that targeted violence or approach occurs.

Paranoia: A scalar measure; the higher the score for paranoia, the less likely it is that the targeted violence or action occurs.

Internally coherent: The scenario must make sense to us. There cannot be big contradictions. The scenario should be a nice, simple, straightforward story. Don't create a scenario based on a formulation that leaves the reader asking, "If this is the plot, then how did that happen?"

Accepted: Would other clinicians and referral sources that know about the case accept this scenario as one that makes sense? Would they see it as a good story?

Reliable: Is the scenario accurate and valid? Would others come up with a similar scenario, or is the story something drawn from left field? If the scenario is tested out, would it produce results?

Identification of the victim: A dyadic indicator; if the victim's identity is named or implied, targeted violence or approach is less likely to occur (a change in direction from the model of S. Smith, 2007).

Mention of love, marriage, or romance: A dyadic indicator; if the messages mention love, marriage, or romance, targeted violence or approach is more likely.

Use of polite language: A dyadic indicator; if any polite language is used in the message targeted violence or approach is somewhat less likely (a change in direction from Smith's model).

Specification of harm to be inflicted on the victim: A dyadic indicator; if any long list of violent actions or any of a diverse set of weapons is specifically mentioned, targeted violence or approach is more likely (a change in direction from Smith's model).

Whether the threatener has contacted the victim before: A dyadic indicator; if the threatener has contacted the target two or more times, targeted violence or approach is more likely.

Note. A scalar measure increases in consistent intervals. A dyadic indicator is either present or not.

poetry or other works of art that could be understood as threatening or inappropriate (e.g., sexual or stalking in nature). These expressions should be explored and understood given the context of the relationship, career aspirations, current mental status, and aggressive intention to harm. There is generally less cause for alarm when a creative writing student shares violent content with a mentor for feedback. It may be more concerning that a student shares graphic and suggestive photography with an admissions counselor who has previously corrected him for inappropriate boundaries. The context is important to understand the potential for risk.

The case of Justin Carter illustrates the potential for overreacting to social media posts. Following an argument with a friend on Facebook about a video game they played together, Carter responded to his friend's comment that he is crazy with "I think Ima shoot up a kindergarten/And watch the blood of the innocent rain down/And eat the beating heart of one of them" (Cooper, 2013, p. 1). He followed the post with "jk [just kidding] and lol [laughing out loud]."

His threat was reported to police and he was arrested and imprisoned for 5 months (Cooper, 2013). The case remains open and highlights the potential for overreaction by police. Although the threat required a police response and further assessment, it is hard to argue that this simple, impulsive Facebook threat merits 5 months in prison. The police invoked a terroristic threatening law, and the prosecutor argued that Carter's free speech ended when his language turned threatening. The speech in question occurred within a few months of the December 2012 Newtown shooting at an elementary school, a fact that would be hard for law enforcement officials to ignore.

Caution should be taken not to overreact to these social media threats. As mentioned previously, the majority of communicated threats do not lead to actual violence (Scalora et al., 2010; Turner & Gelles, 2003). Students might make "threats" as a way of expressing anger, controling or intimidating others, communicating frustrations, or expressing hopelessness. The only way to determine the nature of the violent speech (or text) is to conduct a threat assessment and interview the student to determine the exact nature and likelihood of the threat—again, understanding the threat in the larger context of its occurrence.

However, social media posts and writing may be the only evidence offered as an individual moves to a potential tipping point. Calhoun and Weston (2009) described those simply seeking attention (howlers) and those planning an attack (hunters):

> . . . as a practical matter howlers can become hunters. Some howlers reach a point where something happens to propel them across the line up to take up the hunt. Something tips them across the great divide that separates howling from hunting. We call that tipping point the last straw syndrome. (p. 135)

T. J. Lane reminds us of the importance of taking social media threats seriously. Although doing so led to an overreaction in Carter's case, the underreaction to Lane's writings was a missed opportunity to detect leakage. Lane shot several students at Chardon High School on February 27, 2012. Prior to the attack, he had been involved in several fights and posted the following to his Facebook page on December 30, 2011:

> In a time long since, a time of repent, The Renaissance. In a quaint lonely town, sits a man with a frown. No job. No family. No crown. His luck had run out. Lost and alone. The streets were his home. His thoughts would solely consist of "why do we exist?" His only company to confide in was the vermin in the street. He longed for only one thing, the world to bow at his feet. They too should feel his secret fear. The dismal drear. His pain had made him sincere. He was better than the rest, all those ones he detests, within their castles, so vain. Selfish and conceited. They couldn't care less about the peasants they mistreated. They were in their own world, it was a joyous one too. That castle, she stood just to do all she could to keep the peasants at bay, not the enemy away. They had no enemies in their filthy orgy. And in her, the castles every story, was just another chamber of Lucifer's Laboratory. The world is a sandbox for all the wretched sinners. They simply create what they want and make themselves the winners. But the true winner, he has nothing at all. Enduring the pain of waiting for that castle to fall. Through his good deeds, the rats and the fleas. He will have for what he pleads, through the eradication of disease. So, to the castle he proceeds, like an ominous breeze through the trees. "Stay back!" The Guards screamed as they were thrown to their knees. "Oh God, have mercy, please!" The castle, she gasped and then so imprisoned her breath, to the shallow confines of her fragile chest. I'm on the lamb but I ain't no sheep. I am Death. And you have always been the sod. So repulsive and so odd. You never even deserved the presence of God, and yet, I am here. Around your cradle I plod. Came on foot, without shod. How improper, how rude. However, they shall not mind the mud on my feet if there is blood on your sheet. Now! Feel death, not just mocking you. Not just stalking you but inside of you. Wriggle and writhe. Feel smaller beneath my might. Seizure in the Pestilence that is my scythe. Die, all of you. (GlobalGrind, 2012, p. 1)

The Facebook post is filled with themes of power and control, objectification and destruction; it raises red flags that would indicate the need for further exploration and connection.

Summary

In this first chapter, I introduced some new concepts and left you with more questions that are addressed in subsequent chapters. I've used broad brushstrokes to describe the many ways in which potential violence can be communicated through direct threat, disruptive behavior, passive threat, writing, and social media postings. In Chapter 2, I introduce concepts related to establishing the relationship and setting the conditions for the threat assessment interview. Chapter 4 outlines some of the central threat assessment concepts to better determine the nature and likelihood of violence.

Questions for Further Discussion

1. What is the main difference between threat assessment and violence risk assessment, according to the author?
2. In reading about O'Toole and Bowman's (2011) discussion of potential blind spots, give an example of a time when you experienced a tendency to normalize, rationalize, explain away, ignore, or succumb to icon intimidation during your everyday life.
3. What are some of the challenges related to addressing social media posts and creative writing projects that might contain threats or concerning information? What are some ways to obtain this information from someone being assessed? How might you apply some of the concepts mentioned by S. Smith et al. (2014) included in Exhibit 1.1?
4. Review the section on attack-related behavior mentioned by Calhoun and Weston (2009) that includes grievance, ideation, research and planning, preparation, and breach. Choose one of the cases discussed in this chapter and label some of the attack-related behavior.
5. Compare a time when you experienced a direct communicated threat to a time when you witnessed more subtle threatening behavior. Which concerned you more in terms of likely violence? Why?

Chapter 2

Preparing for the
ASSESSMENT

Chapter Highlights

1. The chapter reviews the importance of paperwork, rapport, and preparation for the assessment. This includes the creation of an informed consent form that covers issues of cost, length and scope, missed appointments, access to testing data, and information sharing.
2. The chapter explains the difference between *assessment* (gathering information regarding a potential threat to others and communicating back to the referral source the nature of the potential threat) and *treatment* (longer term in nature and has a set of behavioral goals to help manage at-risk behavior).
3. Before beginning an assessment, the clinician must gather essential contextual data, including work history, admissions or hiring information, workplace performance or grades, previous treatment history, and parental contact.
4. Ethical considerations related to assessment and the establishment of the assessment relationship are reviewed. Techniques to develop rapport include building on similarities, using Socratic questioning, and lowering defensiveness.
5. The chapter explores diversity as it relates to the assessment through culture and ethnicity, sexual orientation, socioeconomic status, and *microaggressions*, defined as "brief, everyday exchanges that send denigrating messages to certain individuals because of their group membership" (Sue, 2010, p. xvi).

One of my favorite movies is the 1966 spaghetti western *The Good, the Bad and the Ugly* starring Clint Eastwood (Leone, 1967). I like the movie because the unnamed protagonist travels around in his poncho, cigar hanging out the corner of his mouth, and doles out justice. Perhaps I like the movie in part because it served as an inspiration for *The Gunslinger*, my favorite book by Stephen King (2003). The main reason I like this movie, however, is the repeated phrase and running joke, "You see, in this world there's two kinds of people, my friend: Those with loaded guns and those who dig. You dig." And later in the film, "There are two kinds of people in the world, my friend: Those with a rope around the neck, and the people who have the job of doing the cutting." So in this vein, there are two kinds of assessments when it comes to dangerousness to others: there are the more structured, formal assessments and the everyday, ongoing, less structured assessments. Both have value, but each serves a different purpose in the overall goal of preventing violence.

Structured, formal assessments of an individual's potential for harming others often are used to make a decision about the future steps for the individual in question. Is the person able to return to college or the workplace? Should he or she be allowed back into a high school? Are there other risk mitigation steps that should be taken, such as mandated treatment or restricted access to individuals or locations? Formal assessments involve a third party, such as a school administrator, student conduct office official, court, or the dean of students. Often two or three meetings are held during a formal assessment. Clinical tests may be used to establish the presence or absence of mental health symptoms that could exacerbate the risk of violence. In these kinds of assessments, a structured report or letter is issued to the referral source.

Less structured, informal assessments occur frequently within psychotherapy and treatment. These are the everyday observational evaluations of the client's behavior, thoughts, and potential risk to others. Although violence to self or others is not present in all clinical interactions, the clinician should monitor the individual's risk of suicide or threat to someone else. Several licensure requirements and ethics codes guide clinicians and encourage them to ensure that their clients will not hurt themselves or others. For example, the ethics codes of both the American Counseling Association (2014) and the American Psychological Association (2010) require that professionals report danger to a minor as well as share information with authorities if a client makes an imminent threat to harm another. These kinds of observations are akin to the dashboard gauges in your car. They operate continually and influence the driver's immediate "what next" decision. They provide the driver with data he or she needs to adjust speed, fill the gas tank, and check the oil.

Both structured formal assessments and the everyday, less structured observations of a clinician can benefit from an improved understanding of threat assessment principles. In structured assessments, a deeper understanding of risk factors and law enforcement principles can aid clinical staff in developing risk profiles and reports. During everyday, observational conversations with clients, clinicians can monitor their clients' thoughts and behaviors against the threat assessment literature. Like an engine light that alerts the driver to check the engine, an ongoing client who exhibits risk factors or begins to narrow frustration and focus on a target sends a warning sign to the clinician to take additional steps to prevent an escalation.

In this chapter, I focus on structured and formalized risk assessments and some of the steps clinicians can take to ensure that they are anticipating potential problems and doing the necessary groundwork prior to the assessment. Additionally, I explore the importance of taking into account culture, ethnicity, sexual identity issues, socioeconomic status, and issues related to disability.

Difference Between Assessment and Treatment

One of the key issues facing clinical counseling staff is educating the referral source about the ethical and practical differences between mandated assessment and mandated treatment. An assessment is short term in nature and limited to a few sessions. The purpose of a threat assessment is to gather information regarding a potential threat to others and communicate back to the referral source the nature of the potential threat.

Treatment is longer term in nature and has a set of behavioral goals to focus on that are developed by all concerned parties. There is a general agreement that assessment is the less ethically complicated process and more frequently mandated by school administrators and behavioral intervention teams. More controversial are questions around the length, efficacy, and ethics of requiring individuals to participate in mandated treatment. There are certainly ways to perform mandated treatment well and ways to perform it badly. Issues related to treatment are covered in the second half of this book.

Informed Consent

The informed consent form defines the scope of the relationship between the person conducting the threat assessment and the individual who is being assessed; the document clearly spells out the details of the threat assessment process and sets expectations between the two parties involved. The informed consent should clarify what the assessment involves, how long it takes, the cost involved, and general housekeeping rules (e.g., what happens if the person does not keep an appointment).

The following is a list of several broad categories that should be included in the informed consent form. This is not an exhaustive list, and clinicians are encouraged to develop their own form that takes into account specific regional and state requirements. There is a sample informed consent document used for the college and university setting in Appendix A. If you are hiring or vetting a clinician or threat assessment professional to conduct the evaluation, you can review the sample form in Appendix B.

- *Cost.* The document should clearly define the cost of the evaluation to the individual receiving the assessment. There should be no hidden fees that are added onto the assessment (e.g., copying fees or test administration costs). In the event that the evaluation is not being paid for by the referral source (the school, administration, college, or university), efforts should be made to help the individual understand potential charges and what might be covered through insurance.
- *Length.* The length and duration of the testing and interviewing sessions should be explained to the individual before the assessment begins. To some extent, the clinician may be unable to exactly predict how many sessions will be required given the unfolding nature of the interview and the potential for symptoms or behaviors that require further exploration. Efforts should be made to help the student understand the time commitment for the assessment.
- *Release of information.* The informed consent form should contain information about who has access to the evaluation. This includes information about the kind of information that will be shared (e.g., a brief verbal summary vs. a detailed four-page letter) and whether the evaluation will be shared with the student's parents. (Details of sharing previously collected information with the referral source are discussed in more detail in Chapter 3.)
- *Access to testing data.* Many testing companies have ethics codes and guidelines that require raw testing data to be released only to those who have adequate training to interpret the data. For example, raw Minnesota Multiphasic Personality Inventory (2nd ed.; Butcher, Graham, Ben-Porath, Tellegen, & Dahlstrom, 2001) data cannot be released to the individual or the parents in order to obtain a second opinion. Most assessments are released to the referral source either by permission obtained through the signed informed consent form or through a separate release-of-information document.
- *Scope of evaluation.* The informed consent form should outline the parameters of the scope of information that will be collected concerning the target of the assessment. Will the evaluation reach into the student's previous legal history in other states? Will high school records be included if the student has a history of conduct problems? Will parents be questioned in the process? Use the informed consent form to explain clearly the scope of the evaluation.

- *Missed appointments.* Individuals who are referred for a mandated assessment do not always show up for appointments. It is important to communicate at the start of the assessment process the consequences of not showing up for an appointment (e.g., rescheduling, immediate notification of the referral source).

By including these key areas in the informed consent (as well as looking to Appendix A for additional guidance), the clinician creates a pathway of clear communication with the individual receiving the assessment. As mentioned earlier, this is not a comprehensive list, and the clinician should consult with local licensure requirements, regulations, and state laws to ensure that he or she is conducting the assessment in compliance with the required informed consent documentation.

Initial Referral Data

Assessments begin with the gathering of information.

> Part of the skill set of a threat assessment professional is the competence to collect useful and reliable information while interviewing. Interviewing is not about asking questions and ticking off a checklist of required information. Such a clinical "question-answer" interview style seldom proves to be effective. The interview style and the way in which the interviewee is approached are important determinants of the success of the interview. The interviewer needs to establish a trustworthy and professional "working relationship" with the interviewee in order to increase the likelihood of obtaining sensitive information that the interviewee might otherwise be reluctant to share. (Van der Meer & Diekhuis, 2014, p. 60)

S. Smith et al. (2014) stress the importance of ongoing monitoring to guard against relying on data that may no longer be valid:

> Threat assessments have limited shelf lives. In fact, their accuracy and subsequent value can diminish quickly and significantly over a short period of time for a variety of reasons including the threatener's use of drugs, both prescription and over the counter, new stressors in his or her life, interpersonal problems, flare ups from untreated medical and/ or mental health conditions, the influence of the media or other external stimuli, and unanticipated trigger events. (p. 275)

I wrote in the opening to my book *Ending Campus Violence: New Approaches to Prevention* (Van Brunt, 2012):

> There is a poem by the American poet John Godfrey Saxe (1816–87) that tells the story of six blind men who have never seen an elephant before.

It was six men of Indostan
To learning much inclined,
Who went to see the Elephant
(Though all of them were blind),
That each by observation
Might satisfy his mind

The poem continues as each blind man touches a part of the elephant and shares his findings with the others. The first touches the side of the elephant and compares this to a wall. The second touches the tusk and compares it to a spear. The third touches the trunk and compares it to a snake. The leg is compared to a tree, the ear to a fan, and the tail to a rope.

The moral of the poem centers on the importance of being cautious in terms of making assumptions when one does not have an understanding of the entire concept. (p. ix)

Clinicians would do well to remember this poem when approaching the process of assessment. The assessment will always be more informed and thorough if it begins with as much information about the subject as possible. However, assessment is essentially a garbage in/garbage out prospect. It only will be as good as the information that is provided to the clinician performing the evaluation.

When training referral sources on the importance of information sharing with those conducting the threat assessment, I often tell them not to leave it up to the person being assessed to convey the information. Most individuals, if asked to share why they are being asked to comply with a mandated threat assessment, undoubtedly downplay the seriousness of the event and leave out essential information. One could imagine a student sharing, "Me? Oh, I'm here because the school thought I was going to go on one of those crazy shooting rampages you see in the news. I'd never do anything like that. They are just overreacting to something I said in class." The lesson? Make sure the referral source communicates directly with you and conveys accurately and precisely all of the information related to the reason for the assessment.

E. Deisinger, Randazzo, and Nolan (2014) described the importance of connecting with a variety of sources of information for the threat assessment, such as student services, faculty and advisors, administration, police and security, community, human resources, and students. The following is a list of information sources I have found it useful to connect with prior to conducting the face-to-face assessment. This list is more geared toward college and university assessments but gives those working with K–12 students and the community a glimpse of the kind of information that is useful to have on hand prior to the assessment. This is not an exhaustive list but instead a starting place for clinicians.

- *Incident report.* Perhaps the most important piece of information is the first-hand accounts of what happened and what has been documented. This allows the person conducting the assessment to question the student about his or her version of events, test for authenticity and deception, and further explore contextually clues to the student's behavior. In the education community, these often are incident reports. In the community or workplace, these may be police reports or supervisor evaluations or written warnings.

- *Schedule, grade point average, and transcript.* These provide a glimpse into the student's past academic behavior; clues to periods of time that may have been more difficult for the student with regard to grades; and information about the student's current professors, class locations, and frequency. In a workplace setting, these data may be kept through human resources in the employee file. Performance appraisals, harassment complaints, or similar documentation could provide essential information for the person conducting the assessment.

- *Residential life history.* For students living on campus, this kind of information can provide some insight into social interactions; how a student reacts when confronted with rule violations; and information regarding hygiene, sleep habits, and potentially addictive behaviors.

- *Conduct and criminal and judicial history.* This provides some insight into the individual's past behavior on campus as it relates to following the code of conduct and the rules of the institution. Information may shed light on parent involvement, substance abuse or dependence issues, and anger control and aggression. For those in workplace or community settings, past involvement with law enforcement could provide important insight into impulse control, authority conflicts, and illegal activities.

- *Previous treatment.* This would include past outpatient therapy contact, access to inpatient psychiatric records, psychological testing results, and medication history.

- *Parent contact.* For younger individuals, having the ability to talk with the parents and involve them early on in the process of assessment is helpful for a number of reasons: It provides a larger context for the student's behavior, and it also provides an additional layer of risk management (rather than calling them for the first time after the student has engaged again in violent or threatening behaviors).

- *Admissions/hire materials.* Many schools require students to write an essay in order to obtain admission to the college or university. These narrative essays may provide some indication of motivation, insight into past behavior, or hopes for the future. An essay could help the person doing the evaluation have a better context for understanding the student's frustration if he or she is unable to achieve dreams or goals. For those in workplace or community settings, reviewing initial employment documents such as the cover letter, resume, and response to employment questions could provide insight into past contextual information.

- *Social media profile.* Many individuals have a vibrant social media profile that can potentially be accessed through the Internet. Some suggested searches would include www.google.com, www.myspace.com, www.facebook.com, www.youtube.com, Craig's list for the city and state, and www.twitter.com. In yet another rampage shooting, Elliot Rodger demonstrates the importance of attending to social media. Rodger also created a 141-page manifesto and carefully crafted and disseminated his message prior to the attack (Speer, 2014). The social media footprint provided opportunities to identify risk and engage in intervention.

Collecting data is important in terms of both quantity as well as quality. For those conducting the assessment, gathering information from multiple sources provides a richer collection of data from which to examine the potential threat.

Ethical Limitations of Assessment

There are three main ethical concerns in threat assessment. The first has to do with ensuring that the clinician has the training, experience, and knowledge needed to conduct this assessment. Simply reading this book is not sufficient. Most states require some demonstrated ability, past coursework, ongoing training, and supervision in order to conduct these kinds of assessments. Assessors are required to keep up with the literature and to understand multicultural issues that may affect the assessment. Many of the tests used by clinicians require special training and licensure requirements in the state in order to be administered.

The second primary ethical issue is being clear with the individual up front about the nature of your relationship. It would be fair for most to assume, when sitting down with a psychologist, counselor, social worker, or marriage and family therapist, that the person is there to help and has the individual's best interests at heart. In reality, those performing the assessment have two identified clients: the referral source and the individual being assessed. A clear informed consent document can help address this potential conflict.

The final ethical issue is confining recommendations and predictions about future violence to what the research supports. There is a temptation for clinicians performing these assessments to give opinions or conclusions about the nature and likelihood of an individual's risk to the community. It is widely accepted in the threat assessment community that predicting future violence is beyond our abilities. Hart and Logan's (2011) structured professional judgment model, outlined in Chapter 7, provides one approach to ensuring that those conducting the assessment avoid predictions or conclusions that are not supported by the literature.

Establishing the Relationship

In this section, I review the importance of building a connection and relationship with the individual being assessed. In many ways, this art is one of the most important concepts outlined in the book. If the individual lacks confidence, trust, or a willingness to share information with the clinician, the validity of the entire assessment becomes suspect. Like a professor first meeting his or her undergraduate class, it is important to spend time learning about the students, addressing their concerns about the class, and building trust and a sense of community. Any clinician who has provided assessment or treatment can attest to the importance of establishing the relationship and building a sense of trust with the person being assessed.

Establishing Rapport

In the first half of this chapter, I outline the foundational work needed to establish and define the relationship for a formal assessment. Like the foundation of a house, it is essential to have this information in place in order to avoid problems down the line. For clinicians who rush through developing an informed consent or don't take the time needed to gather intake information or define the scope of the assessment, there will be a price to pay in terms of the accuracy and ethical nature of the assessment.

When discussing the assessment with the person being assessed,

> creating proper conditions and setting a proper interview climate when speaking with the subject may increase the likelihood of the interviewee being more willing to share personal insight and useful information. Keywords for the approach in the "threat assessment interview" are objective and neutral, but nevertheless friendly, understanding, and nonjudgmental and subtly supportive approach. In order to find a deeper level of understanding of the person and to be able to "see the world through her eyes," the interviewer will have to be sufficiently attentive. (Van der Meer & Diekhuis, 2014, p. 61)

This personal connection and attention are necessary at the very outset of the assessment. Failure to create the proper conditions and interview climate will result in increased defensiveness and decreased information being shared.

Assessing a student's potential for violence requires first rapport and, eventually, a safe trust-based relationship between the clinician and the student. The relationship communicates a level of concern and caring that allows the student to begin to develop a degree of trust, which is essential when trying to determine what is going on inside the head of the student. Developing trust increases the likelihood that the student will then share the information needed to understand the potential for violence. Without trust, staff and student are locked into opposing sides, each masking and attempting to protect a personal agenda.

This is certainly a challenge when working with individuals who are frustrated, scared, angry, and feeling disenfranchised with the process. Establishing a good rapport requires finding the sweet spot between too hot and too cold. "Too hot" in this context is a clinician who downplays the seriousness of the assessment, who seeks to make a friend rather than work with the person being assessed, and who addresses the individual's expression of concern with glib, superficial redirection and assurance. The "too cold" scenario is one in which the serious nature of the assessment is emphasized to such an extent that the individual responds defensively and fearfully, which leads to a potentially hostile and adversarial process.

Most assessments are mutually beneficial for the student and the evaluator. The evaluator attempts to understand an individual's potential for acting out violently and has to balance both the needs of the individual and the needs of the community. Eells and Miller (2011) described it this way: "The decisions that staff make are difficult on many levels, and always involve balancing the needs of the individual student with the interest and safety of the community at large" (p. 9).

In education settings, the needs of the individual are often related to enrollment in school or achieving some level of academic success in the classroom, determining a career path for future employment, and developing social relationships with those around him or her. Most individuals being assessed would agree that these are the things they would like to achieve as well. The community needs are equally important: the ability of all students to take part in a safe and supportive learning environment and to achieve academic success in a community free of fear, disruptions, and threats to safety. In the event that the individual is not able to remain part of the community, this conversation will be easier to have and understand with a student who feels that the evaluator is trying to find a mutually beneficial outcome.

Establishing rapport with the client is an important part of the interview. Meloy and Mohandie (2014) identified five steps to facilitate that process (see Exhibit 2.1).

The following sections discuss some of the basic skills useful in developing a sense of trust and rapport with the person being assessed. This trust is based on a mutual sense of working together to keep both the individual being assessed and the community safe and ideally has the clinician in a position of advocacy for the target of the assessment.

Stressing Similarities and Building Connections

Building connection with the client is easier when there is a focus on the similarities that exist between the counselor and the client. This

Exhibit 2.1 | **Techniques to Build Rapport**

Smiling. This is a universal gesture of goodwill regardless of culture, nationality, or religion. Research indicates that individuals who receive a smile from another feel accepted and not judged.

Listening carefully. Most people do not listen to each other in an open and patient manner. If the interviewer is attentive, is nonjudgmental, and shows interest in other people, a very positive emotional dynamic will be put in place, even if the interviewee is very distrustful and hates what the interviewer represents (e.g., the Federal Bureau of Investigation, Americans, infidels).

Finding something in common. Identify a characteristic that is shared between the interviewer and interviewee and point that out. It could be marriage, a child, a common geographical area visited, a certain amount of education, or interest in a certain sport. Find it and say it.

Mirroring the interviewee. This refers to mimicking the interviewee's body language and words, which takes attention and practice. If it is done too obviously, it will be noticed and rapport will not arise. It may mean sitting the same way, making similar gestures, using some of the same words, even using similar emotional tones of voice.

Avoiding blunders. Allowing the soles of one's shoes to face another person is considered an insult in the Arabic culture. Displaying a cold and unfriendly demeanor is considered an insult. Conveying impatience, such as glancing at one's watch or tapping one's fingers on the table, is considered an insult. Certain gestures may be an insult. Study the culture and know what the blunders are (Nydell, 1996).

can include simple connections such as hobbies, sports, TV shows, or other interests. The identification of similarities creates a connection between the clinician and person being assessed that lowers defensiveness, lessens objectification, and sets the stage for a sense of mutual goals.

My office at Western Kentucky University, where I served as the director of counseling, was like an explosion of objects arranged by someone with attention-deficit disorder. You would look at one wall and see a picture of the New Orleans staple Café du Monde, a Mephistopheles marionette from Prague, a Tibetan singing bowl, Bob the ficus plant, wooden puzzles, a sand tray, and an hourglass. My bookshelves held figures from the movies *Clerks* (K. Smith, 1994), *The Big Lebowski* (Coen & Coen, 1998), and *The Matrix* (Wachowski & Wachowski, 1999). Lara Croft hung from one shelf; Finn, Jake, and Lumpy Space Princess occupied another shelf. Master Chief from Halo, pictures from my white water rafting trips, a miniature Freud, and a walk-on-water action Jesus filled the other shelf. For me, these objects tell stories about different parts of my life and convey a sense of openness and genuineness to the individuals I saw for assessments and therapy.

I can imagine about half of those reading right now smiling in recognition at the objects strewn about my office. You appreciate this and have your own collection of puzzles, fidgeting toys for your clients, and personal objects around your office. Other readers are engaged in a collective shudder and remember the advice of a supervisor to never put personal objects in the office. This goes double if you perform assessments or if you work in a secure setting like a prison or an inpatient unit.

One lesson I've learned throughout my career is that what works for me might not work for everyone else. As someone who is grounded in Rogers's (1980) humanistic theory with a healthy dose of Yalom's (1980) existentialism, I relish the sharing of whom I am and the immediacy of the conflict that this sometimes brings. It has been my experience that more good than bad has come out of this sharing and that those who I have assessed or provided treatment to have been better because of my sharing rather than harmed by it.

That being said, I realize that sharing personal information with individuals you work with through assessment and treatment, especially in a threat assessment capacity, is not for everyone. There is certainly an element of risk, and it raises a question of maintaining boundaries and protecting your personal space. I encourage clinicians to share only what they feel comfortable with sharing but to be sure to share something. An important element of the assessment process is transitioning the individual from seeing the person doing the assessment as an object or part of the system to seeing the person doing the assessment as a person with a task in front of him or her. I find myself more connected to people when I know something about them. I'm more willing to engage with them, lower my defenses, and share information. A threat assessment interview only heightens and intensifies this depersonalization and objectification from the person receiving the assessment to the clinician. Something as simple as a shared love of animals or a sports team or a fun location pictured in artwork all provide an opportunity for the individual being assessed to see the person offering the assessment as just that, another person.

The limits of self-disclosure, the topic of many a graduate school lecture I have offered to those young hopeful students excited at the prospect of becoming a therapist or performing assessment, are essentially threefold. The first is to avoid sharing anything that would do potential harm to the individual being assessed. This tenet is central in both assessment and treatment. The second is the importance of only sharing information that is resolved for the clinician. A recent divorce, the death of a loved one, or a recent disciplinary action by a work supervisor are all examples of material that should not be shared in a clinical context given the emotional volatility of the information. Finally, clinicians are cautioned against sharing information that steps beyond the boundaries of professional practice. This would include sexual information, inappropriate jokes, or overly personal information.

Lowering Defensiveness

Addressing defensiveness is essential to establishing rapport and to developing ways to increase the likelihood of the individual being assessed sharing details and information with the clinician. Being willing to empathetically listen to the person being assessed helps her or him begin to trust and be willing to share.

In the following sections, I describe techniques I have found helpful when seeking to lower a student's defensiveness or discourage only one-word answers.

Circular Questioning

Robert "Bob" Ross hosted *The Joy of Painting* in the 1980s. I was always amazed at how he was able to take his paintbrush and create these amazing landscapes of happy trees in such a nonlinear manner. It was almost like watching a magician perform a trick. It was hard to see where the pieces all lined up, but it was obvious that the person had the confidence and plan to move forward to create the painting or perform the trick.

Circular questioning (rather than questioning directly off a form) can be an effective way of gathering information while allowing individuals to share their story. This process tends to help lower the defenses of the person being assessed and conveys a sense of respect as he or she shares a story rather than having the story deconstructed onto a form or into a series of questions that only have meaning for the clinician.

I had a student who came in for a threat assessment related to a disturbing video he posted on YouTube. The video depicted the student in a dog cage, with a knife, rapping about his thoughts of wanting to break out and kill others. He had already met with the conduct officer prior to my threat assessment interview, and I rightly assumed he had been asked dozens of questions about his actions. He came into my assessment tired, on edge, and defensive. If I had started my interview with another series of questions related to his potential violence, the answers I would have received would have been monosyllabic "yes" and "no" answers lacking any depth or explanation. Instead, I started with an open-ended discussion of his art, how college had been so far for him, and any plans he had for the upcoming break. By offering a flexible format for him to explore his story, I ended up lowering his defensiveness and communicated that I cared about him beyond the simple question of "Are you a danger to others?" This allowed me to gather more information and build an alliance to help advocate for the student around his future at the college and with the conduct office and behavioral intervention team.

Elephant in the Room

Let's face it, the people we see in a threat assessment capacity are typically either very upset and scared about the process or very angry and annoyed. One central goal of the clinician is to address these emotions in order to obtain some buy-in to the process from the person being assessed. Any resolution involves addressing the individual's frustration and acknowledging the unfortunate nature of the predicament. This doesn't involve agreeing with everything the individual says but instead empathizing with the frustrating situation he or she is in. Clinicians mishandle a threat assessment interview if they ignore the nonverbal frustration or anger being conveyed by the person being assessed (who is forced to comply with the interview itself).

Empathetic Listening

Luckily, most clinicians listen empathically. We spend our lives learning to turn our sensitivity dial up to better detect subtle emotions or nonverbal gestures. Some of us have achieved a circus mind reader–like expertise at understanding what people might be thinking based on their facial expressions. This kind of listening creates confidence in people being assessed that you can handle the information they are willing to share. It may come as a surprise to some, but those being assessed often make decisions about what they will and won't share during an assessment based on their comfort level with the clinician. Take this illustration—If you have a gallon of water to share but the only thing you are given is a coffee mug, you might be hesitant to start pouring because the vessel can't handle it. Now, there are some out there who will pour anyway and the water will quickly overflow the mug. These are the individuals who seem to care less about how they are perceived; they quickly flood and overwhelm most clinicians.

Honesty

Let the person being assessed know when you are concerned or if he or she has shared something that is particularly moving. All of us seek out feedback about our emotions and the information we share with others. People find it refreshing when they get an accurate reflection of what they are thinking or feeling. If the person being assessed says during the interview that he or she has the desire to kill others and watch them suffer, the clinician does the person no good by simply nodding. Some acknowledgement of the disturbing nature of these thoughts is not only helpful but, I would argue, expected by the person being assessed. Obviously, an overreaction such as "You can't say such things" will almost guarantee an increase in defensiveness. A more positive reflection (e.g., "That is hard to hear. It sounds like you have some strong feelings about wanting to harm other people") conveys a sense of appropriate reaction.

Assessment of the Individual

One of the greatest mistakes that can be made during the threat assessment process is failing to take into account the unique worldview and distinctive experiences that have come together to shape the individual being assessed. The clinician who does not understand that the way the client looks at the world is often drastically different than the way the clinician sees the world trips headlong into a minefield of missed understanding, mistaken assumptions, and dangerous blind spots.

The concept of blind spots is well explored by Sue's (2010) work in *microaggressions*, which are defined as "brief, everyday exchanges that send denigrating messages to certain individuals because of their group membership" (p. xvi). Sue, Capodilupo, and colleagues (2007) divided microaggressions into three categories: microassualts, microinsults, and microinvalidiations. By definition, these are often unintended slights that have serious implications and impact those of a different country, ethnicity, culture, sexual identity, disability, or mental illness.

The central challenge in addressing microaggression is found in the understanding that these slights are often unintentional and may even be the result of a person in authority attempting to pay a compliment to someone. This creates the dual problems of a blind spot for the person in authority as well as the common reaction of defensiveness ("Well, that certainly wasn't what I meant. Why do they have to be so sensitive?"). Sue (2010) used the images of thumbtacks and raindrops on his books to illustrate the power of these small, unintentional, everyday microaggressions and to help the reader connect to the larger concept of how the volume and continual nature of these experiences are cumulative for the individual experiencing them. In other words, what matters is not just what an individual just experienced from you but rather that the individual had already experienced on the same day or within a short period. The cumulative effect of microaggressions is considerable over time.

Imagine an office manager in a busy community counseling center who returns to her desk to find a Caucasian and a African American waiting to talk to her about an upcoming appointment. The office manager might ask the African American woman to take a seat in a waiting room in order to determine how to help the Caucasian patient while providing some privacy. By not asking which person was first in line and acting on the assumption that it was the Caucasian person, the office manager commits a microassault. This kind of action is closely related to discrimination and may also involve a direct verbal assault (Boysen, 2012).

Microinsults are actions that disrespect or demean a person on the basis of his or her group status (Boysen, 2012; Sue, Bucceri, Kin, Nadal, & Torino, 2007; Sue, Capodilupo, et al., 2007; Sue, Lin, Torino, Capodilupo, & Rivera, 2009). An example of this could be a clinician who is surprised by a person being assessed who turns out to be gay or has a mental health disorder like Asperger's syndrome. The underlying message from the clinician is that people who are gay or have mental illness behave in a certain way. Again, these comments or observations may come out of ignorance, poor access to teaching or information about ethnicity and culture, or simple stupidity. In any case, the clinician has a responsibility to address these microinsults because they have a strong impact on those they are directed at.

A clinician who compliments an individual for arriving to the appointment on time or says something to the effect that "I am very impressed by how well you speak English" is guilty of committing a microinvalidation. A microinvalidation undermines or denies the experiences of a person of color (Boysen, 2012) or those from a different culture or country. This kind of comment sends the message that "I didn't expect you to be on time today or speak English well"; (Sue, Bucceri, et al., 2007; Sue, Capodilupo, et al., 2007). Another example of a microinvalidation may be a statement such as "I don't really see color—racism is a problem of the past." The speaker (unintentionally, perhaps) coveys the message that the racism experienced by people from a culture other than the speaker's is not valid.

So where does this leave us? The issue of microaggressions in assessment is not easy for clinicians to identify and to handle gracefully. Increased training to identify, intervene, and manage these behaviors and comments is needed. Sue (2010) maintained that knowledge and awareness are key to recognizing and effectively handling microaggressions. It is unlikely that all clinicians will become experts in diversity issues or multiculturalism, but with increased exposure to the importance of this topic it may be that instructors can learn how to successfully engage students in these kinds of discussions.

Culture and Ethnicity

Where does the individual identify as home? How are concepts such as community, family, extended family, holidays, politics, and religion viewed? What is his or her first language? Is language a significant enough barrier to obtaining accurate information during the assessment that it requires a translator or the assessor to have the ability to speak fluently in the individual's own language? The assessor can have a general understanding of experiences common to certain groups (e.g., Middle Eastern students practicing Islam, family and extended family being important to Latino and Hispanic groups, experiences of oppression and slavery in the history of the African American population), but it is essential not to assume that the issues common to a certain group have been important to or experienced by a member of that population.

Sexual Identity

Individuals who are gay, lesbian, bisexual, transgender, queer, or questioning often come to assessment with a history of being bullied, teased, and treated poorly by others. Individuals from these groups often report lower levels of perceived social acceptance, lower levels of psychological well-being, and lower levels of physical well-being (Woodford, Howell, Silverschanz, & Yu, 2012). Clinicians should tread carefully when exploring sexual identification and past events such as the coming-out process, support or rejection from friends and family, and overall social integration. Above all, the clinician should avoid the assumption that a person's sexual identity must be a factor in the assessment. A person's sexual orientation could be a factor to be considered and explored in a threat assessment, but it should not be considered a fait accompli.

Socioeconomic Status

Differences in wealth, health care access, education, and experience should be considered as potential barriers to the successful establishment of rapport. These differences can be overcome when they are addressed with a sense of grace, awareness, and tolerance. Clinicians should develop an awareness of how their individual experiences and privilege (or lack thereof) may create expectations in their conversations with others. These often unseen "ruts in the road" can prevent the clinician from exploring alternative hypotheses and gathering data from a person from a different socioeconomic status.

Disability

Those who come into a threat assessment may bring with them experiences related to either a physical or mental disability. These experiences are often important to understand as they may affect the willingness of the individual to form rapport, share information, or engage in open communications with a person in a position of authority. Examples of disabilities may include deafness, the inability to walk, chronic pain, social awkwardness, sensitivity to light or noises, or a thought disorder. For example, a veteran returning from active duty combat with a history of posttraumatic stress disorder may be reluctant to discuss this with someone who has never served in the military. Until that issue is adequately addressed, information gathering will be hampered.

Summary

In this chapter, I have outlined some key thoughts related to defining the assessment relationship and how to build a relationship with the person being assessed that increases the chances of more open and direct sharing of information. I explored how the issue of microaggressions and developing an appreciation for individual differences can affect the assessment. In Chapter 3, I introduce you to the two case studies that are referenced throughout Part I.

Questions for Further Discussion

1. Why is establishing the informed consent of such vital importance prior to the threat assessment commencing? What are some of the dangers of beginning the threat assessment prior to establishing the informed consent?

2. What are some of the challenges in forming a relationship with an individual for a threat assessment? How might you achieve a balance between building connection and lowering an individual's defensiveness while maintaining adherence to ethics guidelines and appropriate boundaries with the person receiving the threat assessment?

3. What are some of the ways the person conducting the assessment can obtain information from additional sources prior to the assessment commencing? What are some of the ethical and logistical challenges of obtaining this information?

4. Van Brunt reviews some techniques to lower an individual's defensiveness as part of the assessment. These include building connections through similarities and the use of circular questioning. Discuss how these methods might work when conducting a threat assessment. What are some other ways to lower an individual's defensiveness during the initial phase of the assessment?

5. Sue (2010) defined *microaggressions* as "brief, everyday exchanges that send denigrating messages to certain individuals because of their group membership" (p. xvi). What are some examples of microaggressions you have experienced in your life? What are some ways to increase awareness about microaggressions that involve culture, ethnicity, sexual orientation, socioeconomic status, and mental illness?

Chapter 3

Case STUDIES

Chapter Highlights

1. Two case studies, Stacie and Dustin, are presented to provide the reader with detailed threat assessment cases to highlight essential threat assessment concepts later in Chapters 4, 5, 6, and 7. Both case studies are drawn from previous threat assessments conducted by Van Brunt; the names and details have been changed to ensure confidentiality.
2. Following each case study transcript is a sample threat assessment letter addressed to the referral source; it provides the assessor's conclusion about the client's threat level and explains the rationale. Chapter 13 contains information about treatment options for the case studies.
3. Stacie is a student who threatens a difficult and somewhat arrogant professor during class. Stacie has a history of depression and suicidal thoughts. She is remorseful and eager to resolve the matter. The transcript includes Van Brunt's efforts to reduce her anxiety and develop a future plan of action.
4. In the second case, Dustin threatens a previous sex partner during a class and is escorted from the classroom by the police. Dustin has numerous risk factors for violence (weapon possession, objectifying and misogynistic language, substance abuse, a lack of remorse and past impulsive actions) that create a higher risk for future violence. The transcript includes comments from Van Brunt addressing Dustin's defensiveness, poor insight, and lack of cooperation.

In this chapter, I introduce two case studies to help illustrate the core concepts of threat assessments. These cases are also being used as the central scenarios for the New Orleans interviews (Van Brunt, 2014), a two-part video series of threat assessment interviews filmed in 2013 in New Orleans to demonstrate two live role plays of what threat assessments look like in practice. (More details about these videos can be found at http://nabita.org/resources/nolainterviews/.) The cases are portrayed by actors following a set of central talking points and facts drawn from previous individuals I have worked with in threat assessments. Names and details of the cases have been changed to protect client confidentiality.

Each case begins with a summary and is followed with the transcript of the interview conducted as part of the New Orleans interviews. The cases are referenced throughout the book to help illustrate risk and threat assessment concepts. Each case ends with a sample assessment in the form of a letter addressed to the institution requesting the assessment.

The first case study provides an example of an individual who makes a threat with very little validity as an impulsive reaction to arguably rude and cruel comments from her professor. The case involves a discussion of Stacie's mental health background with an important disclosure around a past suicide attempt. Stacie demonstrates a willingness to comply with the assessment and is generally scared and worried about her position in the graduate program.

In the second case study, Dustin (a nontraditional student who made a threat to another student in the classroom) appears for assessment unwillingly. He comes across as arrogant and difficult to talk with. He uses objectified language and offers little assurance that the situation that occurred in class will not occur again. Dustin's past, which includes access to weapons and substance abuse, gives additional cause for concern.

Both cases provide interesting threat assessment vignettes. Stacie's stresses the importance of mental health issues, whereas Dustin raises issues of weapons possession, veteran status, and objectifying women. Stacie is cooperative and forthcoming with information. Dustin is guarded and defensive at every turn. Taken together, these cases provide a useful range of client responses and issues for clinicians to better understand how individuals threaten and then approach the interview.

For the transcripts included in this chapter, I use [] to denote the tone or emotion to help clarify meaning. I use {} to give my reasons for things I said.

Case Study: Stacie

Introduction

Stacie is a graduate student studying photojournalism. She has aspirations of being a photographer and traveling the world to cover wars and humanitarian crises. She has a past history of depression and has been on medication once. She had a college boyfriend and that relationship ended badly. She saw a therapist after that bad breakup; she had some vague, suicidal thoughts but no plan. She has been spending more and more time with Professor Galloway, who is prominent in the department and has traveled extensively doing exactly the kind of work that she dreams of doing.

Stacie was a solid student in her undergraduate work (3.8 grade point average [GPA]) but has struggled more in her graduate work. She finds the assignments poorly defined, and she becomes increasingly frustrated at several professors for their lack of clarity. She has trouble interacting with Professor Galloway on her thesis project. He offers criticism that is arbitrary, is inconsistent, and seems to reflect more of his self-importance than the requirements of the syllabus.

Most students go along with Professor Galloway because his recommendation carries weight in the field and at the university. Behind his back, everyone agrees he is arrogant and difficult to get along with. Most people learn the lesson of avoiding him or placating him in order to proceed. Stacie becomes upset, internalizes her anger, and is tearful when the subject comes up.

Stacie lives off campus with two female roommates. They are supportive of her but have their own lives. They offer support and listen for an hour but aren't supportive beyond that hour (e.g., if Stacie sinks back into her depression or if she starts crying). They suggest she should go back to therapy, "like when she was an undergraduate student and had that bad breakup with her boyfriend." Stacie is thankful for their advice but refuses.

As the semester draws to a close, Stacie struggles with balancing her coursework. She has another professor requiring an enormous paper that takes up all her time. Another class is in the chemistry of photography and requires a great deal of focus. Her goal is to make Bs in all of her classes (a requirement of the graduate program).

Professor Galloway's critique of her final project has been unrelenting. Stacie has been documenting conflicts between a local street preacher and other students on campus. The street preacher attacks gay students, those who dress provocatively, and any Greek students or athletes. Stacie has gotten some good pictures, but none are of the quality required by Professor Galloway.

He singles her out in class and puts a picture she took on the wall through the projector. He talks about her poor composition, lack of imagination, and failure to capture a good picture despite people right in front of her screaming and yelling at each other. He says, "It boggles the mind how you could miss something in this war zone of religious zealotry smashing into sex, drugs, and college hormones. For God's sake, just point the camera and click . . . it's like you go out of your way to get a bad shot here . . ."

Stacie becomes so upset at her professor's embarrassing comments that she mutters back, "It wouldn't be so funny if I cut your brake line, you arrogant prick."

Other students go quiet and Galloway looks at her. He says, "Get the hell out of my class." Stacie leaves in tears.

The student conduct officer requires an evaluation prior to her returning to class. Galloway does not want to let her back, but the dean is clear with him that he does not have that power. Stacie is required to complete a threat assessment prior to returning to class.

Transcript

Brian: Stacie, hi. My name is Brian. I've been asked to sit down with you and talk a little bit about the incident that happened in class a couple days ago with your professor. I wanted to get your take on it. I do threat assessments for the school and after you said what you said, it concerned people and that's what brought me in to talk to you. I've read the reports the school gave me and I've looked over some of those. What I'd love to do though is hear from your perspective about what happened and how we can work together to help you out a little.

Stacie: [anxious] I'm really sorry. It wasn't anything that I meant and I didn't mean anything by it. It's just . . . I don't know if you know anything about Professor Galloway. He's just really, really intense and he started mocking my work in front of the entire class and I freaked out, and I messed up, and I said a stupid thing, but that's all it was. It really didn't mean anything at all. And I'm happy to do whatever it takes to make sure that you know that that's all it was.

Brian: This is something that's . . . You're a photojournalism major? That's one of your goals? *{redirecting to a less anxious topic while I build rapport}*

Stacie: Yeah.

Brian: What got you into that?

Stacie: When I was going through high school a lot of stuff around September 11th was going on and some of the images they had in the aftermath . . . They told the story so much more powerfully than anything I saw or heard on the news. That's when I realized that that's what I want to do with my life.

Brian: Professor Galloway was one of the people who you were taking a photojournalism class with and he was helping you work on some of your projects?

Stacie: It's a portfolio class. You work toward a combination of images that create an entire story. So instead of just one, it's multiple images to try to tell a bigger picture of a specific event.

Brian: I've never been very good at taking pictures or anything. Mine always come out fuzzy and not as well composed. What project are you working on now? Is it a certain final project that you're pulling together, or . . . ? *{building trust by playing down my abilities, giving her permission to have faults and not be perfect}*

Stacie: Yeah. I don't know if you've seen them but there's this preacher guy who tends to hang out around . . .

Brian: Yeah . . . he's always yelling at people. . . .

Stacie: Exactly! But he really fixates on certain groups, certain people, so women who dress in ways he doesn't approve of, anyone who he thinks looks Greek, just a lot of harassment, a lot of screaming, and so you know you have him and his very violent actions. He's always making big gestures and you've got the looks on all the different people who are being hurt by this, the people standing by. Sometimes other people want to get involved and speak up for people and other times they just ignore it and walk by. I just feel like there's a lot of story going on there that can be told.

Brian: I can see in the way you're describing it that you're real passionate about your photos. That's cool. Where did things go south in class? Does he have an appreciation for your work, or are there some struggles there? *{open-ended question coming back to the incident in class}*

Stacie: He doesn't like anything I do. Anything. He loves the concept. He thinks it's a great idea. He just thinks my abilities to take the photos are horribly lacking, that I'm missing the bigger picture, though how much bigger I go I don't understand when it's encompassing all of that. He keeps telling me I need to be more in the moment and that I'm just not appreciating the situation. And it varies from class to class. I'll come in and show him something. I'll be really excited. I'll be looking for feedback. I want to become better. He's amazing. He's a horrible person, but he's amazing. I mean, half of my courses as an undergrad referenced his work. I know I'm not at that level. I'm a graduate student. I want to get there, but he'll come in and tell me that if he were doing it, it would be so completely different and it would be so much better, and I just clearly don't understand this the way he does. Well, then, help me understand. Show me how to be like you. Show me how to make photographs the way you make them and understand them and see them, but don't just tell me how horrible I am and how I should just give up.

Brian: Is he the only professor you've run into these troubles with? Is he . . . ? *{determining if there are other potential fixations or focuses to explore later}*

Stacie: Yeah. I mean, don't get me wrong, Flynn is obscenely hard. The portfolio work in that class is . . . I've literally written almost 100 pages so far, but it's straight across the board. Well, it's like journaling . . . It's a lot of work, but it tends to be reflective work and like journal for five pages this week about what you interacted with and but, it's everyone. She gives it out to everyone. If I'm missing something, she explains what I'm missing. Like the first assignment, I didn't quite get it. She told me, "Oh, no, no, no, I'm looking more for this," and gave me an example. So, it's tough. But when I'm struggling, she helps and she doesn't single me out.

Brian: So it's that embarrassment that was different with Galloway then? He calls you out in front of the class?

Stacie: Yeah.

Brian: I'm sorry about that. *{empathy and connection to her embarrassment}*

Stacie: Thank you.

Brian: I know this has been a rough couple of days for you. You haven't been able to go back to his class. Do you talk with your friends or family, people that you're close with about what you've been going through? How's that been? *{further empathy and assessing supports}*

Stacie: My family's not crazy about the whole photojournalism thing and they thought it was a bit of a waste.

Brian: That's unfortunate, especially since you're so passionate about it. *{lack of support from parents in choice of study}*

Stacie: Yeah. But my roommates are really good. Tony and Jenny are really, really sweet and they've been great. They're not in the department, but they've been with me as I've been going through all this stuff. But they both have a lot of other stuff going on in their lives because they're in grad school too so I feel like there's a limit of how much I can dump on them.

Brian: What do you do to deal with all the stress you've been under? How do you cope? *{assessing positive stress management techniques}*

Stacie: [laughs] Not well, apparently. I mean, the last time I was in therapy they told me to journal and so I have an anonymous blog from back then that I just started updating again. I'm just trying to process all the ingrown frustration and stuff and get it out. And that does seem to help, actually, but a lot of times I just get really freaked out. I have a hard time breathing. You know. I get really tense and after I write some of that stuff out, I can just breathe a little easier and it's not quite as upsetting.

Brian: Kind of feels like a load comes off your shoulders or something.

Stacie: Exactly.

Brian: When were you in therapy before? What was the last time you were in? *{assessing past mental health treatment}*

Stacie: When I was in undergrad, I had a bad breakup. We were together for 2 years. He was my first long-term boyfriend and we had some problems. It didn't go so well when we broke up. They thought I was a little suicidal. They recommended I go to therapy for the rest of the semester. But I got back on track. It all worked out. I took a week or two off classes, but I made up all the work. I didn't need anything. It was all good.

Brian: It sounds like maybe they were more worried about your suicidal thoughts than you were at the moment? *{further empathy and exploration of suicide lethality}*

Stacie: It wasn't . . . It wasn't like I'm going to go jump off a bridge or anything like that.

Brian: Right, right.

Stacie: It was just I mentioned that . . . I mean, it's stupid now in retrospect but you know, that first, exciting I love you. We love each

other and are going to be together forever . . . and then it ends and
. . . bad feelings. And it's like all the plans for what you were going to do after college, your whole life feels like it's falling apart
and you don't know how to put it back together again, you don't
know what you're going to do. Sometimes when you feel like that
it can feel easier just to start thinking that it'd be really convenient
not to have to do this whole thing anymore, you know.

Brian: Does that remind you of where you are now with some of the
same kind of what's next stuff? I would imagine that's a worry
that you have. {making connection to current stress and beginning to
assess current suicide potential}

Stacie: Yeah. It's definitely been reminding me of that whole thing
a lot. I mean like I said before. This is all I've wanted to do since
freshman year of high school. I've known this is what I wanted
to do with my life. I've done my undergrad work, my graduate
work, I'm almost done with my program, and now all of a sudden I'm being told by the premier man in the entire field that I
should just stop now because I'm a miserable failure and there's
no way I'll ever be able to do this. And, I'm just so freaked out by
all this. If I can't get my grades up and get this figured out, then it
doesn't matter what he thinks or I think or anyone thinks because
I'll be dropped from the program.

Brian: Have any of those suicidal thoughts returned for you? Have
you been . . . ?

Stacie: Not really.

Brian: Like not going to jump off a bridge or anything? {using humor
to lighten the seriousness of the question}

Stacie: Exactly. [laughs] Nothing like that. Just the thought that,
"Hey, if that car happened to swerve and hit me, that would be a
load off my mind." [laughs]

Brian: Just feeling kind of like everything's piled up around you and
if someone were to . . . The idea of tuning out a little bit . . .

Stacie: Yeah . . . just something to not have to deal with all, with all
of this stuff.

Brian: You're very eloquent, able to talk about what's going on. The
language that I got in the report said that you threatened to cut
the professor's brake lines. So I'm trying to get in the headspace
of how angry you must have been to yell that. {assessing her
insight between the discrepancy between her easy going nature now in
a supportive environment with her reaction under stress and embarrassment in the classroom}

Stacie: It was stupid. I didn't yell it. That's the other thing. I didn't
yell it. I muttered loudly.

Brian: It was quieter . . . You muttered loudly. Okay. [smiles]

Stacie: [smiles] I muttered loudly. The thing was the professor had
taken one of my shots, which I was actually really excited about.
It was right as the sun was setting behind, so you had this sort

of orange glow, very sort of creepy hellish I thought because there were a lot of reds and oranges and you know, the preacher had his hands up and it was just big gestures and, you know, I thought it was working and he put it up on the projector in front of the entire 36-person class and proceeded to explain how my staging was abysmal because I clearly wasn't taking it from the right perspective to capture all of the emotions, the lighting was horrible and completely forced a separate meaning on the piece that was not there in the actual actions. That I used the wrong camera type. Everything was wrong. So, then, after a full six-and-a-half minutes—I timed it—explaining to the entire class what a complete and utter failure as a photographer I am, how I shouldn't be allowed to be a photojournalist, and how he can't understand how I was able to get this far in the program without someone recognizing it and having me removed . . .

Brian: [surprised] He said that in front of the class? *{reflecting her sense of unfairness}*

Stacie: In front of the class. I don't have the soul to appreciate good photography and clearly should just give up now. And I snapped. And it was stupid, but I didn't realize he was going to stop talking and the entire class was going to be silent at the same time and it came out a little louder than I meant.

Brian: So, if I'm hearing you right, there's no plan to cut his brake lines, no plan to get the brake-line snippers or . . . *{assessing her knowledge needed to carry out the threat}*

Stacie: I don't even know what you'd use for that. I can change a tire and that's about the full range of my . . .

Brian: I'm not very good at any of that either. So the impulsive just overwhelmed the . . . *{connecting to her and confirming how she sees the incident}*

Stacie: It was stupid. It was really, really stupid, and I'm usually good at controlling all of this stuff, like if people are mean or whatever. Someone pushes into me on the subway or whatever, I'm okay with it. It's just that he hates me and I don't know why. And I've tried so hard, and you know he's the reason I came to this school. He's the reason I wanted to come here. We read so much of his work as an undergrad, and it's incredible. The stuff he's done and shot in Bolivia, some of the stuff he's been doing in Serbia. The stories he's told are amazing. And to come here, and have these interactions with him that seem like they would be so inspiring and teach me so much, and have him sit there and mock me in front of the entire class, and even that I could deal with better than telling me that I'm such a complete failure I should never even have been allowed into the program?

Brian: Yeah, that's overly harsh. When you're describing this to me, your emotions are so full to the brim. To, you know, almost the point of being overwhelmed by it. Well, let me tell you, from here, my role really is to assess the threat. It doesn't sound to me as if this was any sort of planned attack that you had on him. *{feedback on the situation to build trust}* Given all the stuff that's going on in the country with the mass shootings and the bombings in Boston and such, we're in a position of . . . we take any kind of threat like this really seriously. *{context about why she was called in and what the concern was initially}* So first, I want to thank you for coming in. I know this has been a rough time already and you came in to talk with me about this and that's important. From here, what I'll do is talk to the dean and let them know the results of what we've talked about. My role really isn't as much of a counselor for you, it's more of giving an opinion back to the dean and letting them know how we move on from here. *{clearly defining for her the next steps and further pointing out that I am not a counselor, but someone assessing her risk}* Professor Galloway, I can tell you from the reports I've read, is frustrated. I have some concerns, I'll be honest with you too, about the way he's treated you. I don't think it's in line with some of the academic standards of the program. My personal opinion on this is that if he has some critical feedback to give you, that's one thing, but to say that you don't have the soul to be a photographer, that's a little different. *{taking a risk here and demonstrating that I understand her frustrations}* And the embarrassment in front of the class is concerning. I'm not defending your actions of muttering loudly . . .

Stacie: It was stupid.

Brian: But it seems like there were two people involved in this. Have you ever had an issue like this before, either? I didn't see anything in college, undergrad as much . . . *{after building trust and sharing my feelings about how she was treated, I redirect again to explore other incidents in her past}*

Stacie: I had one teacher in middle school who was sort of like that where just, I don't know, something about her, she didn't like me. I don't know why. Never figured it out. I loved the subject, always did great, but we didn't click. She would make me redo assignments and she wouldn't make other students redo them. You know, I was able to see my friend's essay and it was significantly worse than mine but she still went way harder on me. I mean I got detention a couple of times, but I just avoided her after that. I never took a class with her again, it was an elective. It wasn't an issue. That's the only other time I've had an issue like this.

Brian: Nothing in college then? With any of the other professors then. You said that, was it Professor Flynn that . . .

Stacie: Flynn is tough. Like, I have several incredibly challenging classes. Flynn and Snooka are really, really tough, but they're fair. Like it's straight across the board. They have high expectations for all the students and they want us to succeed. And if I'm struggling with something, if I'm not understanding, if I mess up the first assignment because I didn't understand it, they'll give me the feedback. They'll say, "Okay, we're not looking for this, we're looking for this. This is how you can improve." And, I mean, it's stressful. I'm doing more writing than I've ever done in my life, which I didn't think you'd be doing as a photojournalist major as much, and the chemistry class. Chemistry of Photography is brutal. I was a straight-A student in my undergrad except for my two required science courses, both Cs. I'm not a science person and that's a bit of a problem, but again, they don't pick on me, tell me I'm a failure. They wanna help me.

Brian: Well, that's where we'd like things to go today. I feel like, you know, my report back when we talk to the dean, you know trying to get you back into class. I know this is a required class for you and I do think there's a bit of work that has to be done at the college level about whether you can go back into Galloway's class, how that might look, whether there would have to be a conversation first, or whether it could be something done online. We'd have to sort that out first. There are a lot of different options there. *{sharing potential options, being clear that these decisions will involve other people besides me}*

Stacie: Whatever. Whatever works. Whatever you guys can get done to get me either back into that class or maybe working with another professor, a separate portfolio review. Just as long as I can finish the semester. Just as long as I don't get flunked out, or get a C or anything that would drop me below the requirements to stay in the graduate program.

Brian: I had a couple of questions to ask. They're just part of the assessment piece. They might feel like non sequitur a little bit, but they're things I have on my checklist I kind of have to go through. *{a bit of a harsh transition, but I have other questions I need to ask to complete the threat assessment}* You didn't really talk about weapons or guns or anything. I know that can be a kind of scary question to ask, but it's one of the things I have to ask related to the assessment. Do you have any guns or firearms? Do you know about guns?

Stacie: I don't have one. I mean I grew up in New England in the countryside so, like I was raised with an awareness of them . . .

Brian: There's a lot of bears out there . . . *{using humor to downplay seriousness of the question}*

Stacie: [smiles] Coyotes, actually. They would come after the chickens a lot. But it was mostly a rifle. Old stuff. It was all my grandmother and grandfather's stuff. I'm vaguely familiar but I haven't even touched a gun since I was 16, maybe. Not really anything I've done since I came to the city. My roommate has a gun in the apartment, but she's got it locked away in the safe somewhere in her room.

Brian: So, is that for protection or what? *{with a weapon in the house, I want to encourage more discussion here}*

Stacie: Uh, yeah. She came from New York as an undergrad. She went to Columbia. There were a lot of issues with attacks, safety stuff. She hasn't had any issues since here. She has a license for concealed carry and I don't think she carries it around or anything. I saw it once, but I think she just keeps it locked up in there in case.

Brian: You mentioned being in therapy before. But were you ever hospitalized for any of those feelings around suicide? *{assessing for more details about past treatment}*

Stacie: No.

Brian: Did they ever start you on any medications or anything?

Stacie: My therapist prescribed something, I forget what it was. I mean I went on it for a couple of months. I wasn't a fan, like it didn't seem like it did anything. Seemed kind of silly to have to take something every single morning.

Brian: Antidepressant, maybe?

Stacie: Yeah, it was an antidepressant.

Brian: It didn't really help a lot? *{reflecting back her comments about it not helping}*

Stacie: No. I mean my issues weren't something that was going to be solved by pills. My issues were . . . I had a broken heart. Don't think they make pills for that.

Brian: How about relationships? Are you in a relationship or anything? You mentioned that one that ended badly in undergrad. Have you been dating recently? Still kind of working through, maybe focusing on studies a little bit more? *{assessing supports and additional sources of stress if there has been a recent breakup}*

Stacie: He was kind of like Professor Galloway, really good at making me feel bad about myself, and . . .

Brian: This was your previous boyfriend? *{clarifying and encouraging more discussion}*

Stacie: Yeah, my previous boyfriend, and that was one of the good things that did come out of the whole therapy thing was that, you know, I need to become more confident in myself and I need to not be as affected by what the people around me think of me, and that's something I've been working on. So I don't really want to jump into another heavy relationship until I'm a little more put together.

Brian: How about drinking or substance abuse?

Stacie: No. I have a glass of red wine with dinner maybe three or four times a month, just socially. I don't really drink anything harder than that.

Brian: If Professor Galloway was to not let you back into class, how would that make you feel? *{assessing frustration tolerance for upcoming process with dean}*

Stacie: Well, do you mean not let me back into class, like I'd have to go work with someone else but I'd still graduate? Or do you mean, like I'd get kicked out of the program?

Brian: Well, I guess that's kind of the question. It's both ways. If he really were to make this a larger issue, would . . . if you weren't in the program anymore, what would happen then?

Stacie: I don't know. I mean I have $60,000 worth of student loans getting me to a degree in photojournalism. It's all I've wanted to do for the last decade. I don't know what else I'd do if I couldn't do that.

Brian: So you'd feel kind of lost then?

Stacie: Yeah.

Brian: I'm not saying that would happen. I'm just . . .

Stacie: Okay, okay.

Brian: I just don't have control over him and if it's the case that, and I don't have reason to doubt it, if it's like you're saying and he's fairly . . .

Stacie: A lot of people in the department will back me up on this. Like the other students in the photography department know that this is a very, very common problem that people complain about him. You know. He treats the students horribly. Some students he loves, he adores, they're great. Other students, he'll mock, he'll belittle. It's really hard to tell what it's going to be but you know, he's written I think over 20 books, all well liked, tons of awards, presents at conferences all the time, has had tenure for like 20 years. What are you gonna do?

Brian: It sounds like that's the heart of the problem for you, too. I'm just listening to you talk about this. There's someone you really admire who has treated you really poorly. *{reflective summarizing statement}*

Stacie: Yeah.

Brian: Well, for our threat assessment, you know, my goal is, like I said, to talk to the dean and let them know what the plan is next. I'm going to share some of the results. I don't see an imminent threat here toward the professor. My worry really is around how we put this back together. It might be that they're going to ask you to do some counseling here for this. *{clarifying the process and sharing my opinion about her risk}*

Stacie: I'm very . . . I'm perfectly happy to do whatever is needed to get me back on track. I mean we're most of the way through the semester. I really don't want to have to restart and you know, start another course over, but whatever it takes to just make sure I'll graduate on time and get done.

Brian: One last thing, and once again, this is a question out of the blue, but you mentioned earlier about the writing that you do. You have an anonymous blog. Is some of that . . . you said you got some of your feelings out that way. What kinds of things are you writing there? *{checking level of fixation and focus on Galloway}*

Stacie: Oh, just description. It's all just descriptions of the stuff going on.

Brian: Like a journal?

Stacie: Yeah, so like I'll explain how he gave us this assignment that said I needed to go, you know, capture a scene, and I thought I did it, and then he told me how horrible it was and made me feel really upset and mostly just describing the things that happen. Almost more like a diary like that.

Brian: Do you have any questions for me about evaluation or anything I can answer for you? *{nearing the end, checking in to see if there are things she wanted to discuss}*

Stacie: What does it look like? What do you see happening here? I'm trying to stay calm. I'm trying to focus. And I appreciate you've been really, really nice about all of this. I just need to know . . . how in trouble am I?

Brian: Well, you haven't been in trouble before, so I mean that definitely helps. You know, I think you said something pretty extreme, but I think after talking to you it seems most likely that you kind of lost your cool and given the scenario and the context of what he was doing, and that's concerning as well, I think that certainly contributed to some of your feelings. *{reflection on events that occurred}* I think if you're willing to stay connected, whether to counseling or just to checking in, other cases like this where I've seen, deans are pretty understanding of it. But, ultimately it's their decision and I'm in a consulting role where I can give my report and my opinion of . . . and do a phone call with them after we're done talking today, probably get you at least closer to a plan. *{giving hope about next steps}* But the only part I'm worried about, if the professor's really adamant that you don't return to class, they'll have to work with the department head to come up with some kind of creative middle ground to get you back into finishing the program. *{being clear about the professor's reluctance to have her back}* But, you know, we've done that before, so the fact that you're willing to come in here and talk and work with us is important.

Stacie: Okay.

Brian: Well, thanks for coming in here and talking with me.

Stacie: Thank you so much.

Brian: You're welcome.

Sample Threat Assessment Letter to Referral Source

Dean's Office
University of Education
1 Academic Circle Drive
College Town, USA

To Whom It May Concern:

This is a summary of my interview with Stacie following the incident where she threatened to harm her professor by "cutting his brake lines." I have completed a risk assessment and find Stacie to be a low risk for potential violence to her professor.

During our interview, Stacie was apologetic and remorseful for her statement. She shared that she was frustrated with Professor Galloway's critique of her work in front of the class and said something impulsively because she was angry and embarrassed. She denies any knowledge of Professor Galloway's car and denies having any automotive knowledge necessary to cut his brake lines. She has no past conduct history at the university, and law enforcement confirms no previous criminal history in this state.

Stacie received counseling in the past following the conclusion of a turbulent romantic relationship. She was placed on an antidepressant medication briefly but stopped taking it because she didn't like the way it made her feel. She has no past inpatient history. She denies any current suicidal feelings but reports a return of some depression symptoms as she struggles more with her classes.

Stacie lives with two roommates with whom she gets along. This has been a stressful semester for Stacie, and she has had trouble keeping up with her graduate courseload. She often becomes tearful and sad at home, testing the limits of her roommates' support. Stacie shares that one of her roommates has a firearm in the apartment but it is kept locked away with the ammunition stored separately. Stacie has little firearm knowledge.

Stacie denies similar outbursts in the past and claims this was a unique experience brought on by frustration in the face of a harsh and unyielding critique by her professor. Stacie's violent threat seems to be motivated by a desire for a release or expression of her frustration and in an effort to defend herself from further attack. She expressed remorse and guilt following her outburst and is eager to find a resolution to be able to continue in her program.

I would recommend some form of mediation between Professor Galloway and Stacie, prior to her return to class, to resolve the tension. If Stacie were unable to return to class due to an academic restriction, I would advise the exploration of an Incomplete or explore the ability of Stacie to complete the coursework from home or with another professor in the department. Without mediation, future contact between Professor Galloway and Stacie will likely exacerbate the risk of further conflict.

Of additional concern is Professor Galloway's directness in his critique. While this is not my field of study, I would suggest there may be more effective teaching methods in lieu of public embarrassment. This, of course, is Stacie's report and additional confirmation from other students should be obtained before any corrective action is taken with regard to Professor Galloway's teaching techniques. In either case, some mediated conversation between Stacie and Professor Galloway is recommended.

While this violent outburst in class seems to be a unique experience with a low likelihood of resulting violence, it may be useful to help Stacie reconnect to counseling in order to help her process the event and the stress she has experienced this semester. A secondary goal of this counseling could be the potential to further explore her frustrations with Professor Galloway and look for additional prosocial ways for her to express and redirect her frustrations in the future.

It might also be helpful to address the class that witnessed the critique of Stacie's work and the resulting threatening outburst. This would be most effective if the message came from the conduct office, who might explain how any threats like this are handled, along with counseling to offer support for any students in need. As mentioned earlier, it would be helpful to explore the intensity and tone of Professor Galloway's critique of Stacie prior to any mediation or conversation with the class.

During the initial assessment, Stacie mentioned an online blog she kept that discussed her feelings about the incident. Further access to this document would be important to better understand her motivations and potential for future escalation.

Respectfully Submitted,

Dr. Brian Van Brunt, LPCC
Director of Counseling

Case Study: Dustin

Introduction

Dustin is a nontraditional sophomore student who is studying nursing at a community college. He currently works as an emergency medical technician (EMT) in the local community. He wants "that easy emergency room nurse job so I don't have to drive around anymore and pick up the sickies . . . I want them to come to me."

Dustin was in the army for 2 years before being discharged for a chronic knee injury that first occurred in basic training. He has been in numerous arguments and appeals with Veterans Affairs (VA) to have his physical therapy covered and to go back to school.

Dustin does well in class, mostly because of his street knowledge as an EMT and first responder in the military. The coursework is easy for him; the problem lies more in his attention to detail in the classes and his attendance. He has a 2.8 GPA. He has no mental health history (no therapy, medication, or inpatient stays). He has one past assault charge from a bar fight with a bouncer that ended in 6 months probation.

Dustin feels distant from other students and often comes across as having a chip on his shoulder or being angry. He shares in the interview, "You know that scene in the Hulk movie where David Banner says he is angry all the time. That's me. I'm always just a hair's breadth away from pulling the god-damned trigger."

Other students see Dustin as a kind of loose cannon, capable of just about anything. Most give him a wide berth. His social life includes a series of volatile sexual relationships with women at the college. None has lasted more than a hook up or two, and all have included the potential for rough sex and violence. Dustin sees himself as a bit of a sadist and enjoys being in positions of control. He doesn't seem to have these same kind of problems at his EMT jobs—Dustin says, "Everyone gets it there. We have a dark sense of humor. No PC bullshit."

Three weeks before the end of the semester, one of the girls he slept with makes a joke about his injury and him being less than a man to one of her friends during a classroom lecture. The instructor does not hear this initial comment.

Dustin yells at her, "You are a fucking cunt. Shut your god-damn ignorant mouth or I'll shut it for you." The instructor is very concerned about the potential for violence and feels this is a potential Title IX reporting issue as well. The instructor asks Dustin to leave the class and he refuses. Crossing his arms and says, "I've paid to be here. I'm not going anywhere."

The police remove Dustin from the class after the outburst and lack of compliance. They determine that there is no immediate risk of harm. The dean requires him to complete an evaluation, prior to returning to campus, to determine his risk of violence to others.

Transcript

Brian: Dustin, my name's Brian and I'm here to talk to you today about what happened in class the other day. I'm hired by the university to assess the threat of the situation; you know, people are concerned about you and concerned that maybe this is the tip of the iceberg and there might be something else going on. I can imagine that it's not a fun situation for you to be sitting here across from me. I appreciate you taking the time to come in.

Dustin: I didn't have a choice.

Brian: That's true. *{agreeing to lessen tension}*

Dustin: I'm here. I want to get this over with. I want to get back to class and continue on with the program. I'm here because they told me I had to be here in order to get back to class so I just kind of want to get this over with.

Brian: {I note his dismissive attitude toward the assessment} That's fair. I tried to put myself in your position and I feel like if I did something like that and felt like the school was coming down on me, it would be a bad place to be, so I appreciate you coming in and kind of meeting me halfway. Can I hear from you like—I've got reports. I've gotten all the police stuff—what I'd rather hear at this stage is what, in your words, what happened. Maybe give me a little perspective so I can try to understand. *{attempting to lessen tension, build connection and seek his opinion on what happened}*

Dustin: I was dating this girl. Okay. Not dating. Okay. I met her in class. We ended up going out drinking as a class. I ended up fucking her. Ended up hanging around with the group of classmates and she just mouthed off in fucking class. Fucking cunt. Seriously, man. She mouthed off in class. She made a comment behind my back. She didn't think I heard it. She was talking to one of her girl-friends in fucking class and I told her she should keep her mouth shut or I was going to do something about it. Teacher just heard that. He didn't hear her mouth off or her provoke me. And the next thing you know they tell me I need to leave class and I'm like, "No, I'm not leaving class. I pay to be here." They're already giving me enough crap about my freaking attendance and now they want me to leave another class when I'm actually there? I actually have time. I work 24-hour shifts as an EMT full time. I skip some of the classes occasionally because it's a rotating schedule. So sometimes it conflicts with my school schedule so I have to miss some. If I just go in and take the damn tests I can get out of there. That's how it is. And then they want me to miss more classes because this girl . . . this fucking cunt . . . gives me crap about . . .

Brian: {I note his objectification of women and dehumanizing language. Waiting to further build rapport to challenge these ideas} Is it fair to say that you're balancing a lot of stuff right now? From what I'm hearing, the way you're describing this, you were already at . . . the glass is already kind of at the tippy-top full and this was just another thing on top of it. *{attempting a rather basic summary statement about his stress level}*

Dustin: I'm not balancing anything. I'm doing fine.

Brian: Okay. *{taking time to let him talk more as he rejects even reasonable, basic summaries of his situation. I note the basic lack of understanding of him being asked to leave class when threatening versus being asked to attend classes. Seems like he is baiting me}*

Dustin: It's their problem. They're giving me crap. If they'd just let me go in and take the damn tests I can pass them. My classes are great. My freaking grades are awesome. They're just giving me crap about the attendance, about class participation. That's dropping me to like a freaking 70. Every single exam I get a 95 to 98. I've been there, I've done that. I know what's going on. I wouldn't go wiping someone's ass . . . you know. These kids in there don't know anything, don't know any of the medical stuff, the physiology, haven't seen any of these injuries, they don't know how to handle it, and yeah, they need to be there. I'm working the street. That's class. I'm in there. I can take the tests. I pass them. That's not a problem. They give me a bunch of crap about it, about not being there, and then they tell me I can't go back to class until I come in here. That's going to drop my grade even more. It's all because of that fucking cunt.

Brian: {I again note his misogynist language and objectification of others} Can I ask you a question? What got you involved in the EMT stuff to begin with? *{redirect to another topic that is less charged for him}*

Dustin: I was in the military. I served a couple years and I was a medic over there.

Brian: Similar kind of stuff? Similar kind of EMT stuff over there that you did compared to here? How is it different? *{trying to engage in open-ended questions}*

Dustin: Well, I mean, you got more gunshot wounds than you have on the street over here.

Brian: I suppose that's true.

Dustin: It's more motor vehicle accidents over here and more gunshot wounds over there. That's pretty much what it is. You know. It's a good adrenaline rush. You always know somebody's got your back over there. It's the same thing over here when I'm working as an EMT. You know somebody's got your back. So yeah, similar in that regard. In class, I feel like I've got to watch my tongue. You get a little dirty on the street. You know. You understand each other. Same thing as when you're overseas. Things get dirty and you know who's there for you. Over here, you don't know. You don't know who has your back, so you're always watching out. And that's what class is. It's a freaking bureaucracy.

Brian: *{I note some reduction in defensiveness. I proceed cautiously to encourage more of the same}* I don't want to assume this, but from the way you describe this, it sounds like this wasn't a real long-term relationship with this girl. It was someone that you met . . . a little shorter . . .

Dustin: [laughs] Yeah, yeah, long-term relationship with that whore. No man, it was not a long-term relationship. Sweet piece of ass, but man, once she starts talking, you just don't want to listen, man.

Brian: *{encouraged by laughter and letting down of some guard}* You kind of laughed at the long-term stuff. Do you not have a lot of interest in pursuing a long-term relationship or are you just kind of enjoying . . .

Dustin: Nah, man. Nah . . .

Brian: . . . you like the way it is now . . .

Dustin: Dude. 24-hour shifts. All over the place. Not gonna have a relationship and I don't really want one. They're all whores, man. They always want something out of you. They want something and I'm not going to give it to them. I'll give them what I want to give them.

Brian: *{more casual language addressing me indicates a strengthening in rapport. More objectifying language toward women}* From my perspective, it seems like you got pretty upset, pretty angry, at her in class for . . .

Dustin: She wouldn't shut her mouth. Of course I got angry at her.

Brian: Does that happen a lot in other areas of your life? Or is this an isolated . . . *{attempt to assess other potential threats or aggressive behavior}*

Dustin: What do you mean? There are a couple times but I mean seriously man. You're lucky I didn't get into a fight with the guy in the car that cut me off on my way over here as a matter of fact. Fuck it. Yeah man. It does happen. It happens every now and then. There was one charge since I got out. Got it dismissed. Bouncer started crap. Started trying to muscle me and my friends because we were being too loud in a bar. I took care of it. And the next thing you know, the cops show up and it got dismissed. I just left the bar. I just don't go back to that one. But if you push my buttons, I'm gonna react, man. [angry now] You push my buttons, I'm gonna react. It's not my fault more people push my buttons. Fucking whore in class pushed my buttons.

Brian: *{I note the return of anger at being challenged}* And that's what happened with her in class?

Dustin: That's exactly what happened with her. She's saying crap right behind my back. She's two rows behind me . . . two seats behind me . . . and she's talking to one of her friends about my . . . performance. I'm gonna say something to her. You push my buttons. I'm gonna react. I'm not gonna be sitting there taking that shit from her. Somebody cuts me off, I'm gonna say something about it. You do something about it when somebody pushes you.

Brian: *{I note his reactive anger to others getting in his way}* This time, it's resulted in you getting into some heat, some problems. Having to take time out of your day to come over here.

Dustin: It's not my problem. It's their problem. That's all. I just wanna get back to class and get on with my life. That's why I'm here.

Brian: *{I note the defensiveness has returned again}* Well, let me tell you what the college is concerned about, and you're probably . . . *{an attempt to separate concern}*

Dustin: [sarcastically laughs] Tell me what the college is concerned about. Go ahead, tell me.

Brian: *{I attempt to soften the conversation}* They don't know you very well. That's part of the issue at hand. And having you come in here and meet with me helps because it gives us a little more perspective on who you are and now I know a little more about Dustin. I clearly don't know a whole lot about your life, but the fact that you were willing to come in and talk to me is a good sign.

Dustin: Willing is a real choice word, man. I was told to come in here if I wanted to go back to class.

Brian: *{he ignores everything and goes back to being forced in to see me. I acknowledge his frustration and reframe}* So maybe feeling a little . . . arm-twisted . . . to come in here and do the talk. I appreciate that. Again, you coming in. In this day and age, I'm sure you follow the news, all the craziness that's going on at colleges, all the stuff that happens. There's a concern because we don't know you that well and because we don't know what this could lead to next, with the kind of language you used in class, with the yelling, it gets people worried. And that's what brought you in here today. *{lengthy explanation to once again explain why he is here}*

Dustin: You work on the street. You use some language people don't like. I think that's kind of what it is. That's all. I called her what she was. That's all I did. And if they don't like my language . . . What do you think I'm going to do? You think I'm gonna fucking lose it? I'm not gonna lose it. If I was gonna lose it, I would've lost it. I didn't attack the cops that came in to remove me from the classroom. I stayed under control. I went out of the classroom with them. I'm here right now. If that doesn't show control, I don't know what does. I'm not freaking bringing a gun back in the class. Bringing a gun into class. Is that gonna get me in trouble if I start talking about that or what?

Brian: {*he offers some tentative statements about not harming others, immediately followed by mixed statements about what he would do if he wanted to do it. I redirect*} I think the issue at hand is trying to assess, trying to help me figure out, like you said. I want to go back to something you said a little earlier. What *you* want is I think the important piece here. You want to be in a position to be back in class and finish the goals that you're on. {*redirect to his goal to get back into class, attempting to have him meet me halfway*}

Dustin: Yeah.

Brian: {*assessing weapon knowledge and access*} So, you mentioned guns. Let's talk a little bit about that. You said you've never been to class with a gun or you'd never be in a position of coming in and shooting people.

Dustin: No, I would not.

Brian: But, you've been in the military. I'm guessing you have guns, or have some gun knowledge.

Dustin: Yeah, been in the military. I own a bunch of guns, yeah. When you're over there, you sleep with your gun. You have it next to you when you take a shit. You bring your gun with you. When you go to the mess, you bring your gun with you. You eat with it. You breathe with it. If you don't have your gun, something's gonna happen. And when the shit happens, if you can't handle it and you don't have your gun with you, then you're not prepared. That's just it. Straight from basic all the way up to where we're in the field. You don't go anywhere without your rifle.

Brian: {*less defensiveness from him, I wonder about his experiences there and his adjustment back*} How has it been switching between being over there and being here?

Dustin: Difficult. Can't go into a post office with a gun. Can't go in a bank with a gun. Well, without them seeing ya. Can't walk onto campus with a gun. I think that's stupid. I mean I hear what's going on, but those are for crazy people, man. I'm not crazy. I'm not going on a thing . . . I just need it. That's all. You need to have it with you in order to protect you. Look, I don't got it on me. I'm not armed. I didn't bring it to the counseling session, okay. I'm trying to follow the rules here. {*I note his attempt at doing what is right, though I'm concerned that bringing a gun into counseling and classes was a considered option for him}* I'm not supposed to have it when I'm in the ambulance. I think that's stupid, too. Type of crap that I run into out there. Run into the middle of a motor vehicle accident and you pull up. People are fighting. That can turn on you in a second. You get a domestic violence call and you go in there because a neighbor calls and says that somebody's injured and you go there. Cops aren't there yet. You're the first one on the scene. You need something to protect yourself. I don't carry it anymore. Got spoken to. It just leaves you feeling a little more vulnerable, you know. That's all.

Brian: *{I note the trauma experiences and ongoing trigger events in his work}* So, it's an adjustment coming back, trying to get used to this. Sounds like it's been a rough time for you.

Dustin: Man, there's still a piece of me over there. You just kind of don't leave it always behind. But that's not why I'm here. *{vulnerability quickly covered by defensiveness}*

Brian: We're here to determine if you're a threat.

Dustin: I'm a threat. People know I'm a threat. I'm not a threat right now. And I'm not a threat in that class either, okay? *{mixed messages again about his dangerousness}*

Brian: One of the other things the professor asked you do was to leave after the outburst and you had some trouble with that. Ended up having things escalate . . .

Dustin: Because she . . . because she gives me crap about not coming to class. So I'm actually in class and then she tells me to leave class. *{he comes back to this odd argument claiming to not know the difference between required attendance and leaving class when threatened}* That's the reason why my grade is so low. I need to get a passing grade in order to get my degree. If I could just take the tests, send me off to a different room to take the tests, that'd be fine, but she wants me there. So then, because of that fucking cunt behind me, the teacher then yells at me and tells me to get out of the class. I'm not gonna leave. I pay to be there. That's my job on the line. I'm trying to get out of being an EMT. It doesn't pay shit. I can barely pay rent. I've had to fight my way . . . in order to get school paid for by the VA. It's stupid. It's stupid that I've been fighting this entire time to get school paid for in order to get my benefits and then she's telling me to get out. Man, I'm living from hand to mouth at this point. If I get the nursing degree I can work in an emergency department. They make more money. That's why I'm doing this. I gotta do what I gotta do to get there. *{multiple mentions of stress he is under and vulnerability}*

Brian: *{I attempt to go back to an early summary about his stress level}* Dustin, you don't know me very well, so I don't expect you to trust me; in fact, I'd worry about you if you came in and were immediately trusting everything I said. I think being a little curious about who I am and what's going on is important. I said earlier on it seemed like you were having trouble balancing things and I don't think you agreed fully with that.

Dustin: No, I don't.

Brian: {I push forward, attempting to be more direct and genuine} Okay. I keep listening to your story though and it sounds like, man, if I had the kind of things that you have to try to balance in my life, you know, work, and different expectations, and the money issue, you know, I don't even know how you left the military, what happened there, why you transitioned back, you just have a lot of stuff going on. I'm struggling to try to understand how that *doesn't* impact your life. I mean that stress would be a lot for any man to handle.

Dustin: You do what you gotta do to get by. Just like you said. Any man does what he's gotta do to get there. That's it, man. *{a reduction in defensiveness but little admission of the stress related to the situation he is in}*

Brian: {exploring military exit} Why did you end up getting discharged?

Dustin: A knee injury. Medical. Honorable medical discharge. Tweaked it in basic initially and then we were doing a house clearing and I ended up tripping going down the stairs. Feel like an asshole for it. But I tripped going down the stairs and it popped completely. Wore a brace. Tried to get back on and then finally after going to orthopedics, and various other things through the VA, you know, they sent me back, and they gave me the discharge. Clean. Got a good record but now I've had to fight for all these benefits in order to get the disability, just to try to get the medical bills paid for, you know. The VA doesn't do anything. First of all, their doctors suck. They don't have any good orthopedic doctors who are actually able to patch this up, so most days I'm just wearing a brace when I'm on duty.

Brian: {continuing his story, assessing daily stress} So the pain's still there with the knee . . .

Dustin: Oh yeah. When I woke up yesterday, I couldn't walk. I'm using a cane some days just to get up and down the stairs.

Brian: Wow, that must be pretty brutal.

Dustin: Yeah. But you deal with it. It's pain. Whatever. *{vulnerability followed by defensiveness}*

Brian: I've not been in the military myself, but I've watched some of those news shows about the benefits and the problems that people have had after getting discharged. It sounds like that fits with your experience.

Dustin: Yeah. Man. News shows. That's an understatement. Phone calls. Letters. Appointments. Just one thing after another in order to make sure I've got the correct benefits. Then I had to fight in order to get the school paid for. My job isn't going to pay for me to leave them, to become a nurse and stop being an EMT. If I wanted to do a paramedic, they might help with that, but because I want to be a nurse and not a paramedic . . . I don't want to ride around in a truck my entire life. I don't wanna be climbing up and down stairs picking up fat people {*objectification, dehumanizing language again*} in order to actually get them into . . . I need to actually have something that's in one location and get it done. Let them bring them to me. My work won't pay for that so now I have to fight for the GI Bill in order to get the school paid for. And you know, just like they're giving me crap about the knee trying to get an outside doctor, they're giving me crap about going to school because I have the medical discharge and I gotta prove that it's honorable and it's just phone call after phone call after phone call. And nobody knows anything, so it's just been going on for years.

Brian: {*I note his ongoing chronic stress dealing with the knee pain and accessing services*} Did you ever have to go to counseling or anything through the VA? Deal with any of that stuff? Any type of mental health things?

Dustin: Nah. Man. You get the discharge when you come back. They sit down with you for two seconds, and of course your sergeant tells you right before you get out, "Okay, don't say this, don't say that," just so you can get it done with so you can get back. You know. You're not suicidal. You're not gonna kill anybody. You're not gonna do anything else. You're not hearing voices. You're sleeping okay.

Brian: Your rubber stamp.

Dustin: Yeah, exactly. And that's what I'm hoping to get done here. Just let me go back to class.

Brian: Have you ever been in counseling before?

Dustin: Nah.

Brian: No medications or anything like that?

Dustin: No. No medications. No. I mean I take the painkillers for the knee, but that's about it.

Brian: Any problems with the painkillers, or do they work pretty well?

Dustin: Nah, man. I don't want to get addicted to them or anything like that. That's what booze is for.

Brian: {*I note the potential for substance abuse. Defensiveness seems to be lowering some*} So, some supplemental painkillers I'm hearing . . .

Dustin: Nah, man. No, no, no. There's no problem with painkillers. It's more of a pain in the ass. The VA won't . . . has a hard time even giving me medications for anything for the knee. They have all sorts of different limitations for how many they're going to give you, how long you can take them, and then since I've been on them for awhile, it's chronic, and it's just all sorts of problems. It's not even worth it. It's not even worth it. Take high doses of ibuprofen and I'm feeling fine and that's pretty much all it is. That and the knee brace is what get me through.

Brian: I'm noticing your tattoos. Sounds like over there or over here where you got 'em? *{building rapport, exploring visible tattoos for meaning}*

Dustin: Both. Pretty much over here. Got a couple of small ones.

Brian: Which ones?

Dustin: Man, I'm covered in 'em, man. Which one? This one? I've got a tiger. Got it all around. Got a half-sleeve. Got a couple half-sleeves. Got a back piece.

Brian: Those look like ravens or birds or something.

Dustin: Yeah, man. They're crows. Crows and ravens, both. Got some fire and wind. Dude, I'm not here to talk about my tattoos though. *{defensiveness returns as he realizes he is opening up}*

Brian: Yeah, yeah. My bad. *{I demonstrate it is okay to be wrong hoping to encourage more vulnerability}*

Dustin: Is that gonna get me back to class? If you wanna buddy-buddy with me and get me back to class that way, that's fine. But man, I just wanna get out of here. I'm tired of this. I see you're trying to help me relax. I see you're trying to help me relax with this. I'm relaxed. I'm in control. I just want to go back to class and get this over with. *{interesting response to my vulnerability toward him with an immediate attack. He discredits my motives, lacks trust}*

Brian: *{attempt to reconnect}* See it's interesting. I think if I were teaching the class, and we were just talking, or hanging out, I don't think you and I would have a whole lot of problems.

Dustin: I'm not going to hang out with my teacher from class. Trust me.

Brian: I think if I were . . .

Dustin: Oh, you. You teach it?

Brian: If I were teaching your class, it seems like when you get upset though that's where the problems are. We're both kind of relaxed here. We're having a conversation. You seem relaxed. I'm relaxed. I think it's when it gets tense. When stuff builds up. When you felt disrespect . . . was it disrespect, you know, by her? Talking about . . . was it your sexual performance in class? That's a little harsh to hear. *{attempt at a summary of the conflict Dustin finds himself in}*

Dustin: Dude, she's mouthing off to this fucking cunt behind her. She's talking to her friend. She makes a joke. Something about my limp. Because I was bringing my cane with me that day to top it all off. And she mouthed off behind me and of course the teacher didn't hear any of that.

Brian: So she was mouthing off about . . .

Dustin: [worked up] She was mouthing off. No. Who? Which one was mouthing off? Oh, the teacher started mouthing off to me after this bitch mouthed off to me. And after she was talking to her friend she said, "I'll say whatever I want." And I said, "No you fucking won't. You won't say any shit about me."

Brian: So she was making fun of your leg. Making fun of your disability.

Dustin: I don't know what she was making fun of. She made a comment. All I heard was, "He's limp." That's all I heard from behind me. And then she snickered to her friend. And then I told her she's not going to say that stuff and get away with it. That's what I told her.

Brian: {attempt to move toward a solution together} So here's our conundrum. You go back into class. Will this happen again?

Dustin: She keeps her mouth shut. No. It won't happen again.

Brian: {I comment on his unrealistic suggestion at a solution} It's really hard for me to control that.

Dustin: Well, maybe she should be in this counseling session instead of me. Maybe the one who opened up her mouth and started to provoke me because I fucked her one night should be in this counseling session and maybe she should deal with her daddy issues.

Brian: But she's not here now. *{redirection}*

Dustin: No, she's not.

Brian: You're here now.

Dustin: Well, you know what? Maybe she should have been told to leave class. Maybe she should go to a different class. I don't know why I have to come in here because of her mouth.

Brian: {attempt get his attention and reframe the problem} Can I be straight with you about why that happened? I mean you seem like you want it straight. I mean I don't know that you like it . . .

Dustin: Be straight with me, Doc. Go ahead, be straight with me.

Brian: {I try more direct challenge as any vulnerability on my part brings an attack} Well, I think when you responded the way you did to her, you know, it made it into something different. Then the professor saw and now you are where you are. I mean you've worked with people before. You know. You worked for the army. You've been under supervision with your EMT job. Then it becomes a failure to comply. A university official asked you leave the classroom. You refused. Police had to be brought in.

Dustin: I followed the police. I left when the police came in. I didn't start swinging. I didn't take it to the next level.

Brian: {I continue to push} That's my worry, Dustin. If you started swinging, I don't even think we'd be having the conversation. I just don't think you'd be at school anymore.

Dustin: That's why I didn't swing. She's giving me mixed messages. The teacher's telling me I need to come into class. Then she's telling me I need to get out of class. Get into class. Get out of class. Which is it? Which is going to help my grade? You know what? You give me an A, you give me the grade I deserve, you know what? I'll leave class and I won't come back. I don't have a problem with that. But if somebody's mouthing off behind me, I'm going to do what's necessary to protect myself.

Brian: {restatement of why his solution won't work} And that's where we're stuck. Because I can't control whether people are going to mouth off or not.

Dustin: Get her into counseling. Tell her to keep her mouth shut. Maybe get an agreement going on here. You know. That teacher is not my superior officer. I don't have to listen to everything she says.

Brian: This one girl. Is there something special about her that's been . . .

Dustin: [laughs] There was nothing special about her. *{degrading, objectifying language}*

Brian: So it's more the circumstance that you found yourself in, her disrespect for you.

Dustin: Yeah. That's exactly what it is. Again, if somebody disrespects you, you assert your authority and you get that respect. Especially from some dumb woman behind me who's mouthing off. Okay. We're going back and forth, man. You know.

Brian: It's a tough thing to decide. It's a difficult situation. Because from where I'm sitting, it sounds like you're very dedicated to school. You're interested in being here. You want to finish.

Dustin: I want to make something of myself, man. I've done it so far. I'm not gonna stop.

Brian: {summary of the dilemma} Yet, if you want to go back to class, and this happens again, it sounds like the same response would happen again. So I'm stuck with how we can set it up so it doesn't happen that way again.

Dustin: {offers more useful solutions} Sit her in a different part of the class. Don't have her sit two rows behind me. I'll move my seat. I'll sit in a different corner. But again. It has to do with me being sent in here because she mouthed off. Again, it's her freaking problem. Tell her to be quiet. I'll be quiet. I just want to get this done. I need to just get back to class. I've already missed a week and a half at this point between the times you guys can actually squeeze me in here.

Brian: {encouraging him to reflect on what he might lose} It's taken some time to get you in here.

Dustin: {describing his stress and worry about returning in good standing} Class is three times a week and I've already missed a week and a half. I've missed four classes because of this. And I'm already getting crap. I'm trying to get the assignments done but I think because she's upset at what happened . . . she's taking her sweet ass time in order to get me the assignments so I can keep on going on with the school. I just want to move on.

Brian: {focusing on the next step} Well, thinking about that moving on, it's part of the challenge I think for us. To be honest with you, I think we have a couple of options. Part of the experience here is I'm going to do a write-up based on what we talked about, and share some of the information back with the dean, and then I think the dean's going to make a decision about whether or not . . .

Dustin: So it's not your decision?

Brian: I consult with him. It's based on some of our conversation, but it's not my decision directly, no.

Dustin: What's your opinion? Can I go back to class? It's not your decision, but what are you gonna tell her?

Brian: {*Dustin expresses a need, from a vulnerable position. I am aware I need a careful response here*} Well, that's a good question. I feel like it's a little tough for me right now to kind of net out what I would say because I feel stuck here. I feel like you're really trying. We don't totally agree on the whole balancing thing, but from my perspective it seems like you have a lot of shit on your plate and you're trying to juggle that . . . {*using some of his language to connect*} trying to balance all these different things and it's hard. So you know, I see on one hand, you working almost to capacity to be able to reach your goals and I appreciate that, I like that. On the other hand, I feel like one misstep from this other woman, and you go pretty quick. I don't know if you feel like a zero-to-sixty guy, you know? We haven't really talked about anger or how you feel about things, but you know it seems like if someone gets in your face, you said someone cuts you off in traffic, I mean you go from peaceful, easy feeling to a needle in the red. At least from where I'm sitting. I don't know if that's right or not. {*I request clarification from Dustin*}

Dustin: You lose your temper when people do stuff, and you do what you gotta do. If somebody pushes my buttons, I lose it. But I can control it when I have to. Like you said. Like I told you before, I'm a man. You do what you gotta do in order to get by, in order to get what you gotta get. But you know what? If somebody provokes me in class . . . I didn't swing at her. I didn't swing at the guy coming here who cut me off. I can hold it together when I need to. Yes, do I lose it occasionally? Yeah. Man, everybody loses their temper occasionally.

Brian: {*exploring social connections*} Dustin, tell me a little bit more about your friends at work. The EMTs and people you hang out with. How would you describe those relationships?

Dustin: Man, they got your back. That's pretty much what it is. You're all seeing the same things. You're doing the same things. Some of it's not pretty. You need people who have your back, who are gonna be there when you need them. Again, if I'm getting into something with a guy in a multivehicle accident that's gonna be fighting me, I need to know that somebody has my back on there. When I run into a house, you know, because there's something going on, I need to know someone's got my back. It's the same thing as an EMT. You gotta know when you're rolling up on something that you know, somebody's there for you, reads your mind, knows what you need next. And that's what it is. I mean it's . . .

Brian: Did you ever get a chance to hang out with them outside of work? Do you guys have a . . . *{explore quality of friendships}*

Dustin: Yeah, we go out drinking . . . Don't wear our uniforms. It's the only people I really have time to hang out with. I mean I've got class how many nights a week. You know. And at the same time, and I'm banned from all my classes until we get this done, so . . .

Brian: Frustrating spot to be . . .

Dustin: Yeah. I've been drinking a little bit more this week because I've had a little more free time, but other than that, you know. You're working 24-hour shifts . . . certain number of hours, not 24 hours straight. But those are the only people I have a chance to hang out with. I'm there. I'm at class. I'm at home. That's it.

Brian: *{assessing substance abuse}* Can I ask what an average night of drinking looks like for you? Are you a beer guy? Or a hard liquor guy? Or a shot guy?

Dustin: Yeah. All of the above. Depends on who's buying, man. I'll drink anything. It's perfectly fine. Why? You getting into whether I have an alcohol problem or something? Is that where you're going with this one? *{Dustin sees through this and calls me out on my questions}*

Brian: Little bit, yeah. *{a genuine reply}*

Dustin: Yeah. I don't have a problem. I don't drink on duty. I don't drink in class. Okay, I'll have a couple before class. But seriously, she's sitting there. She's droning on for ages, man. You gotta have a couple in you sometimes just to kinda cruise through class. But I'm not an alcoholic. I don't go to meetings. That's not how that works.

Brian: *{calling him out on his drinking behavior}* Did you just subtly tell me that you go to class drunk sometimes?

Dustin: Ahh, man. It's more buzzed. I'm not drunk. You don't go in drunk. I know this stuff is boring as hell. If I'm just sitting there. I'm not a doodler. I don't doodle. So I've got to have something to numb me out a little in class. Whatever.

Brian: *{assessing how others see his drinking}* Did you ever have any of your friends or family say that you have an alcohol problem? Call you on it?

Dustin: No. I don't really have any family that I'm in contact with anymore, and I drink with the people I work with, after work. So no, man. Nobody knows me well enough in order to tell me that I have an alcohol problem. Trust me.

Brian: Do you ever worry about that?

Dustin: No. I don't drive drunk.

Brian: *{subtly assessing for trauma reactions}* I would imagine in that kind of career, you see a lot of results of that. The multivehicle accidents and such.

Dustin: Yeah, man. Of course. I'm not gonna be one of those guys. Do I drink? Yes. Do I have nightmares? Yes. But whatever, man. *{defensive response}*

Brian: {assessing for additional substance use} Do you ever mess around with anything stronger than alcohol?

Dustin: Nah, man. Just booze. Just booze. Told you the painkillers when I first got the first injury, but they stopped prescribing that to me and I'm not gonna go shooting that shit in the street. I'm not gonna go trying to get that stuff. And, more trouble than it's worth trying to do it through the EMTs and the paramedics or anything like that. I'd lose my job. You gotta make it by. So I'm not doing anything. So alcohol's the way I go. That's pretty much it.

Brian: Do you EMTs have drug tests or something?

Dustin: No, no. But they watch what drugs they have. The paramedics have certain cases and they have their drugs. So I'm not gonna go trying to steal any of those drugs or get one of them to do it. Honestly, if I wanna get into the emergency department, I'm not gonna be trying a substance abuse problem or anything like that. I don't want anything on my record for substance abuse either. I do not use drugs, okay? Is that clear? *{defensive again and showing insight into the ramification of the assessment process}*

Brian: {addressing his ability to see through subtle questions} I appreciate your honesty with that kind of stuff. I feel like sometimes when we're talking here that you kind of, I don't know whether it's you being in the military or being an EMT, but you see through any potential ruse I have for a question. Like you kinda almost know the question behind the question in my head.

Dustin: Dude, I'm on the street.

Brian: There's no fooling you, I guess.

Dustin: I'm on the street, man. You know what people are gonna ask. I know how to get the answers that I need from the person I'm talking to on the street. Are you trying to butter me up or something like that? Because, yeah, no, I know what they're doing. Yeah. I don't have a substance abuse problem. Let's just leave it at that. I'm not drinking right now. I don't have anything. I'm not having anything right now. I'm sober when I'm in here. Do I have some before class occasionally? Yes. Do I drink when I'm off duty? Yes. Do I drink to go to sleep occasionally? Yes. Do I take sleeping pills? No. *{defensive, challenging reaction remains consistent throughout assessment}*

Brian: {attempt to engage Dustin on a different level, assessing his ability to see my perspective} I feel like I'm kind of stuck sometimes with you. Like, back to the tattoos for a second. It's hard for me to notice something and appreciate it and just want to talk to you about it without feeling like you think I'm trying to butter you up or trying to get inside your head or shrink your brain or something.

Dustin: We know why I'm here.

Brian: True.

Dustin: I'm here for you to assess me and determine whether I can go back to class. So, what's with all the crap and the bullshit and everything around it talking about my mom and dad and stuff like that? We're here to figure out whether I can go back to class. And I asked you before whether I can go back to class and you kind of gave me a wishy-washy answer on that. What do you need to hear so I can go back to class? I need to go back to class. I don't want to flunk this semester because of a week and a half's worth of missing classes for tests that I know I can pass because of some dumb bitch that said something in class. That's all.

Brian: {trying a different approach and challenging his objectified language to test his ability to hear critical feedback} That's not as helpful to get to back to class. I can tell you that, and I don't know if it's just part of the EMT world or the military world, but that kind of language in the higher ed world . . . it sticks out. You know, when you use that kind of language to describe women, it worries people. It's out of step. I'm sure you've noticed that at the college. People aren't using that kind of language as much, maybe I don't know. But when you refer to women as bitches, and whores, and cunts, it's . . .

Dustin: It was the girl I slept with. I know what she is. I did not refer to the teacher as that. I did not refer to the dean as that. I'm in here. I don't refer to my boss as that. I toe the line. I know when to keep my mouth shut. But somebody that I've slept with? You know what? I'm gonna call her what I want. I've seen her naked, okay? I fucked her. I know what it's like. I can call her what I want. {I note this strange entitled attitude} If somebody has a problem with that. I'm not shouting that in class . . . unless she provokes me. But you know what? I'll sit on the other side of class. I'll keep my mouth shut. Is that what I need in order to get back? Because that's where it is. I need to get back to class in order to move on with my life.

Brian: {responding to his question about what happens next} Let me be direct because I know you thought I was kind of ditching your question before. For me, I was just trying to learn a little more about you, but I can see why it feels like I'm being wishy-washy or moving away from it. I'm not quite sure yet. There's a lot of . . .

Dustin: {upset at the idea he may not be able to return} Wait. So wait a second. So you're telling me you're not being wishy-washy by telling me you're not sure? That's a funny way to say . . .

Brian: Well . . .

Dustin: No, go ahead. Talk. Talk.

Brian: Thank you. And that's why we're just thinking of some different language. Can I not know and not be described as wishy-washy? For me, wishy-washy feels like I'm all over the place and I'm kinda not figuring things out. For me, I just, I haven't decided yet what I would write. I think I'm still getting to know you a little bit. You've got a lot going on in your life, and trying to sum this all up in a half-hour talk is hard. So let me answer the question that you asked before because you've asked me a couple times now. I'm not quite sure yet, but what I'd like to do is I'd like to meet with you again, and I'd like to talk to the dean. [Dustin begins to interrupt again] And . . . hang on a sec. . . Talk to the dean in the middle and say . . .

Dustin: Can I go back to class?

Brian: Well, that's what I'm getting to. I think if you can come back in and we can do this again, and talk a little bit more and get to know each other a little bit more that we could be in a position of getting you back in . . . some kind of moving forward with that. I don't know that you can go back in the classroom right now.

Dustin: [upset at the prospect of not passing this semester] It took me a week and a half to get this freaking appointment. It happened last Monday. I tried calling on Tuesday. Right now, it's Thursday a week later. So I'm missing a week and a couple of days of class. If I can go back to class, I will come in here for another appointment. Whatever it takes. Because I just need to get back in there because she's already giving me crap about missing it and if my attendance. . . Again, she doesn't answer my emails. I can't show up to her door in order to talk to her about it until I get in here first.

Brian: {*addressing his concern about failing the class because the school banned him from class*} Yeah. Let me say this. I can say that you're not going to be penalized for missing class because you're in a threat assessment process and you have some conduct things going on, okay?

Dustin: So those days aren't going to be knocked off for attendance problems?

Brian: We will work with you around that, and that's what the dean's going to help you with. I don't know all the details on that, but if you're held up here and you can't go back to class until you finish this interview and I talk to the dean, I can't see how we're going to punish you for that. If you're putting in the good faith, which you are, you're coming in and talking to me, that's a good place to start. What I don't want to have happen, Dustin, to be honest with you, is having you showing back up to class, and have her still sitting next to you and she says something, and . . . {*attempting to move the interview to a close*}

Dustin: I told you, she'll sit in the back corner, I'll sit in the front corner. Opposite corners. I won't say anything to her.

Brian: {*unfortunately, I fall into his argument here*} So you guys are walking out together . . . she mumbles something under her breath . . .

Dustin: You know what? If she's tailing me off campus, she's got a bunch of other problems going on that we're gonna have to deal with. In class. Again. Is she coming here? Does she have an appointment coming to see you or what?

Brian: {*regaining control and being firm*} I can't really talk about that one way or another. She wasn't the one who made a threat in class and that tends to be what I specialize in is talking to people about threats.

Dustin: What can we do? So, can I go back to class if I say that I'll meet with you next Thursday? I'll meet with you next Thursday if I can start taking my classes this next week. *{searching for me to give him an answer}*

Brian: It's not up to me.

Dustin: I don't have a . . .

Brian: And I'm sorry about that. It's up to the dean.

Dustin: How long is the dean going to take to get back to you on this?

Brian: *{attempting to reassure him I am attending to this right now}* I'm going to call her right after our conversation's over today and I'll share with her my opinion about what's going on, and let me tell you what that's going to be. *{summary of problems}* That you're someone who's . . . and this is my opinion so you can definitely chime in if you don't agree, but this is how I see things . . . you're someone who's stressed; you've got a lot of stuff going on in your life. This was a one-time incident where you got upset at another girl in class and you're looking at ways to get back into class and to finish off the semester well so that you can reach your academic goals. And my feeling is that if you can connect up with someone, whether it's someone like me, or another counselor, someone to talk to you for a little bit, just to kind of make sure things are good for the rest of the semester, I think we can get you back in. But I can't promise that, and that's really going to be the dean's . . .

Dustin: *{interesting desire for connection with me, despite the defensiveness throughout the interview}* Am I going to be seeing you, or am I going to have to start this whole damn thing over again with somebody else? So I'm going to have to get assessed by somebody else next week? Is that what you're telling me, or what?

Brian: You'll see me next week. We'll meet again. You talked a little bit about your family. I'm curious about your family. I'd like to talk about that.

Dustin: You want to go into my childhood. No. Not right now. We'll have a . . .

Brian: [sarcastic joking] We'll have you lay down on the couch and . . . no, it's not going to be like that.

Dustin: You better be joking, bro.

Brian: Here's the thing, Dustin. I feel like you've put me in a bit of a stuck place and I want to get to know you and I want to understand where you're coming from but any time I try to do something nice or I'm seeming curious, I think you're wondering, why is this guy doing this? You're a little suspicious. Which, I don't know, if I'm in your shoes, maybe I feel that way too. *{attempting to address the defensiveness}*

Dustin: Yeah. Because you could tell them not to let me back into class and they won't let me back into class and there goes my shot at becoming something better, man. So, yeah, I'm a little suspicious of you, you gotta say that, man.

Brian: That's fair. And I personally don't think you're holed up in your apartment with an air AR-15 assault rifle waiting to do stuff. Do you have an AR-15 assault rifle? *{probing around weapon knowledge and access}*

Dustin: Yes, I have an AR-15, man. Yeah, I have a couple of guns. But I'm not gonna . . . I'm not waiting to do stuff. I'm not going anywhere other than the shooting range with it. I told you that. I follow the rules. I don't bring my guns on campus. I'm not going on a shooting spree. I'm in control. I have a job. I have a career. I look where I'm going. I have somewhere to go. I wanna become a nurse. I told you all that, okay? I'm not gonna be going into class shooting, okay? *{somewhat reassuring}*

Brian: *{trying to summarize next steps}* Yes. So I would say that's where we'd head from here. I'm going to talk with the dean after our conversation and let her know that you've agreed to come back in and talk with me once again. I would guess that she'd be pretty comfortable knowing that you're coming back in again. She'd see that as being cooperative. That we could work out something. Maybe there's a chance that you could do that class online. That you can catch up on some of your assignments. We'll talk about all that. I don't know . . .

Dustin: The . . . young woman . . . look, see I didn't call her that [other word]. *{interesting movement toward cooperation here near the end of session, perhaps aware now that he hasn't been as cooperative as he should have been so far}*

Brian: I appreciate that . . .

Dustin: See, I'm working with you. She's only in two out of the four classes I'm taking this semester. Can I go to the other two then? Because I'm not gonna run into her at that point, or what?

Brian: *{finding a middle ground; compromise}* That seems reasonable. Let me check with the dean on that.

Dustin: I don't want this stopping every single fucking thing that I've got going on in class, just because of one class . . . two classes that she's in because we had one outburst in one of them.

Brian: *{reframing the entire set of concerns beyond how he spoke to the student}* I understand that. And to me, the part I want you to understand is the reaction to her was concerning. The other reaction we're concerned about is when the professor asked you to leave class, that's the other piece, you know, that the dean's gonna talk to you about. There's an issue, in the conduct, with the failure to comply. When the university asks you to do something, you have some responsibility to do . . .

Dustin: Yeah, but she's also asking me to come to class. So she's asking me to come to class, then she's asking me to leave class. You can't have it both ways and still give me a grade. *{return to this argument again}* You know what? I'll do it all online. I'll answer the questions online. I'll take the tests online. I don't have a problem with that. In fact, I would love to do that, but she's telling me to come to class, then when I come to class, she tells me to get out of class.

Brian: We'll try to find the middle ground there.

Dustin: Yeah. There's gotta be somewhere in there for me to get . . . I need to take that class. That's a requirement.

Brian: {attempting a compliment} I know you feel like I'm buttering you up here, but I appreciate you. This is not an easy time to come in and talk to me. I get that. Some doctor's in here trying to figure out if you're good to go or not. You've had a lot of other people in your life telling you things, in the military, in the EMT job. I appreciate you hanging with me in this setting and talking through some of this stuff. That's not easy.

Dustin: [a bit sarcastic] I appreciate you. Let me take my class. And telling the dean, telling the teacher that I could take my class. I would appreciate that. Just let me back in there and we will be good to go. I will come back here and I'm not getting all touchy-feely with you, but just let me back and start taking these classes again. And do an online thing. I don't care. I just want to get grades. I need to do this.

Brian: Okay. Thanks for taking the time today.

Sample Threat Assessment Letter to Referral Source

Dean's Office
University of Education
1 Academic Circle Drive
College Town, USA

To Whom It May Concern:

This is a summary of my contact with Dustin, who was referred for a threat assessment following a verbal threat made to another student in the classroom. I have completed this assessment and feel there is some reason for concern regarding Dustin's threat and the potential for violence in the future.

Dustin has a history in the U.S. military serving in the army as a medical technician. He was honorably discharged from service and works as a full-time EMT while completing his coursework to become an emergency department nurse. His grades are adequate, with a GPA of a 2.8 in the program.

Dustin projects an entitled attitude during the interview and feels this entire process is beneath him. He feels justified making the threat because he "slept with the girl in question" and shows little insight or remorse for his actions. He failed to comply with the instructor's request to leave the classroom and was escorted out by police. Dustin has a past criminal record following a fight with a bouncer that resulted in 6 months probation.

Dustin is at risk for engaging in impulsive violence in response to stressful or irritating social interactions. Dustin's motivation for violence seems rooted in his arousal response, to release or express himself or control or change the environment. He escalates quickly and challenges others he finds himself in disagreement with.

Dustin has a strong work ethic and shares few problems with his work colleagues at the ambulance service. He alludes to this positive experience at work to be a result of the blue-collar nature of his coworkers and the darker, gallows humor they share in the face of tragedy and the chaos of emergency medical response. There is also a discrepancy between Dustin's desire to help others through his career choices (soldier, EMT, nurse) and his general comments supporting a rather negative view of other people. This is an area in need of further exploration.

Of particular concern is Dustin's objectifying and misogynist language that flows through the entire interview. He sees women as objects for his pleasure and demonstrates little ability to empathize with their thoughts, feelings, or concerns. During his threatening conflict with the female student, he demonstrates a lack of guilt or anxiety related to the incident. These serve as disinhibitors toward future violence.

Dustin's lack of attention and appreciation for the seriousness of his language serves as a destabilizing factor. His drinking to excess and admission to showing up to class intoxicated also create a destabilizing factor for future violence. Dustin shares an extensive knowledge of weapons based on his military background, and he owns several firearms. He does not include shooting or gun violence in his threats and gives little evidence that he would use a firearm to attack others.

It is unlikely Dustin has a desire to change his behavior, but rather has a desire instead to stay enrolled and complete his study. This external "carrot" may be useful as a motivator for Dustin to engage in therapeutic treatment to address his impulsive outbursts, objectified feelings toward women, and poor frustration tolerance in the face of difficult circumstances.

While there does not appear to be an immediate risk of violence to the female he threatened in the class, it would be advisable to attempt some kind of mediation between the two, with the student conduct officer, prior to Dustin returning to the classroom. Also of importance is addressing the class that witnessed his outburst and escort out by law enforcement, as well as the instructor who was placed in a difficult position of having to stop the lesson and react to this crisis event.

Given Dustin's difficulty empathizing with others' perspectives, the mediation will be a delicate process that should seek to balance challenging his behavior with the promise of being able to continue his program and have the incident dealt with internally at school rather than publicly in the community (which may threaten his EMT job).

Further treatment to address the anger, impulse control, objectification, and depersonalizing language should be required as a condition for Dustin to return to the program. Given the nature of his threat and subsequent escort by police from the classroom, it may be warranted to explore an Incomplete or the option to finish the coursework in another class, under the supervision of another professor, or online from home. Central focus points of treatment should be focus on active listening, reducing objectified language, increasing tolerance for different opinions, and exploring other options when he encounters the temptation to yell or threaten someone in the future.

While there is a low likelihood of immediate violence based on Dustin's evaluation, there remains a level of concern given his lack of remorse, history of impulsive action, and fragile willingness to get back into class (but only based on his terms). Future monitoring, treatment, and mediation are key to preventing an escalation in this situation.

Respectfully Submitted,

Dr. Brian Van Brunt, LPCC
Director of Counseling

Summary

In this chapter, I provided detailed transcripts of two threat assessments. Stacie's case provides insight into how to assess past mental health treatment issues such as suicide, social support assessment, and exploration of an incident with a person who is anxious and worried about the potential outcome. Stacie is cooperative throughout the assessment, and further connection to treatment is a relatively straightforward matter.

It would be essential for the clinician to gather additional information regarding the online blog that Stacie mentions during the assessment. Obtaining direct access to this document is critical in developing a formulation of violence as well as understanding her thoughts related to Professor Galloway.

In contrast to Stacie, Dustin provides an overview of one of the most difficult individuals I have ever encountered. His objectifying and misogynistic language throughout the interview is difficult to hear and raises concern for future depersonalization toward a target. Dustin shares a rather concerning history with firearms, has a military background that assisted him in learning how to use the lethal weapons, and shares that he considers bringing them to class and work. Dustin also shares a substance abuse history and a general unwillingness to comply with the threat assessment process willingly. He often becomes defensive and aggressive to questions.

In Dustin's case, further exploration of his motivations to work in the helping profession would be useful. There is something of a contradiction in his distaste for other people and his pursuit of careers in the helping profession such as soldier, EMT, and nurse. Additionally, someone should further talk with the potential secondary target (the professor) to better ascertain if there is additional information that might be useful to mitigate a future potential threat or attack in response to her involving law enforcement.

For the rest of the assessment section of the text, I will use these cases to help illustrate threat assessment concepts. Chapter 13 offers some insight into how Stacie and Dustin may go through mandated treatment following their assessments.

Questions for Further Discussion

1. During Stacie's assessment, Van Brunt moves more slowly to the incident in order to lower her anxiety and increase her willingness to share more information. Discuss some of the challenges to this approach.

2. Stacie mentions an online blog that she keeps about her feelings related to Professor Galloway. What are some ways to gain access to this blog? What kind of information found in the blog would increase concern? What kind of information might decrease the concern?

3. Dustin is a difficult individual to build rapport with during the assessment. What are some ways you might try to address his coarse language, defensiveness, and general argumentative opinions?

4. Dustin talks about his work performance, past military service, and difficulty with other people. How relevant is his behavior in the workplace and military to his current behaviors in the classroom? What are some additional questions you might have about these activities related to his current behavior?

5. How would you approach ending the interview with Dustin? Are there additional questions you would ask? How might you handle the follow-up around his substance abuse in the classroom, his brief mention of a weapon in the classroom, and the potential for threat against his professor for calling the police? Are there other ways to connect Dustin to potential treatment?

Chapter 4

Central Threat
CONCEPTS

Chapter Highlights

1. This chapter reviews a dozen or so essential threat concepts that form the foundation for the assessment. These concepts are foundational, rather than hierarchical, and are presented with examples to demonstrate how they are assessed in practice.
2. *Action and time imperative* refers to the immediacy of the potential attack. *Fixation and focus* address the narrowing of attention on a specific person, place, or system. In the context of a threat, *organization* and *disorganization* are terms used to refer to the internal consistency, preparation, and structure of the attack plan.
3. *Legacy tokens* are writings or media content prepared by the perpetrator to share a message; the content is intended to be found after the attack.
4. *Costuming* is an attacker's acquisition of military attire prior to an attack.
5. *Objectification* and *depersonalization* are methods used by an aggressor to dehumanize people who are targeted. This tendency is often observable during the threat assessment through the language and vocabulary chosen by the aggressor (person being assessed).

For years, I understood violence from a mental health perspective; I had received some threat assessment training from the National Association of Forensic Counselors (http://www.nationalafc.com) and the National Behavioral Intervention Team Association (www.nabita.org) and during my graduate studies in testing and assessment. In August 2011, I attended the annual conference of the Association of Threat Assessment Professionals, which brought together law enforcement, the Los Angeles Police Department, district attorneys, Federal Bureau of Investigation staff, the Secret Service, the Naval Criminal Investigation Service, and numerous threat assessment consulting firms and human resource departments to focus exclusively on threat and violence risk assessments.

For those interested in a better understanding of what to look for in term of workplace violence and risk, *Threat Assessment: A Risk Management Approach* (Turner & Gelles, 2003) offers an easy-to-read overview of several critical factors related to threat and risk assessment. (For a list of useful questions to ask when hiring or vetting a threat assessment professional to conduct an assessment for your workplace or college, see Appendix B.)

This chapter covers several key factors related to identifying and assessing dangerousness. The first of these is assessing the immediacy of an attack. The fixation and focus an individual has toward a particular target is also an important risk factor to assess: The closer and more focused an individual becomes on a particular person, place, or system, the more likely the attack. The organization or disorganization of an attack also becomes an area for exploration. How detailed and prepared is an individual to carry out a systemic and structured attack against an individual, system, or group? *Legacy tokens* are writings or media content prepared by the perpetrator prior to the attack that are typically designed to be found following the attack as a way to share a message. Individuals who plan targeted violence often engage in *costuming*, acquiring a uniform or military attire prior to an attack. The attacker might be motivated by a desire to blend in with law enforcement or to adopt the persona needed to carry out the act of aggression. Objectification and depersonalization are discussed as potential risk factors that allow the aggressor to dehumanize the intended victims. The seeing of another as separate from oneself is one of the building blocks necessary prior to carrying out a rampage shooting or other extreme violent event.

Action and Time Imperative

The action and time imperative relates to the impending nature of a potential attack. The *action imperative*, according to Turner and Gelles (2003),

> refers to the need on the part of the person to take personal action to resolve the situation . . . the person has determined that all other avenues (administrative, legal, criminal, etc.) are not going to help with the resolution. (p. 97)

The issue for the clinician is to determine the suspect's desire to act on the threats being made. In the case of Stacie (see Chapter 3), her threat seemed to lack a sense of planning or urgency. In fact, it would be reasonable to suggest that her threat was made impulsively and in direct reaction to an embarrassing statement made by Professor Galloway. However, one cannot assume that she was simply responding in an angry manner to a hurtful or embarrassing comment by the professor and drop the exploration of the incident. Even though that might be the most likely scenario, the clinician should explore where the statement itself came from. Was this, perhaps, a brief unprotected defensive window where Stacie was less guarded and let slip a private fantasy? Has she researched what car Professor Galloway drives? Has she looked on YouTube for informational videos about cutting brake lines? Could she possibly be planning some action against her professor? What evidence is there to support the scenario of a defensive, angry, impulsive statement with no attachment to reality? What supports this statement as potential leakage, or the "tip of the iceberg," for a more detailed fantasy or rehearsal of a plan to harm someone whom Stacie views as a mortal foe of her academic progress?

In terms of the time imperative, there is little evidence that Stacie has a sense of urgency to carry out a potential action against the professor. The entire premise of "cutting brake lines" presumes the person is unaware of the threat and would not check first to ensure the car has not been tampered with. However, following the dean's involvement, Stacie may now have a sense of urgency given that her threat may have compromised her course grade or her academic standing in the graduate program. Whereas the threat itself may not have any real danger behind it, the time imperative to retaliate against Professor Galloway or the school may be increased given the trouble she now faces.

In our other example with Dustin (Chapter 3), the threat against another student is immediate and pressing. Without intervention by the professor or campus police, it would be reasonable to assume that Dustin could very well have escalated to violence against the female student. There is a demand for her to comply with his direction to stop talking as well as a threat with a clear action and time imperative—if she chooses to continue talking about him, he will act.

In *Ending Campus Violence: New Approaches to Prevention* (Van Brunt, 2012), I highlighted several case examples where the action and time imperative are integral in understanding the individual's desire to commit violence.

In 2002, Robert Steinhäuser killed 16 and injured seven before committing suicide during the Gutenberg-Gymnasium shooting. He had been expelled from school and had concealed his expulsion from his parents for 6 months. His ruse would have been discovered as soon as the exam results were published. These pending exams created both the action and time imperative for him to act prior to his parents finding out about his expulsion.

The 1996 rejection of Frederick Davidson's second thesis defense at San Diego State University, and the requirement to successfully defend his thesis to secure a job, created a pressure to act immediately to punish his committee and then kill himself. The date of the second thesis defense became the time imperative for Davidson's attack. His lack of degree and job prospects drove his action to punish those he saw as responsible for his failure.

For the clinician conducting a risk assessment, attending to the external events that create a time pressure for the individual help assesses the sense of immediacy of a pending attack or violent event.

Examples of external stress events in educational settings are listed here:

- Failure on a key exam or test
- Dismissal from a program because of test scores or performance issues (such as a nursing or teacher education program)
- Suspension or expulsion following a conduct action
- Separation from an athletic team for an injury or poor conduct
- Lack of financial aid or housing options
- End of a job or internship tied to academics
- Looming graduation

Other external events might create an action or time imperative:

- Ending of a significant (or perceived-significant) romantic relationship
- Public dissemination of a closely held secret (e.g., sexual orientation)
- Life-threatening medical condition or chronic pain/injury
- Sudden change in family or home life (parents' divorce, financial disaster)

Overall, the action and time imperative address the immediacy of a potential attack. While there may be additional concerns and risk factors to mitigate, the action and time imperative are often the focus of law enforcement professionals when determining the need for direct intervention.

Fixation and Focus

Turner and Gelles (2003) suggested that individuals with a fixation and focus to their threats present a higher risk than those who lack these traits. *Fixations* are strongly held beliefs and obsessions about a certain group being responsible for the pain or suffering an individual is experiencing. Fixation relates to the degree of blame and how it is attributed; a group of individuals is stereotyped in a grandiose or sweeping manner. Examples of statements that reflect fixation include "Everyone from the Northeast is an elite, NPR-listening, Obama-loving liberal" or "All those from the Southeast are racist."

George Sodini (Van Brunt, 2012), a 48-year-old man who killed several women at an LA Fitness aerobics studio in Pennsylvania, desired to date much younger women and saw the resulting rejections as evidence that the women were the problem. He worked hard on making himself more attractive to younger women, and their rejection of him fed his conviction that they were responsible for hurting him. Sodini's misogyny and objectification of women then became a fixation that fueled his eventual violence.

If one detected in Stacie a fixation toward her professor or others in authority, exploration would be necessary to determine whether some deeper theme in her life might offer an explanation of why her anger may be especially present with someone like Professor Galloway. The first hypothesis here would be that he is simply an arrogant, power-hungry individual who crossed paths with a student who chose a different way of interacting with him besides capitulation or "going along to get along." It would be important to look for other evidence of her interactions with people in positions of power or authority. Perhaps there is some evidence of her having past problems with teachers in high school, her parents, or her intimate relationships.

With Dustin, there does appear to be a pattern of temporary relationships and a tendency toward objectification, or at least dismissiveness, with women. His threat, however, seems impulsive in nature, and there is little evidence of him actively seeking out women to put down or be in conflict with. In fact, the evidence seems to be that Dustin seeks out sexual relationships with women. Although there may be some dominance or control elements to these relationships, his threat in this instance seems more in reaction to a perceived attack or insult from a woman. The intensity of his response is of concern, as is his lack of appreciation for decorum and the rules of the classroom.

Focus is a further narrowing that occurs when an individual with a particular fixation begins to zero in on an individual, system, or location. Jason Hamilton displayed this level of fixation and focus in 2009 when he blamed his mathematics professor for a failing grade and took two shots at him with a .30-06 rifle (Van Brunt, 2012). He held a particularly entitled fixation and belief that his professors owed him a particular grade. This fixation then narrowed toward a single professor with whom he argued about his grade.

It is unlikely that Stacie has a fixation that all professors at her college are mistreating her, but she does develop a focus on Professor Galloway. We would be more concerned if we learned that Stacie kept a journal outlining ways she fantasized about hurting Professor Galloway, or if she kept a website insulting him anonymously and encouraging other students to contribute their frustrations.

With Dustin, it would be interesting to explore if he has had hostile verbal outbursts with other women he has dated before. Is this an isolated incident or a larger pattern of behavior from him? In other words, is there a particular focus on this one girl in class? Does that stand in contrast to his general fixation on women being more submissive and objectified in his worldview?

Sodini was fixated on the idea that more than 30 million women in the world had rejected him; he brought his frustrations into focus on the seven women he shot, killing three at an aerobics class in an LA Fitness club. It is this narrowing of focus and attribution of responsibility and blame that becomes an area of chief concern (Van Brunt, 2012).

Imagine that Stacie is separated from the program for her threat. She loses her financial aid and any chance at graduating and pursuing her career. Perhaps she becomes increasingly frustrated and develops a fixation on all graduate professors who lord their power over the weak in order to achieve some kind of dominance and fleeting sense of power. As time passes and her options for returning to her program diminish, she begins to narrow her fixation on the professor, who becomes the epitome of arrogance and singularly responsible for all of her problems. She begins to study him more carefully, where he lives and what his habits are. She thinks about trying to make him as miserable as she has become. This would be a demonstration of fixation and focus.

To better assess the presence of a fixation or focus in an assessment setting, the clinician establishes a rapport that helps reduce the defensiveness of the individual being assessed (see Chapter 2). For a student like Dustin who has an objectified view of women, the counselor performing the assessment must wrestle with finding the balance between building trust and losing boundaries. For example, if Dustin were to ask me, "So doc, tell me. Are you a tits or ass kind of guy?" I would have to be careful in my response. Although my temptation would be to launch a diatribe about objectification and depersonalization, doing so would have the effect of communicating to Dustin that this kind of language is not something that is tolerated in session. If the goal is to explore Dustin's objectification of women, shutting down this potential source of connection closes off the likelihood of further inquiry. Likewise, responding to Dustin's question by choosing one body part over another creates the potential for an unprofessional and boundary-violating relationship. In this specific case, I would recommend a middle of the road response such as, "I like everything about women. I don't think I could decide between the two." The response is distasteful, but it might secure gathering Dustin's trust without furthering the misogynist, objectifying exploration focused on my sexual preferences. Instead, this response encourages him to share more of his feelings with someone he now sees as a potential "guy's guy."

Female clinicians have the same challenge when assessing someone like Dustin. It would be easy to imagine Dustin engaging a female therapist in a potential flirtation or testing her willingness to tolerate his beliefs. My advice here is the same: I would encourage redirection, limited self-disclosure, and focus on balancing professionalism with creating a nonjudgmental environment that allows for maximum information gathering.

In treatment, addressed in the second half of this book, these goals shift slightly. The focus now becomes teaching the client and shaping enlightened, prosocial behavior. Challenging sexist or misogynistic viewpoints becomes an essential part of the therapy. At the assessment stage, information gathering becomes the prime focus.

Organization Versus Disorganization

Individuals with disorganized thoughts often do not have the same heightened risk as those with organized thoughts. Disorganization demonstrated in the person being assessed is reflected in his or her lack of planning and emphasis in a nonlinear manner. Here the person becomes frustrated at a variety of life stressors, and the points of conflict are often arbitrary. Although an individual who engages in multiple conflicts and finds various potential targets for his or her diatribes raises public safety concerns, the risk profile becomes heightened when an individual demonstrates a linear and logical pattern.

Dustin's frustrations with his female classmate represent a disorganized context for his threat. Although he makes the threat specifically to one person, further exploration of Dustin's past helps recognize that this is a larger pattern of thoughts and behavior. Like the spinning top on the table, Dustin reacts to whatever happens to be in the environment closest to him at the time. His threat, "Shut your god damn ignorant mouth or I'll shut if for you," requires follow-up and the creation of sanctions related to his behavior in order to retain his status in class as well as at the college. It does not, however, seem to possess a deeper sense of fixation and focus on this one girl.

Dustin's scenario lacks any evidence of a significant mental health component. There are no intrusive thoughts or delusional beliefs. There is certainly some objectified language and antisocial thoughts but little evidence of a major mood disorder or a disturbance that would rise to a personality disorder at this time. Some whose threats have a quality of disorganization are clearly fueled by a diffuse sense of frustrations, delusions, paranoid thoughts, and hallucinations that create a disparate set of potential targets. They become enraged at their surroundings and lack any linear threat or sense of disturbance to any consistent target. Imagine an individual who is upset at his parents for not giving him all of his entitlement paycheck money to spend the way he would like, his doctor for continuing to prescribe the same antipsychotic medication that has upsetting side effects, his teachers in school for being inflexible with accepting late assignments, and parking enforcement on campus for issuing him more parking tickets than other students. The disorganization of the threat pattern counteracts the creation of a linear attack plan; he smacks into those around him with a disorganized sense of focus and quickly moves to the next thing.

This is not to say that all those with mental illness find themselves so distracted as to prevent constructing a linear and organized plan to commit violence. In May 2003, Biswanath Halder was a troubled individual who developed several rather paranoid and delusional ideas that Case Western Reserve University was conspiring against him. Halder sued another student whom he accused of "hacking" his computer account and deleting files for a multi-million-dollar business plan. The psychologist who evaluated Halder said, "He was fighting cyber criminals, by striking at the university he made the world a safer place. His goal was to 'liquidate' the university. He says, 'By doing what I did I saved mankind'" (Van Brunt, 2012, p. 255). His thoughts were clearly delusional and paranoid, but they were organized along his own internal logic whereby attacking the school would save mankind.

Jared Loughner, who posted a video of himself burning a flag prior to his shooting of U.S. Representative Gabrielle Giffords of Arizona (Van Brunt, 2012), demonstrated some organization and logic in his plan to attack the government based on his delusions around the need for a new currency in the government. There was an organization to his delusional and paranoid thoughts around the concept that the government, and those in authority, were operating illegally and threatening his rights. There was also a fixation and a focus on Representative Giffords that moved him forward in his attack. His fixation and focus shifted over time from his frustration and anger toward the faculty at Pima College, to his belief that the bookstore was being operated with an illegal currency, to his anger over other students' illiteracy and ignorance (of their manipulation by the government). Finally, his attack demonstrates a level of action and time imperative with his separation from college and the subsequent timing of Giffords's political rally to Tucson.

I am often asked for more clarity around the issue of disorganization and organization related to threat, as many of the thoughts and behaviors can seem similar and only develop into a concern under certain contextual scenarios. The Loughner case describes both an initial disorganization in the potential violence toward others as well as a later sense of organization as the attack crystallized and culminated in Tucson. Loughner displayed a wide range of odd and strange behavior that could well be described as threatening and challenging during his interactions with instructors, other students, and campus security. These thoughts and behaviors, seemingly driven by his schizophrenia, lacked a sense of linear planning, focus, or fixation on any particular target. When he was asked to leave school until he completed a mental health evaluation, his disorganized thoughts and behaviors shifted toward a more organized plan of attack fixated and focused on Giffords. The action and time imperative became engaged when he learned of her visit to nearby Tucson; the opportunity to "give life" to his plan of harming the government came to fruition.

Legacy Token

The *legacy token* is a manifesto, written text, online blog, video project, piece of art, diary, or journal created prior to an attack and left for someone to find after the attack. It clarifies the motives of the attacker or better defines the attacker's message of infamy. The legacy token merits study by those involved in violence prevention because it can help them be better prepared to engage others who intend to harm. One of the most compelling legacy tokens was disseminated on the morning of Anders Breivik's attack (Van Brunt, 2012). Breivik set off a bomb killing eight people in Oslo, Norway, before continuing onto Utøya and gunning down 69 youths at a labor party camp in July 2011. He claimed these events were marketing for his 1,500-page manifesto outlining a coming war against the Muslims. The manifesto also included detailed plans on how to make bombs and obtain weapons, and it included a journal account of the months leading up to the shooting.

In this manifesto, Breivik (2011) wrote:

> I just bought Modern Warfare 2, the game. It is probably the best military simulator out there and it's one of the hottest games this year. I played MW1 as well but I didn't really like it as I'm generally more the fantasy RPG kind of person—Dragon Age Origins etc. and not so much into first person shooters. I see MW2 more as a part of my training-simulation than anything else. I've still learned to love it though and especially the multiplayer part is amazing. You can more or less completely simulate actual operations. (p. 1408)

Another example of a violent person creating a legacy token comes from Duane Morrison, who took hostages and shot at students at Platte Canyon High School in Bailey, Colorado (Kelley, 2006). Morrison entered the school building claiming to carry a bomb. He carried a backpack containing duct tape, handcuffs, knives, a stun gun, rope, scissors, ammunition, and two sex toys. He took six female students hostage and sexually assaulted them, later releasing four. When police broke open the classroom's door with explosives, Morrison opened fire with a semi-automatic pistol before shooting a hostage. He wrote in his suicide note:

> Please forgive me for the terrible things you have heard or are about to hear. Suicide is sometimes an embarrassment to family members, so for this I truly apologize for any hurt I may cause all of you. To me suicide is a final release from an empty and painful life that has never had any meaning for me. I'm tired of living, and for the past 15 years I'm tired of living in pain. Constant pain. (Van Brunt, 2012, pp. 25–26)

Unlike Breivik (2011), Morrison's legacy token attempts to offer an apology and explanation of his horrific actions. Both Breivik and Morrison clearly were writing to a posthumous audience. As with a suicide note, those who plan violent attacks have spent time creating a lasting legacy token to either explain their actions or influence their media profile following the attack. In this sense, the legacy token becomes something of the killer's press kit.

All of these legacy tokens provide the clinician assessing an individual the opportunity to detect potential leakage prior to the attack. The clinician should look for evidence of a desire on the client's part to communicate potential motivations concerning the attack or to control the message after the attack. In fact, the conversations and communications between the clinician and individual being assessed may be categorized as a potential legacy token. The individual may see the assessment as a potential future source of information about his or her motivations for violence.

James Holmes (Elliot, 2013) in his 2012 Aurora, Colorado, attack selected a movie theatre for the stage for his performance. It is reported that prior to his attack he mailed a notebook to his psychiatrist that offered a foreshadowing of the attack. The desire to be known and to communicate the motivations and influence the media message is often strong in those who commit mass violence. Although not every person who is required to complete a threat assessment will share their legacy tokens with the clinician, an awareness and exploration of the existence of these as a violence risk factor should be part of the clinical investigation.

Clinicians should be vigilant for legacy tokens that they may come across when performing assessments. (Technically speaking, this would be evidence of leakage if detected prior to the attack.) Clinical staff should have an awareness of existing legacy tokens from past crimes to better understand the potential for violence.

Costuming

Costuming is the process of creating a persona or mask that defines or hides the true identity of those planning violence. There are two explanations for the type of clothing and accessories mass shooters choose. First, this is an individual who is dressing tactically to complete a mission. Few online stores or military surplus shops that sell tactical vests, knee pads, thigh rigs, and harnesses offer colors in red, pink, or yellow. Choices are more typically black, olive drab, and camouflage. Colors and styles are designed to allow for easy access as well as to blend into surroundings. Shooters choose these items for similar reasons.

The second reason shooters outfit themselves in this style of tactical gear is more psychological in nature. Meloy et al. (2011) referred to this as *identification warning behavior*:

Identification warning behavior—any behavior that indicates a psychological desire to be a "pseudo-commando" (Dietz, 1986; Knoll, 2010), have a "warrior mentality" (Hempel, Meloy, & Richards, 1999), closely associate with weapons or other military or law enforcement paraphernalia, identify with previous attackers or assassins, or identify oneself as an agent to advance a particular cause or belief system. (p. 265)

An example of this is found in the story of Kimveer Gill (Doug, 2006), a stony-faced man who killed one person and wounded 19 before killing himself while in a shootout with police. Dressed in black as a self-described Angel of Death, he brandished a Berretta Storm 9-mm rifle. Pictures of Gill can be easily found on the Internet (standing in his black trench coat holding an evil-looking gun) using the search terms "Montreal Shooting" and "Kimveer Gill."

Prior to his attack, Gill described himself on the website www.vampirefreaks.com in his profile this way:

His name is Trench. You will come to know him as the Angel of Death. He is male. He is 25 years of age. He lives in Quebec. He finds that it is an OK place to live. He is not a people person. He has met a handful of people in his life who are decent. But he finds the vast majority to be worthless, no good, conniving, betraying, lying, deceptive, motherfuckers. Work sucks . . . School sucks . . . Life sucks . . . What else can I say. Metal and Goth kick ass. Life is like a video game, you gotta die sometime. (Van Brunt, 2012, p. 253)

He posted dozens of pictures of himself, mugging for the camera as he brandished an assault rifle and other weapons. "Head to toe, all black. Boots as black as tar. Cloak lashing to and fro with the wind," he wrote in one entry. Gill was invested in how he saw himself prior to his attack. He shared these fantasies on a website through an avatar prior to the attacks. These writings provide an opportunity to detect potential leakage for the clinician performing a violence risk assessment.

Few images of the costumed anti-hero resonate as strongly as Jared Loughner (Couch, 2011). He shaved his head and left an iconic mug shot of himself as a crazed killer. Hours before the attack, he had pictures developed of himself posing with his handgun in a red g-string. The time and effort he spent on taking these pictures provide some insight into how he wanted to be seen by the media. These efforts to costume and control image are another possible source of leakage potentially discoverable prior to an attack.

Objectification and Depersonalization

Distancing oneself from a target is a common technique used in order to avoid any lasting emotional connection that might distract from completing the mission at hand. This technique is used by the U.S. military and law enforcement to train soldiers and officers, when shooting, to avoid seeing the target as a person but rather to focus on center mass torso shooting. Grossman (1996) discussed these phenomena related to the training in his book *On Killing.* He argued that soldiers are loathe to kill, yet this aversion has been overridden through sophisticated methods.

Cho's writings (and the video manifesto he sent to NBC) contain this objectifying language. Cho leaves us with vivid images of himself holding guns and a hammers demonstrating, prior to his attack, his desire to destroy those he held responsible. Jared Loughner attacked Giffords as a representative of the illegal system of government he ranted against. Pekka-Eric Auvinen in 2007 and Matti Saari (following in his steps) in 2008 took part in two devastating attacks in Finland. Both wrote extensively about their disdain for humanity and their desire to destroy humanity.

In May 1998, 15-year-old Kipland ("Kip") Kinkel was suspended pending an expulsion hearing from Thurston High School for being in possession of a loaded, stolen handgun. He killed his parents to "spare" them the embarrassment before returning to school. He parked two blocks away from school and hid several weapons and 1,127 rounds of ammunition under his trench coat. He shot two while entering the school and then shot another 24 students in the cafeteria. After firing 50 rounds, 27 hits resulting in two deaths, Kinkel was tackled by another seven students and then was arrested by police (Curry, 2003; Hammer, 1998; Hornblower, Faltermayer, Grace, Monroe, & Woodbury, 1998; Sullivan, 1998).

Kinkel left some journal writings prior to the killing spree that shed light on his romantic frustrations:

> I don't understand any fucking person on this earth. Some of you are so weak, mainly, that a four year old could push you down. I am strong, but my head just doesn't work right. I know I should be happy with what I have, but I hate living . . . I am evil. I want to kill and give pain without a cost. And there is no such thing. We kill him—we killed him a long time ago. Anyone that believes in God is a fucking sheep. (Van Brunt, 2012, p. 12)

For the clinician conducting a violence interview, the lesson provided by the preceding examples is the importance of attending to objectifying language that depersonalizes those whom the person being assessed is potentially targeting. In its basest form, this can be as straightforward as using words like *whores, bitches,* and *sluts* to describe women. Individuals may use hate speech and racial slurs that provide evidence of objectifying feelings toward groups that are different from their social, ethnic, or cultural group. This could also include teasing and bullying of overweight, gay, lesbian, bisexual, or transgender individuals by using objectifying and depersonalizing language. The clinician might be tempted to challenge and reshape these negative ways of seeing others; the focus here is on the insight that such language provides regarding the individual's deeper beliefs that their thoughts, beliefs, and feelings are not as important as his or her own. We see this in Kinkel's language calling those who believe in God "fucking sheep." This exact terminology is echoed in T.J. Lane's social media post prior to his attack in 2012, "I ain't no sheep. I am Death" (GlobalGrind, 2012, p. 1).

Dustin offers many examples of objectified language that provide insight into his lack of respect and disdain for women. He sees them as objects for his pleasure and uses misogynistic insults and language to convey a sense of control and power over them. The not-so-veiled threat to "Shut your god damn ignorant mouth or I'll shut if for you" contains demeaning language, disrespectful treatment, and insults, all of which provide insight into Dustin's depersonalization of women. When trying to understand his potential for violence, it is important to take this perspective into account. If he sees the women he dates as so different from himself, if he sees them as weak, objects to be used for his pleasure or recipients of his sexual gratification, then it is reasonable to assume he lacks a sense of empathy and care for their perspective. This increases the risk of violence.

However, some additional factors reduce the risk. He seems to lack a fixation and focus on this target. There is disorganization to his impulsive threatening behavior. Although there is immediacy to his threat, there seems to be no action or time imperative in terms of a future attack. Dustin seems to have a negative view of women, which he expresses vocally when challenged. The targeted risk for this one student does not appear to be a critical area of response in Dustin's case. Dustin would likely benefit more from ongoing treatment to address his objectionable and misogynistic language that reflects a larger problem being able to empathize with half of the world's population.

There is little evidence of objectification in Stacie's case. In fact, one might regard her as demonstrating an overdependence and empathic desire to understand and be liked by Professor Galloway. Conversely, one could assume that Professor Galloway may have some tendencies to objectify students like Stacie by reducing them to something less than human in his cruel critiques.

Jared Cano's cell phone video clip, recorded as part of his thwarted 2011 attack at Freedom High School in Tampa, Florida, is full of examples of objectified language. He begins the recording with "For those of you retards . . .", emphasizing how he sees his audience as people of substandard intelligence and different from him. He ends the clip with the statement "If you don't like it just find a way to find people like me and just line us up and shoot us . . ." (GlobalGrind, 2012, p. 1). This statement contains a sense of hopelessness and desperation in regard to a positive future. It's as if he understands how broken he is but remains unable to improve his condition. Suicide and death become alternative endings to his fantasy rehearsal of becoming a campus shooter.

Summary

This chapter described essential concepts related to assessing violence. While teaching these concepts, it makes sense to list them in separate sections and discuss each individually to ensure that it is clearly defined. I have found, however, that many of these concepts naturally coalesce during an actual threat assessment. In trainings, I compare these magnified moments when several risk factors come together to the individual strands of a rope. It is when these individual strands, or risk factors, come together that the threat assessment begins to take shape and provide a larger picture of the risk.

In the next chapter, I review some additional concerns and risk factors related to violence. It will be helpful to remember this concept of magnified moments and use the metaphor of strands of a rope coming together as a way to understand how the additional dozen risk factors in the next chapter interact with the central threat concepts introduced here.

Questions for Further Discussion

1. The action and time imperative helps the threat assessment professional better understand the immediacy of the potential for violence. What are some suggestions Van Brunt offers to better assess the immediacy of an attack?
2. What are some ways to assess focus and fixation during a threat assessment? If there is a threat to a particular person, place, or system what requirement do you have to share this information with the target? How does the immediacy of the attack (action and time imperative) affect your decision to alert the referral source of the potential for danger?
3. Some individuals are very organized in the planning of an attack. Others have a more diffuse focus on multiple targets. Discuss the potential for risk in both of these scenarios.
4. The presence of costuming may present the opportunity to detect leakage prior to an attack. What are some ways to assess a topic like costuming or the creation of a legacy token prior to an attack from an individual who may be reluctant to share his or her plans?
5. In what ways do you see objectification and depersonalized language used in everyday communication within our society? How does this contribute to a culture that lacks empathy and understanding?

Chapter 5

Additional Threat
CONCEPTS

Chapter Highlights

1. Additional threat concepts are reviewed in this chapter to provide a textured understanding of risk factors present in cases of extreme violence. These concepts build upon the foundational ones reviewed in Chapter 4.
2. *Weapon access and knowledge* is important to explore in the context of the threat assessment; so too is *bomb materials knowledge,* which establishes the ability to carry out the attack.
3. Understanding how the individual approaches authority figures contributes to the overall likelihood of future negative interactions. *Fading supports* such as absence of friends and family, lack of finances, and academic distress are also explored as potential risk factors.
4. Langman (2009b) offered a typology for those who commit rampage violence: *traumatized, psychotic,* and *psychopathic.*
5. *Mental health* is explored in the context of the threat assessment. Concepts such as social isolation, delusional and paranoid thoughts, depression and suicide, irrational thoughts, social isolation, and bipolar condition are discussed as potential risk factors.

This chapter continues the discussion of threat concepts reviewed in Chapter 4. If that list provides a rough sketch that helps the clinician identify a pattern of concern, the threat concepts described in this chapter provide additional details to the sketch (shading, shadowing, and context). All of these concepts should be viewed as interwoven within the context of the overall picture rather than separated out and addressed only on an individual basis. It is the gestalt, that the sum of the parts is greater than the whole, that provides the most useful conceptualizations.

Knowledge of and Access to Weapons and Bombs

When I worked with younger children in an outpatient setting, I visited Toys "R" Us once a month to browse the toys and look for what was new and different in the toy world. In assessing violence, it is important to have knowledge of weapons so that you can knowledgably converse with those you are assessing and so you understand the significance of references the person being assessed might make to weapons.

In the second case study in Chapter 3, Dustin told the clinician that he had weapons at home. He talked a bit about his experience as a veteran and shared how the military expected him to carry his gun wherever he went while he was on active duty. The adjustment back to the nonmilitary life has been a challenging one for him. Although his threat does not explicitly involve the use of a weapon, the clinician performing an assessment on Dustin regarded his weapon knowledge as a potential risk factor.

When assessing gun knowledge, clinicians should understand that the person being assessed might interpret any question about weapons as an expression of concern that he or she might shoot someone. A defensive or incredulous response would be reasonable in some cases. Efforts should be made to inquire about weapons through a more Socratic and naturalistic inquiry method. Perhaps talking about video games, hunting, regional gun culture, or recent news events related to firearms would be a less direct way to ascertain the individual's knowledge about and possession of firearms.

The following is a short list of weapons that are commonly used in attacks; I provide it here as a starting place for those without much firearm experience. One of the best ways to learn more about weapons is through the many YouTube clips dedicated to describing how the weapon is loaded and the benefits and negative qualities of each gun and rifle.

- *Glock handgun.* This weapon is commonly seen as a streamlined and modern handgun capable of holding 17 bullets in a standard-sized magazine. The gun can have different calibers (e.g., 9 mm, 10 mm, .40, and .45). Generally speaking, the 9 mm caliber is the smallest and cheapest to purchase. It is commonly used at the shooting range and is easy to maintain.
- *Sig Sauer.* A German handgun known for its efficient design.
- *Smith and Wesson.* This American-made weapon is most commonly a revolver known for its reliability.

- *Colt Python.* This is a popular revolver in the Resident Evil video game series and *The Walking Dead* (Darabont, 2010) TV show. It holds only six bullets but is valued for its accuracy and stopping power.
- *Desert Eagle.* An Israeli-made handgun that is available in a .50 round caliber, this gun was made popular because of the enormous kick it gives when fired. The gun is also popular in the Call of Duty video game series.
- *FN P90.* This bull-pup style carbine fires expensive ammunition; it was made popular in the movie *Stargate* (Synder, 1994) and the Call of Duty video game series. The rifle is very recognizable because of its compact size and high magazine capacity of 50 rounds laid out across the top of the rifle. The FN pistol uses the same ammunition and was the weapon of choice by Major Nidal Hasan, the psychiatrist who killed 13 and injured 29 in the 2009 Fort Hood shooting (Owens, 2009).
- *AR-15.* This rifle became popular after it was used in several of the recent large shootings—at the Newtown, Connecticut, elementary school (used by Adam Lanza) and at the Aurora, Colorado, movie theatre (used by James Holmes). It is often the type of weapon that features in debates between gun enthusiasts and those seeking to reduce access to firearms in the United States.
- *Crossbow.* This weapon is featured on many of the Call of Duty video games and is seen as a more elegant way to kill opponents with skill rather than the power of traditional weapon. It has been popularized by its use by a lead character in the TV series *The Walking Dead.*
- *EOtech.* This company manufactures a high-quality set of optics and holographic weapon sites that are used in many popular TV shows, movies, and video games.
- *Hollow-point bullets.* These bullets have a distinctive wound pattern and tend to break up into smaller projectiles on impact; they are sometimes referred to as *cop killers.*
- *Airsoft.* The guns are popular with college students and often result in conduct violations when they are found on campus. Hobbyists who play intricate military games frequently use these toy guns.

The client's knowledge of bombs and explosives should be assessed, a point that was convincingly made during the April 15, 2013, Boston Marathon bombing. As with weapon access, the challenge for the threat assessor is to use subtle techniques to assess the individual's knowledge and awareness in this area, because the person is not likely to share information about his or her plans if asked directly.

The individual being assessed may be experimenting with different chemicals and explosives and may spend time watching Internet videos, reading manuals related to building trip-wire traps, or making his or her own explosives. Eric Harris and Dylan Klebold created several pipe bombs and smaller devices during their 1999 attack at Columbine High School (Gibbs et al., 1999). California State Northridge student David Everson shared with his counselor a desire to kill, leading police to discover bomb-making materials and a shotgun in his room (Dobuzinskis, 2011). Michael Evans was arrested in 2006 in Puyallup, Washington, after sending another student an instant message that expressed a suicidal desire "to finally go out in a blaze of hatred and fury" (Van Brunt, 2012, p. 14). Evans had two rifles, two handguns, a copy of the *Anarchist Cookbook*, and a homemade bomb (Associated Press, 2006).

The following list (not intended to be exhaustive) of explosives-related terms have come up in threat cases that I have reviewed or conducted.

- *C4.* A military-grade plastic explosive, C4 is used because it is relatively stable. Often referenced in films, movies, and videos as a commonly known explosive, its availability is highly restricted.
- *Radio controlled (RC) car.* Related to C4 and made popular in the Call of Duty video game, RC cars are strapped with C4 explosive and a video camera. They are available to the player to drive around and "explode" when triggered.
- *Anarchist Cookbook.* Popular in the 1970s, the cookbook contained information about how to make bombs and illegal drugs and ways to subvert the phone company. Made available on the Internet, it has been downloaded and studied by several involved in bombing attacks and school assaults.
- *Pressure cooker bomb.* This explosive device (created with a pressure cooker, shrapnel, and an explosive charge) is a low-tech, low-cost method of creating a device; it was used in the April 2013 Boston bombing.
- *Dirty bomb.* A dirty bomb is made with some kind of radioactive material designed to contaminate a larger area. The concept was made popular by many TV shows, movies, and video games.
- *Pipe bomb.* This small, contained explosive is made out of a plumbing or polyvinyl chloride pipe and other basic materials that may be available through hardware stores and fireworks outlets.
- *Little cricket.* These bombs (used during the Columbine attack) are made from CO_2 cartridges, explosives, and fuses. They may be mentioned by those who study past attacks and plan copycat attacks of their own.

Evidence of Attack Plans

Predatory violent attacks are rarely impulsive or unplanned. Those who plan these attacks often spend weeks, months, and sometimes years acquiring the data needed—drawings of the target, detailed blueprints, photo surveillance—to carry out their assault. The person being interviewed may have an obsession with a particular target considered to be responsible for his or her ill fortune. As with assessing weapon or bomb knowledge, it behooves the clinician to question carefully in order to ascertain access to items that would assist the planning of an attack, such as schematics, a journal, and a list of objectives.

Examples of this have already been mentioned; a brief reminder suffices here. Jared Cano, the Tampa, Florida, high school student who had a hit list, recorded a cell phone video of himself and had detailed attack plans written on a crude spiral notebook (Teicher-Khadaroo, 2011). On January 30, 2001, Al DeGuzman planned a Columbine-style school shooting at De Anza College. An employee at a Longs Drugs store developed pictures of DeGuzman posing with his guns and homemade bombs. She and a coworker called police. DeGuzman was arrested when he returned for his photos. Police found DeGuzman's bedroom stacked from top to bottom with sophisticated handmade bombs and a map of De Anza College, marked with locations where bombs would be placed.

Both of these cases are important for clinicians to understand. They illustrate the fantasy rehearsal and planning that went into planning the attacks. And in both cases, planned attacks were thwarted when a vigilant person who came across the information notified law enforcement.

Attitude Toward Authority and Society

At the heart of most violence lies the separation of the individual from the society. Those who turn toward violence see themselves as different and unconnected from those around them and often begin to isolate and fantasize about their difference and how it can be reconciled. Some become overwhelmed by this difference and experience depression and isolation; they become lost in a sense of meaninglessness. Others channel their perspective into unique or extraordinary lives marked by nonconformity and artistic vision. Still others become disillusioned by society and authority and seek to define themselves as the anti-hero, struggling and pushing against the greater community and those in authority.

More than any of the other risk factors discussed to this point, antiauthority sentiments and feelings of isolation from the larger society can be rather subjective qualities to assess. What teenager doesn't struggle against the oppressive nature of authority of parents and teachers? This defining of oneself as a unique individual is part of a normal developmental process. However, the distancing of oneself repeatedly or in a manner that involves the police or law enforcement may indicate a larger area of concern. Similarly, if the individual uses objectified language or sees himself or herself as superior or entitled to rule or dominate others, this is an additional area of concern.

The following examples of areas to assess as part of the threat assessment interview process provide a starting point to ascertain the person's attitude toward society and authority.

Judicial and Arrest History

Has the individual been involved in previous rule or law breaking behaviors in school or the community? Can these records be requested from school officials or obtained through a background check? It is essential to assess the client's history with law enforcement through means other than direct self-report.

Past Impulsivity

Past impulsive behavior may be risk taking in nature, in response to limits set by parents or authority figures or incidents of poor judgment. These behaviors are considered risk factors for future impulsive decisions. Clinicians should assess this through self-report as well as confirming narratives with school officials, conduct officers, police, and family. They should review when the person being assessed acted impulsively and what the potential triggers or contributing factors were that increased the potential for impulsive action.

Substance Abuse/Dependency

Substance abuse and dependency are also contributing factors that must be assessed as part of potential dangerousness. The clinician should determine how often the individual is using and what substances are used. As mentioned earlier, this process is more effective when using circular, nonthreatening questions after the establishment of a rapport. The clinician should determine the frequency and duration of use, contributing factors to use, violence and impulsive or risk-taking actions related to abuse, periods of sobriety, range of substances used, and the common emotional state when using. The individual being assessed should be told that substance use negatively affects the evaluation.

Attitudes Toward Authority

Authority figures include teachers, police, religious figures, and court officers. Counselors should assess how the person being assessed interacts with authority and how these past behaviors may be predictive of future interactions. Has the student been involved in past legal actions? How does he or she react to those who enforce the rules but have little power to punish (movie theatre clerk, parking attendant, religious community elders)? Is there a tendency to test these lesser authority figures with noncompliance because it is possible to escape consequences? Can these be seen as grooming or practice behaviors increasing the likelihood of greater challenges to stronger authority figures in the future?

Fading Supports

Think of a building under repair and surrounded with scaffolding. The scaffolding provides support while the underlying structure is being repaired. I find the concept of scaffolding useful when thinking about risk factors that originally are supportive to the individual and offer structure, support, and consistency during the good times. The removal of these supports becomes a risk factor during times of increased stress. The clinician should assess the following areas to better understand how the lack of these supports can increase the risk of violence.

Absence of Friends and Family

From a sociological perspective, many environmental factors help individuals to conform to the overall societal expectations regarding social norms. Friends and family are two of the most central and important factors in influencing and communicating community expectations. These two groups also serve as a sort of shock absorber for individuals during times of trouble, depression, stress, and transition.

We are still learning new things about the shooting in Newtown by Adam Lanza (Weizel, 2013) that occurred on December 14, 2012. We do know that Lanza had no friends and was socially isolated and described as a "shut in" by the media. He rarely communicated with his mother and had little contact with other family (Kleinfield, Rivera, & Kovaleski, 2013).

Lack of Finances

Financial stress is a risk factor for violence. Financial stress can increase a sense of hopelessness and despair in the person being assessed. The lack of a positive future may contribute to an impulsive, violent action. This can be a contributing factor that serves as a multiplier effect on other risk factors. In the case of Stacie, described in Chapter 3, it is conceivable that her anger and frustration over a future separation from the college could easily be exacerbated by the lack of financial aid and other monetary resources she requires to attend graduate school. Although it has not been directly mentioned, one can assume that both Loughner (Tucson shooting) and Holmes (Aurora movie theatre shooting) became more focused because they were not enrolled in a university and experienced mounting pressure to work or find a new career.

In a more subtle and subjective comparison, we can all relate to the increase in stress when under financial pressures. When there isn't enough money to pay the rent, buy food, or buy the goods needed for daily living, the increase in tension is substantial and unavoidable.

The clinician should assess how financial stress affects the individual's overall wellness and life functioning. Has there been a recent change in finances? Are there pressing financial goals or deadlines that create an action or time imperative toward action (such as removal from a dormitory because of failure to pay)? Have these been sudden financial changes, or ones that have built consistently over time?

Additional Loss of Supports

Beyond friends and family, a loss of supportive people in an individual's life can add to the stress he or she experiences and create further frustration, tension, and hardship. Teachers or instructors may report growing frustration with a student's poor classroom performance or difficulty with assignments, leading to a distancing from the student. An administration may grow weary of trying to proactively work with a student who seems to continually push against the rules and regulations of the institution.

The end of a relationship (or the inability to begin a relationship with a person of interest) can be devastating to an individual's desire to connect and to feelings of self-worth and self-esteem. An example of just how upsetting such rejection can be made the news on January 21, 2009, when Virginia Tech student Zhu Haiyang was arrested for murder. He had apparently hoped to marry fellow student Yang Xin, and he lashed out when she said she planned to marry someone else (Slater, 2009). He beheaded her in the Au Bon Pain café on campus. Police responded to Zhu holding Yang Xin's head and took him into custody. A psychologist who evaluated Zhu testified that severe mental illness ran in his family and affected his upbringing. Zhu was sentenced to life in prison without parole.

Another Example

In April 2009, Henry Ford Community College student Anthony Powell shot and killed another student he had tried to date but who had rejected him (Runk, 2009). Prior to the attack, Anthony posted numerous YouTube video clips about his frustrations with women, atheists, and others with whom he disagreed.

Declining Academic Progress

Poor academic progress in both primary and secondary school can also increase the potential despair and hopelessness of the person being assessed. If the individual is failing classes, feeling bad about future goals, or facing an imminent grading decision, these factors may increase the risk for violence in the presence of additional risk factors. We see this as a clear risk factor in Stacie's case study (see Chapter 3). The potential for a failing grade in Professor Galloway's class causes her profound distress. Left unchecked, this could lead to a violent outburst or impulsive action toward the professor, the registrar, or those who would enforce her removal from her larger graduate program in photojournalism.

In January 2010, Jason Hamilton fired several shots at his math professor because he was upset over a failing grade in her class. He defended his actions by claiming to be depressed and to have Asperger's disorder (Martine, 2009). Robert Flores shot and killed his three professors before committing suicide in October 2002. He was in danger of being expelled from his program for falsifying internship hours during his nursing practicum. As a nontraditional student, he often complained of mistreatment and a lack of empathy from his professors. He wrote, "I guess what it is about is that it is a reckoning. A settling of accounts . . . and arrogance of authorities. . . . The University is filled with too many people who are filled with hubris. They feel untouchable" (Van Brunt, 2012, p. 15; see also Rooney, 2002).

James Holmes purchased a high-power rifle as part of his arsenal of weapons in the Aurora, Colorado, attack on July 20, 2012. He purchased the rifle at Gander Mountain in Thornton, Colorado, after learning on June 7 that he had failed an oral exam. Although other factors may have also influenced Holmes in his attack, there is a clear connection between his academic failure and the movement toward his attack plan.

Mental Illness and Violence

Although those who are mentally ill are *not* more likely to cause violence (Choe, Teplin, & Abram, 2008), it is hard to avoid looking at the news stories and noticing that almost every person who picks up a gun and commits violence in a school or mall shooting has a history of mental illness. Where does that leave the issue of mental health when assessing an individual's potential for violence?

In my book *Ending Campus Violence: New Approaches to Prevention* (Van Brunt, 2012), I highlight a number of cases where mental illness was a factor in shooting and mass casualty violence cases. The following attackers struggled with depression: David Everson at California State, Jason Hamilton at Northern Virginia Community College, Anthony Powell at Henry Ford Community College, Steven Kazmierczak at Northern Illinois University, Pekka-Eric Auvinen in Finland, Asa Coon at Success Tech Academy, Seung-Hui Cho at Virginia Tech, Victor Cordova at Deming Middle School, Jacob Davis at Lincoln High School, Evan Ramsey at Bethel Regional High School, Jillian Robbins at Pennsylvania State University, James Kearbey at Goddard Junior High School, and Robert Poulin at St. Pius X High School.

Still others struggled with possible schizophrenia: James Holmes (2012, killed 12) at the Aurora, Colorado, theatre; Jared Loughner (2011, killed 6) at the Tucson, Arizona, rally; Jiverly Wong (2009, killed 13) at Binghamton; Steven Kazmierczak (2008, killed 6) at Northern Illinois University; Latina Williams (2008, killed 2) at Louisiana Tech; Douglas Pennington (2006, killed 3) at Shephard College; Biswanath Halder (2003, killed 1) at Case Western Reserve; Peter Odighizuwa (2002, killed 3) at Appalachian School of Law; Michael McDermott (2000, killed 7) in Wakefield, Massachusetts; Andrew Wurst (1998, killed 1) in Edinboro, Pennsylvania; Michael Carneal (1997, killed 3) at Heath High School; Wayne Lo (1992, killed 2) at Simon's Rock College of the Bard; Arthur McElroy (1992, killed 0) at University of Nebraska-Lincoln; Patrick Purdy (1989, killed 5) at Cleveland Elementary School; Edward Allaway (1976, killed 7) at California State University; and Walter Seifert (1964, killed 11) at the Cologne School.

That many campus shootings involve a student with some form of mental illness is hard to deny. Nevertheless, I would argue that mental illness should not be our concern here; instead, we should focus on the risk factors previously identified that may overlap with existing mental health concerns. For example, the fact that someone has severe and recurrent major depression is not cause for alarm. Instead, it is the person who is isolated, hopeless about his future, and in constant emotional pain. Although the symptoms are common to both the diagnosis and the risk factors for violence, we are interested more in the behaviors, emotions, and thoughts rather than the diagnostic code.

Students who are isolated and disconnected from others have a difficult time feeling part of the community. Isolation is different from shyness, solitude, or a preference for limited social interaction. Isolation usually comes from a feeling of separation, difference, teasing, fear, or anxiety. Isolation from the community is a negative warning sign that should be flagged by threat assessors.

Cho displayed many of these social difficulties throughout his life. From the Virginia Tech Review Panel (2007, N-3) report: For all of his 23 years of life, the most frequent observation made by anyone about him was that he had absolutely no social life. During all of his school years he had no real friends. He had no interest in being with others. In fact, he shied away from other people and seemed to prefer his own company to the company of others. His few attempts to reach out to females at college were inappropriate and frightened them.

In an ideal world, the student would choose to have friends and be in social contact to whatever his or her individual personality preference might tolerate (realizing we each have different social needs for connection and friendship). In many school and educational settings, students may be isolated from others because they are different; bullies respond to them with cruelty; or others have difficulty in understanding their odd, strange, or socially maladjusted behavior.

Langman Typology

Peter Langman (2009a) reviewed a number of high-profile rampage school shootings and developed three main categories of rampage school shooters related to mental health concerns: traumatized, psychotic, and psychopathic. He added an important caveat that is essential for us to understand: "Most people who are traumatized, psychotic or psychopathic do not commit murder" (p. 79). This concept is supported by Choe et al. (2008), who found that most people with mental illness are much more likely to be the victims of a violent crime rather than the perpetrators of one. Let's look briefly at the categories.

Traumatized

Langman described traumatized shooters as coming from broken homes and having suffered physical or sexual abuse (or both). Each shooter in his study had one parent with substance abuse problems and at least one parent with a criminal history. In 1997, Evan Ramsey was teased and bullied by other students and often addressed as "Screech," a character from the TV show *Saved by the Bell* (Engel, 1989). His mother had lived with numerous violent men. Ramsey was abused physically and sexually when in foster care. It was reported that he attempted suicide at 10 and suffered from depression. He went to school on the bus and entered the building with a shotgun borrowed from a friend. It was reported that more than 15 students knew of the attack and two helped him work the shotgun. He killed one student and injured two others. He then shot and killed the principal and considered suicide. He put the gun to his head but then surrendered, saying, "I don't want to die" (Cornwell, 1997).

Langman noted two key factors that separate traumatized shooters from other traumatized individuals: father figures who engage in illegal use of firearms and peer support for the attacks (e.g., friends who encourage the individual to go on a shooting rampage).

Psychotic

Langman noted that unlike traumatized shooters, rampage shooters of the psychotic type come from stable homes with no history of abuse. Many have some form of schizophrenia-spectrum symptoms. Examples here are Seung-Hui Cho from the Virginia Tech shooting and Dylan Klebold from the Columbine attack. Langman noted that a sense of paranoia was common among all psychotic shooters; some also experienced grandiose delusions, auditory hallucinations, and disorganized thoughts.

Psychopathic

Rampage shooters display a lack of empathy, a sense of superiority, and contempt for others. Langman described them as having skill in impression management, pleasure in deceiving others, and sadistic delight in inflicting pain on humans or animals. Those studied had intact families with no signs of abuse. In October 1975, Robert Poulin raped and killed a fellow classmate before burning his house to the ground and going to his high school and shooting six others, killing one and then committing suicide. He tricked the classmate over to his house and wrote in his journal, "I don't want to die before I have had the pleasure of fucking some girl" (Cobb & Avery, 1977, p. 160).

Langman noted that many of these shooters had obsessions with weapons and families with a history of legal firearm use, and some had recruited peers to support them in their attacks.

Yet most people who are traumatized or who experience psychotic or psychopathic symptoms do not commit murder (Langman, 2009b). The *Report to the President on Issues Raised by the Virginia Tech Tragedy* stated, "Most people who are violent do not have a mental illness, and most people who have mental illness are not violent" (Leavitt, Spellings, & Gonzales, 2007, p. 5). Mental illness alone, like profiling, is not a reliable predictor as to who the next shooter is likely to be. In fact, Seung-Hui Cho, of the horrific Virginia Tech shooting, was evaluated on three different occasions and in each case was deemed to be depressed and anxious but not at risk of hurting himself or others.

The practical question remains: Which mental health symptoms should be a concern when they overlap with existing violence risk factors? I have listed a few examples below of mental health symptoms that overlap with existing risk factors for violence. These should be areas of further exploration for the clinician.

Social Isolation

Social isolation occurs in various disorders such as autism spectrum disorder as well as depression, social anxiety, and avoidant personality disorder. The inability, or lack of desire, to form social connections with peers creates a sense of isolation for the individual being assessed. This isolation keeps the individual away from others and reduces the potential for leakage or other observations. In the Adam Lanza shooting at Newtown in December 2012, Lanza's isolation kept him away from others who could have expressed concern about his thoughts of violence or shared their concerns with the authorities. However, it is important not to unfairly target those with social anxiety disorders and see them at risk for campus shootings or violence simply because they have trouble getting along with others; this is not the case. Each risk factor, including social isolation from peers and family, should be considered in the greater context of the threat assessment evaluation.

Manic or Impulsive Thoughts

In bipolar illness, there is a tendency toward manic thoughts, emotions, or impulsive actions. These actions are very rarely dangerous, but the tendency to experience grandiose ideas or harbor intensified emotions is increased. When I conducted a threat assessment at a university I worked at, the student first came into my office demanding to use my computer to shut down her Facebook account. (She had tried unsuccessfully to do this shutdown initially on her phone.) It turns out she had bipolar disorder and the stress of the threat assessment evaluation and conduct interview had brought on a manic phase resulting in her symptoms. She was difficult to understand and attributed her behavior (in a rather odd non sequitur) to her Russian heritage. She was fidgety and had trouble sitting in her chair. Although we never want to profile someone solely based on his or her diagnosis, her impulsivity in my office gave useful insight into the violent shouting outbursts she had in class that resulted in her being sent to my office. Individuals with bipolar disorder may experience extreme mood swings that impact their decision making and increase the risk of violence to self or others. This is particularly of concern when the individual is disengaged from treatment or noncompliant with a medication regimen.

Delusional or Paranoid Thoughts

The detachment from reality that accompanies delusional or paranoid thoughts can cause concern particularly when it is paired with a fixation or focus on a certain target. The person, place, or system may be woven into the delusion of paranoia and may be seen to require punishment or destruction. More often than not, the patient experiencing the thought-disorder symptoms has a rather disorganized sense of threat that is diffuse and spread to a great number of potential recipients. A greater area of concern arises when the threat becomes linear and consistent in nature. (Again, most people with a thought disorder have enough to manage merely keeping their own reality and daily life activities intact without planning some larger attack on a person, place, or system.)

Depressive and Suicidal Thoughts

As mentioned earlier, the concern is less the diagnosis or presence of depression; the concern is the hopelessness, isolation, and desperation that accompany mental illness. The person who has no positive options in the future and feels as if life is not worth living is in a very desperate place. It would be easier to imagine that someone like this, detached from any hope or positive connection, might be willing to harm others as well as commit suicide. Meloy, Hoffmann, Roshdi, Glaz-Ocik, and Guldimann (2014) described it this way: "Suicidal ideation appears to be a strong behavioral marker for last resort warning behaviors. . . . This warning behavior is described as an increasing desperation or distress through declaration in word or deed, forcing the individual into a position of last resort" (p. 45).

I attended an Association of Threat Assessment Professionals seminar where a presenter introduced the idea that homicide and suicide were really only half a second and 90 degrees apart. He asked us to imagine a disgruntled employee coming into the office with a gun to kill himself in front of his boss. As he stands there, the thought of "Why should I just kill myself? I should take you with me" would be easily accommodated in his plan quickly by turning the gun on the supervisor first before shooting himself.

Again, it is important not to overreact; people who are depressed and are being assessed for risk of violence should not be profiled as mass shooters. Instead, the clinician should carefully assess the level of hopelessness and desperation as they relate to future action and harm to self as well as others. However, Mohandie (2014) had this observation:

> Many of the common patterns observed among school violence offenders mirror the commonalities of suicidal individuals as observed by Shneidman (1996): (1) solution-seeking, (2) cessation of consciousness, (3) unbearable psychological pain, (4) frustrated psychological needs, (5) common emotion of hopelessness/helplessness, (6) cognitive state of ambivalence, (7) perceptual state of constriction, (8) common action in escape, (9) common interpersonal act is communication of intent, and (10) consistency of life-long styles. Violent actions, fantasy, and planning offer a grandiose, omnipotent attitude to counteract feelings of hopelessness and helplessness in homicidal (and sometimes concurrently suicidal) individuals. (p. 128)

There is an important link between suicide and other forms of violence.

Irrational Thoughts

One of the most challenging areas of overlap for threat assessment and mental illness is found in the understanding of the irrational and often contradictory thoughts and obsessions possessed by some who commit violent acts. This becomes both a concerning and hopeful experience. It is concerning because the logic and nonlinear thoughts expressed by some who plan rampage violence seem to be so warped and out of place when measured against those who think rationally and in a linear manner. It is hopeful in that there remains an opportunity to engage with these individuals early in their pathway toward violence in order to intervene and challenge their assumptions about the world and their target.

Few demonstrate this more succinctly than Texas clock tower shooter Charles Whitman, who killed 16 people and wounded 32 others on August 1, 1966, before being shot and killed by an Austin police officer. He began by murdering his wife and mother at their homes. An excerpt from his suicide note reads:

I do not quite understand what it is that compels me to type this letter. Perhaps it is to leave some vague reason for the actions I have recently performed. I do not really understand myself these days. I am supposed to be an average reasonable and intelligent young man. However, lately (I cannot recall when it started) I have been a victim of many unusual and irrational thoughts. (Bowden, 1999, p. 74)

Wellington Menezes de Oliveira went to the Tasso da Silveira Municipal School in Rio de Janeiro, Brazil, introduced himself as a former student (he was), and said that he had a desire to see the school's history. He proceeded to roam the halls, shooting children at point-blank range. Nearby police entered the school and shot the gunman in the leg, causing him to fall down the stairs. He then committed suicide. He left a letter stating that he planned to commit suicide. In a video shot 2 days before the shooting, he stated,

The struggle for which many brothers died in the past, and for which I will die, is not solely because of what is known as bullying. Our fight is against cruel people, cowards, who take advantage of the kindness, the weakness of people unable to defend themselves. (Van Brunt, 2012, p. 19; see also Barbassa, 2011)

Although Menezes de Oliveira struggled with the trauma of his mistreatment during his childhood at the school, his thinking that old trauma can be remedied by assaulting and killing children with whom he had no connection is clearly irrational. This flawed logic provides an opportunity for a clinician to challenge his beliefs prior to the attack and attempt to show him another way to resolve his feelings.

Amy Bishop shot three people dead and wounded another three on February 12, 2010, in Huntsville, Alabama; it was reported that she was upset because she had been denied tenure. Previously, she had assaulted another woman at the International House of Pancakes because she took the last booster seat for her child. She shouted, "I am DR. BISHOP!" and demanded the chair. It is likely that Amy Bishop suffered from additional mental health problems; she had a history of overreaction and irrational thought about how people should treat her and what she deserved. Throughout her story there are reports of her expectations around tenure; her desires to be at a more prestigious school; and a general disappointment with her life and goals despite a job, relationships, and family that would have been the envy of others, particularly in a difficult economic climate (Wallace, 2011).

The diagnosis of mental illness is less important in the cases of Bishop, Menezes de Oliveira, and Whitman. We should attend more to the irrational thinking and beliefs that drew these shooters inexorably toward tragic and horrific action. In each case, the potential existed for early intervention and treatment that could have helped move these killers off the pathway toward violence and instead helped them locate other ways to address their grievances with their past injuries and the perceived social injustices.

Summary

In this chapter, I reviewed several risk factors to violence related to weapon and bomb knowledge and acquisition, attitude toward authority and society, and fading supports. In the following chapter, I review risk factors for violence outlined in the literature before beginning a discussion of structured professional judgment in Chapter 7.

Questions for Further Discussion

1. How might you assess an individual's knowledge of weapons, bombs, or schematics without increasing his or her immediate defensiveness and thus limiting the information that is communicated? What are some ways to increase your knowledge about weapon or bomb making in order to be able to ask more appropriate questions and understand potential leakage?
2. How does an individual's attitude toward authority or the large society give insight into his or her potential to commit violence? What are some ways to separate those who have a healthy respect for individual rights (and thus stand against authority) from those who may be planning a more significant attack?
3. Social isolation and fading supports such as teachers, professors, staff, and supervisors who may have previously served as advocates are seen as additional risk factors. What are some methods the clinician performing the threat assessment can use to better assess the presence (or absence) of these factors?
4. Van Brunt argues that those with mental illness are more likely to be the victim of a violent crime rather than the person perpetrating the attack. Yet, it is hard to avoid the high occurrence of school shootings by those with mental health disorders. Where is the balance between these two positions?

Chapter 6

Risk Factors Identified in the LITERATURE

Chapter Highlights

1. The field of risk and violence assessment is not a recent development. For decades, groups such as the U.S. Postal Service, Federal Bureau of Investigation (FBI), U.S. Secret Service, Association of Threat Assessment Professionals, and Department of Education have provided lists of risk factors and materials useful for assessing potential threat. This chapter reviews these risk factors.

2. In 2011, the U.S. Postal Service updated its 2006 set of risk indicators as part of its *Threat Assessment Team Guide*. In 2002, the FBI created a four-pronged approach to threat assessment in response to the Columbine High School massacre in 1999. The FBI document includes recommendations to assess the personality of the student, family dynamics, school dynamics, and social dynamics.

3. Turner and Gelles (2003) wrote a seminal book on workplace violence titled *Threat Assessment: A Risk Management Approach*. In 2006, the Association of Threat Assessment Professionals created the *Risk Assessment Guideline Elements for Violence (RAGE-V)*. In 2011, ASIS International and the Society for Human Resource Management published *Workplace Violence Prevention and Intervention*.

4. Following the Virginia Tech shooting in 2006, G. Deisinger et al. published *The Handbook for Campus Threat Assessment and Management Teams* (2008). In 2009, Randazzo and Plummer wrote *Implementing Behavioral Threat Assessment on Campus: A Virginia Tech Demonstration Project*.

5. Meloy et al. (2011) wrote an essential article "The Role of Warning Behaviors in Threat Assessment: An Exploration and Suggested Typology." They identified the following warning behaviors: pathway warning behavior, fixation, identification, novel aggression, energy burst, leakage, last resort, and directly communicated threat. O'Toole and Bowman (2011) discussed concerning, threatening and dangerous behavior in their book *Dangerous Instincts*.

No profile or collection of risk factors predicts future violence. In the 2010 FBI Law Enforcement Bulletin, Albrecht wrote, "Threat Assessment Teams aim to assess dangerousness, not predict violence; only the perpetrators ultimately know their intentions" (p. 16). This is important and speaks to the need for clinicians and those performing threat assessment to be wary of claims that some expert system can identify potential threat with certainty. Although no single list or profile will identify the exact probability that an individual will actually commit violence, it is still useful to pull together in a single chapter the threat assessment work of the U.S. Postal Service, the Association of Threat Assessment Professionals, Gelles and Turner, and the FBI.

The parallel here for the clinician is the suicide risk factors used when assessing potential for self-harm. The presence of any single risk factor does not predict suicidality. If an individual possesses a firearm, has had past suicide attempts, or has a history of mental illness, these are risk factors for suicide: They increase the risk of suicide but they do not predict suicide (or even a suicide attempt). The loss of someone important, a sense of hopelessness and depression, and the writing of a suicide note all suggest increased risk, but they do not foretell an attempt. The risk factors for a heart attack are similar. We understand factors that increase the risk, such as obesity, smoking, and family history, but these factors do not predict with certitude when a heart attack is imminent.

Clinicians conducting threat assessments should have a familiarity with the research and past cases related to threat in order to have a better foundational knowledge of the factors that could exacerbate the risk of violence. In my 2012 book *Ending Campus Violence: New Approaches to Prevention*, I used the risk factors and more than 100 violence cases to develop a single list of risk factors useful for college administrators, staff, members of the Student of Concern (SOC) and Behavioral Intervention Teams (BIT). These 35 factors are called the Structured Interview for Violence Risk Assessment (SIVRA-35) and are included in Appendix C.

U.S. Postal Service Threat Assessment Team Guide

In 2011, the U.S. Postal Service updated a set of risk indicators as part of its Threat Assessment Team Guide from 2007. I have chosen a few examples here to help illustrate the type of risk factors the U.S. Postal Service attends to with its employees.

- Past history of violent behaviors (e.g., physical assaults on others)
- Having a concealed weapon or flashing a weapon
- Fascination with semi-automatic or automatic weapons and their capability to cause great harm
- Odd or bizarre beliefs (magical or satanic beliefs or sexually violent fantasies)
- Perceived loss of options
- Inspiration of fear in others (exceeding mere intimidation)
- Obsessive focus on grudge—often quick to perceive unfairness or malice in others, especially supervisor
- Direct or veiled threats of bodily harm
- History of poor impulse control and poor interpersonal skills (p. 29)

Some of these risk factors are provided to the clinician prior to the interview as part of a police or incident report. Other items will require exploration to determine their relevance for a specific individual. For example, in the case of Stacie introduced in Chapter 3, one of the relevant risk factors is the perceived lack of options. She worries about the ability to continue in her program, and Professor Galloway seems reluctant to have her back in class. In Dustin's case, he shares a history of previous impulse control problems from past bar fights and other explosive outbursts. In both cases, however, it is reasonable to assume a lack of grudge toward their targets at the present. Stacie still sees Galloway as a kind of mentor figure; Dustin seems ready to move on quickly to the next sexual conquest. There may be some desire on Dustin's part to intimidate or instill fear in others in order to gain dominance. Neither Stacie nor Dustin appears to be fascinated with weapons. As you can see, having a deeper understanding of just some of these factors can influence the nature of the threat assessment and provide the clinician with added insight into what questions to ask and what areas to assess.

Risk Assessment Guideline Elements for Violence (RAGE-V)

As mentioned previously, the Association of Threat Assessment Professionals put together a document titled *Risk Assessment Guideline Elements for Violence (RAGE-V;* 2006). I have included the full document in Appendix D; here I note some risk factors of concern:

- Beliefs, revenge, entitlement, grandiosity, need to force closure
- Drug use: methamphetamine, cocaine, alcohol, steroids
- Head trauma
- Criminal history, including history of violence, homicide, stalking, threats, assaultive behavior, violation of conditional release
- Prior voluntary or involuntary commitments

- Past suicide attempts, or suicidal ideation, to include suicidal thoughts, statements, gestures, and attempts
- Adverse responses to authority and limit setting
- History of mental problems that compromises coping or enhances the appeal of violence: depression, paranoia, psychopathy, bipolar disorder, personality disorders (narcissistic, paranoid, borderline, antisocial), and perceptions of injustice or insoluble problems

In Chapter 3, Dustin demonstrates an air of entitlement to say whatever he wants to say in class to the girl with whom he had sex. He doesn't empathize with others and views the entire threat assessment process as a hassle. He demonstrates an adverse reaction to the limit setting by the professor, and the result is police involvement.

Turner and Gelles

Turner and Gelles (2003) identified several risk factors for workplace violence that should be at the forefront of any threat or risk assessment.

Verbal Cues
- Direct and indirect threats
- Threatening/harassing phone calls
- Recurrent suicide threats or actions
- Hopelessness
- Boasts of violent behavior or fantasies
- Frequent profanity
- Belligerence
- Challenging or intimidating statements

Bizarre Thoughts
- Paranoia
- Persecutory delusions with self as victim
- Delusions in general
- Command hallucinations
- Significantly deteriorated thought process
- Obsessions
- Signs or history of substance use/abuse

Behavioral Clues
- Physical altercation/assault upon another person
- Inappropriate weapons possession or use
- Physical intimidation
- Following and surveillance of targeted individual
- Short-fused, loss of emotional control, impulsive
- Destruction of property
- Deteriorating physical appearance and self-care
- Inappropriate displays of emotions
- Isolated and withdrawn

Obsessions
- Self as victim of a particular individual
- Grudges and deep resentments
- Particular object of desire
- Perceived injustice, humiliations, disrespect
- Narrow focus—"sees no way out"—"no other options"
- Publicized acts of violence
- Weapons and destruction
- Fairness
- Grievances and lawsuits (pp. 17–18)

On Valentine's Day 2008, Steven Kazmierczak stood in front of a terrified lecture hall. He had horrific images of a skull impaled with a knife tattooed on one arm and a depiction of the Jigsaw killer from the *Saw* (Wan, 2004) torture film on the other (Keen, 2008; Sander, 2008; Vann, 2008). He fired his shotgun with a blank look on his face. It was his moment of fame, his moment of meaning. People watched him, attended to him. He was present, noticed, and important. He had done something that mattered. He killed five and injured more than 21.

Kazmierczak had studied weapons and violence. He experienced delusions, belligerence, and paranoia. He had depression and recurrent thoughts of suicide. He had experienced bullying, discrimination, humiliation, and disrespect. All of these details were identified by Turner and Gelles as risk factors.

FBI Four-Pronged Approach

The FBI (O'Toole, 2002) suggested a four-pronged approach to threat assessment: (a) the personality of the student, (b) family dynamics, (c) school dynamics, and (d) social dynamics. This approach was designed primarily for use with K–12 schools, although its relevance to the higher education environment is clear.

O'Toole (2000) reminded readers:

> It should be strongly emphasized that this list is not intended as a checklist to predict future violent behavior by a student who has not acted violently or threatened violence. Rather, the list should be considered only after a student has made some type of threat and an assessment has been developed using the four-pronged model . . . No one or two traits or characteristics should be considered in isolation or given more weight than the others . . . (p. 15)

The four-pronged approach consists of the following:

Prong 1: Personality of the Student
- Leakage
- Low tolerance for frustration
- Poor coping skills

- Lack of resiliency
- Failed love relationship
- "Injustice collector"
- Signs of depression
- Narcissism
- Alienation
- Dehumanizes others
- Lack of empathy
- Exaggerated sense of entitlement
- Attitude of superiority
- Exaggerated or pathological need for attention
- Externalizes blame
- Masks low self-esteem
- Anger management problems
- Intolerance
- Inappropriate humor
- Seeks to manipulate others
- Lack of trust
- Closed social group
- Change of behavior
- Rigid and opinionated
- Unusual interest in sensational violence
- Fascination with violence-filled entertainment
- Negative role models
- Behavior appears relevant to carrying out a threat

Prong 2: Family Dynamics
- Turbulent parent–child relationship
- Acceptance of pathological behavior
- Access to weapons
- Lack of intimacy
- Student "rules the roost"
- No limits or monitoring of TV and Internet

Prong 3: School Dynamics
- Student's attachment to school
- Tolerance for disrespectful behavior
- Inequitable discipline
- Inflexible culture
- Pecking order among students
- Code of silence
- Unsupervised computer access

Prong 4: Social Dynamics
- Media, entertainment, technology
- Peer groups

- Drugs and alcohol
- Outside interests
- The copycat effect (pp. 16–24)

As one of the most detailed lists of risk factors, the FBI four-pronged assessment is a useful checklist to have on hand during an interview in order to fully assess the multiple spheres of an individual's interactions with others. The nearly 30 personality factors all occur with prior school shootings and provide a detailed account of risk factors. As with any list, however, the danger of false positives lurks and creates problems for those attempting to separate true violence risk from developmental changes and normal teenage angst. The FBI addresses this by suggesting that the assessment be used only following some kind of threat. One could easily imagine a teenager with poor coping skills, a sense of narcissism, and an exaggerated sense of entitlement who fails at a love relationship. While the student may have five clear risk factors, in the absence of a threat, this may simply be normal behavior for a teenager or college student. As with all threat assessment checklists, exercise caution with overplaying the existence of risk factors apart from the context of a potential threat.

ASIS Workplace Violence Prevention and Intervention Standards

ASIS International and the Society for Human Resource Management published *Workplace Violence Prevention and Intervention* (2011), a set of standards designed to help security and human resource personnel prevent and intervene in potentially dangerous scenarios. They advised organizations to remain alert to the following problematic behaviors:

- A history of threats or violent acts, including threats or violence occurring during employment and a criminal history suggestive of a propensity to use violence to project power and to control others or as a response to stress or conflict.
- Threats, bullying, or other threatening behavior, aggressive outbursts or comments, or excessive displays of anger.
- Verbal abuse or harassment by any means or medium.
- Harboring grudges, an inability to handle criticism, habitually making excuses, and blaming others.
- Chronic, unsubstantiated complaints about persecution or injustice (a victim mindset).
- Obsessive intrusion upon others or persistent unwanted romantic pursuit.
- Erratic, impulsive, or bizarre behavior that has generated fear among co-workers.
- Homicidal or suicidal thoughts or ideas.

- A high degree of emotional distress.
- Apparent impulsivity or low tolerance of frustration.
- A fascination with weapons, a preoccupation with violent themes of revenge, and an unusual interest in recently publicized violent events, if communicated in a manner that creates discomfort for co-workers.
- Any behavior or collection of behaviors that instill fear or generate a concern that a person might act out violently. (p. 22)

Though focused primarily on workplace settings, these risk factors echo similar thoughts and behaviors that have occurred in a variety of rampage attacks.

Meloy, Hoffmann, Guldimann, and James

Meloy et al. (2011) published an article outlining eight warning behaviors, described as "factors which constitute change, and which are evidence of increasing or accelerating risk" (p. 260). This list is particularly helpful because it addresses key behaviors that place individuals at increasing risk for engaging in violence.

1. **Pathway warning behavior**—any behavior that is part of research, planning, preparation, or implementation of an attack (Calhoun & Weston, 2003; Fein & Vossekuil, 1998).
2. **Fixation warning behavior**—any behavior that indicates an increasingly pathological preoccupation with a person or a cause (Mullen et al., 2009). It is measured by:
   (a) increasing perseveration on the person or cause;
   (b) increasingly strident opinion;
   (c) increasingly negative characterization of the object of fixation;
   (d) impact on the family or other associates of the object of fixation, if present and aware;
   (e) angry emotional undertone. It is typically accompanied by social or occupational deterioration.
3. **Identification warning behavior**—any behavior that indicates a psychological desire to be a "pseudo-commando" (Dietz, 1986; Knoll, 2010), have a "warrior mentality" (Hempel et al., 1999), closely associate with weapons or other military or law enforcement paraphernalia, identify with previous attackers or assassins, or identify oneself as an agent to advance a particular cause or belief system.
4. **Novel aggression warning behavior**—an act of violence which appears unrelated to any targeted violence pathway warning behavior which is committed for the first time. Such behaviors may be utilized to test the ability of the subject to actually do a violent act (de Becker, 1997), and may be a measure of response tendency, the motivation to

act on the environment (Hull, 1952), or a behavioral tryout (MacCulloch, Snowden, Wood, & Mills, 1983).

5. **Energy burst warning behavior**—an increase in the frequency or variety of any noted activities related to the target, even if the activities themselves are relatively innocuous, usually in the days or weeks before the attack (Odgers et al., 2009).

6. **Leakage warning behavior**—the communication to a third party of an intent to do harm to a target through an attack (Meloy & O'Toole, 2011).

7. **Last resort warning behavior**—evidence of a violent "action imperative" (Mohandie & Duffy, 1999), increasing desperation or distress through declaration in word or deed, forcing the individual into a position of last resort. There is no alternative other than violence, and the consequences are justified (de Becker, 1997).

8. **Directly communicated threat warning behavior**—the communication of a direct threat to the target or law enforcement beforehand. A threat is a written or oral communication that implicitly or explicitly states a wish or intent to damage, injure, or kill the target, or individuals symbolically or actually associated with the target. (pp. 266–269)

Handbook for Campus Threat Assessment and Management

G. Deisinger et al. (2008) originally suggested these investigative questions in *The Handbook for Campus Threat Assessment and Management Teams* drawn from the original U.S. Secret Service document (Fein & Vossekuil, 1998). The questions are summarized and adapted below from E. Deisinger et al.'s (2014) more recent chapter:

1. What first brought the person to the assessment? Do these conditions or situations still exist? Does the person of concern feel that he or she is being addressed?

2. Have there been any communications suggesting ideas or intent to attack others?

3. Has the person shown inappropriate interest in campus/workplace/school attacks or attackers; fixation on weapons; other mass violence or terrorism; obsessive pursuit, stalking or pursuit of others?

4. Has the person engaged in any attack-related behaviors?

5. Does the person have the capacity to carry out an act of targeted violence?

6. Is the person experiencing hopelessness, desperation, or despair?

7. Does the person have a trusting relationship with at least one responsible person?

8. Does the person see violence as an acceptable, desirable, or only way to solve problems?

9. Is the person's conversation or "story" consistent with his or her actions?

10. Are other people concerned about the person's potential for violence?
11. What circumstances might affect the likelihood of violence? What would increase the risk? What would decrease the risk? (pp. 122–123)

Virginia Tech Faculty/Staff Guide

In 2009, Randazzo and Plummer wrote *Implementing Behavioral Threat Assessment on Campus: A Virginia Tech Demonstration Project.* The report included a flyer that is distributed to the community to assist faculty, staff, and students to know what kind of behaviors should be reported to the threat assessment team. Although they noted that their list should not be considered exhaustive, they suggested that the community report the following concerning behaviors:

- Unusual or abrupt changes in behaviors or patterns;
- Extreme reaction to a loss or traumatic event;
- Preoccupation with weapons, violent events, or persons who have engaged in violent acts;
- Uncharacteristically poor performance;
- References to harming others or planning a violent or destructive event;
- Evidence of depression, hopelessness, or suicidal thoughts/plans;
- Inappropriate responses such as prolonged irritability, angry outbursts, or intense reactions;
- Strained interpersonal relations, isolating behaviors, or low self esteem;
- Significant change in life circumstances such as loss of job or relationship. (p. 124)

Concerning, Threatening, Dangerous

I'll end this chapter with one of my favorite concepts from Mary Ellen O'Toole and Alissa Bowman's book *Dangerous Instincts* (2011): concerning, threatening, and dangerous behavior. It is worth noting that O'Toole worked as an FBI profiler; this list of behaviors, though not exhaustive, provides an excellent place to start when considering a person's risk:

> Impulsivity, inappropriate or out-of control anger, narcissism, lack of empathy, injustice collecting, objectification of others, blaming others for failures or problems, paranoia, rule-breaking, use of violence, thoughts and fantasies of violence, drug and alcohol problems, poor coping skills, equal opportunity coping skills, and thrill seeking. (pp. 181–182)

One of the terms that I have found helpful in understanding those who develop plots of revenge and intricate schemes to inflict harm on others is the *injustice collector*. O'Toole described this individual as "a person who feels 'wronged,' 'persecuted' and 'destroyed,' blowing injustices way out of proportion, never forgiving the person they felt has wronged them" (O'Toole & Bowman, 2011, p. 186). These individuals keep track of past wrongs committed against them and are often upset in a manner that exceeds what would typically be expected. They hold onto past slights, many back as far as childhood, and see the world from this singled-out view. Additionally, they often have poor coping skills to deal with their frustrations.

However, it is important to remember that moving from idea to action remains exceedingly rare. Calhoun and Weston (2009) put it this way: "The vast majority of people suffering some sense of injustice do not cross that great divide to seeking violence. Perhaps only the actual attack demands as much fortitude and determination as deciding to do it" (p. 55).

Summary

The full challenge of threat assessments should be apparent after reading this chapter: Not only do dozens of risk factors exist, but many state agencies, threat professionals, law enforcement agencies, and academics have developed their own threat protocol and processes. This complexity can leave the clinician slightly overwhelmed with choices. The purpose of this chapter is not to overwhelm but instead expose the clinician to some of the wide variety of literature and conceptualization in threat assessment.

Perhaps you find yourself in the same place I was in when choosing a therapeutic approach during graduate school. The phrase *technical eclectic* was a popular one denoting a therapist who had no single theory but drew from a range of techniques and approaches found across dozen of fields. I present a number of approaches to threat assessment not to confuse the matter or overwhelm but instead to offer a wide overview of the scholarship and thinking currently available in this field.

Chapter 7 provides a methodology for thinking about risk that will prepare the clinician as he or she gets ready to generate a report.

Questions for Further Discussion

1. What are some common factors that stand out when reviewing the different risk factors stressed by each of the major groups in this chapter? Consider creating a list of risk factors as you read through the chapter and create a personal list of questions to use in a threat assessment.
2. How do the risk factors for school violence differ from those in workplace settings? In general, what are some of the considerations that are different when assessing a student in K–12 or college versus an individual in the community or workplace?

3. Discuss the term *injustice collector* as it applies to threat assessment. Give some examples of where you have observed this in your personal life. How might you assess injustice collecting tendencies during a threat assessment?

Chapter 7

Structured
Professional
JUDGMENT

Chapter Highlights

1. This chapter reviews the concepts of *structured professional judgment* (Hart & Logan, 2011; Hart et al., 2011) as it applies to violence risk assessment. This approach to risk assessment and management consists of seven steps: gather information, determine the presence of risk factors, determine the relevance of risk factors, develop a good formulation of violence risk, develop scenarios of violence, develop a case management plan based on those scenarios, and develop conclusory opinions about violence risk.
2. Gathering information is key to conducting an accurate threat assessment. The information is drawn not only from the clinical assessment but from the referral source, the community, law enforcement, educational settings, and the workplace.
3. Determining the presence of risk factors (see Chapter 6) is the next step in the process. The identified risk factors are then assessed for their relevance to the case at hand.
4. The development of a comprehensive formulation of risk consists of assessing the potential motivators, disinhibitors, and destabilizing elements as they influence the potential for violence.
5. Once these initial steps are completed, the structured professional judgment model moves to develop *potential scenarios for violence* that are individualized, narrative, diachronic, testable, amplitive, and fertile. These scenarios are then used to guide case management and develop conclusory opinions about violence risk.

One of my favorite parts of working as a consultant is the ability to travel and attend trainings around the world on violence and threat assessment. In April 2013, I was able to attend the launch of version 3.0 of Historical Clinical Risk-20 (HCR-20), a well-respected clinical tool that assesses violence through a review of an individual's historical, clinical, and risk factors. During this weeklong training event in Edinburgh, Scotland, I was able to attend a session on structured professional judgment run by Stephen Hart, a co-author of the HCR-20 (Douglas, Hart, Webster, & Belfrage, 2013). The charismatic and affable Dr. Hart walked the audience through the process of threat assessment focused on the needs of the individual, case management, and a detailed discussion of clinical formulation.

Hart's work moves away from prediction models and instead illustrates the potential exacerbating factors that could cause violence, as well as those inhibiting factors that reduce violence risk. To illustrate the model concepts, I use the cases of Stacie and Dustin (see Chapter 3).

The structured professional judgment process can be outlined in seven steps: gather information, determine the presence of risk factors, determine the relevance of risk factors, develop a good formulation of violence risk, develop scenarios of violence, develop a case management plan based on those scenarios, and develop conclusory opinions about violence risk.

Before reviewing these seven steps, I remind the reader of advice offered by Beck (2008):

> There is no substitute for clinical judgment in assessing the risk for violence and in making the many decisions involved in treatment. Actuarial methods are helpful . . . but only as background. For example, it helps to know that young people are more often violent than older people, men are more often violent than women, that people brought up in violent circumstances are more likely to be violent than those brought up in safety, and so on. However, knowing all the actuarial data will not in the end serve to reduce the necessity for making a clinical assessment of risk. The person in the clinical encounter is unique; the circumstances of his or her life are unique and may be changing, rapidly or slowly, in ways that affect risk. It is in the clinician's responsibility, difficult as this may be, to learn about the person and the circumstance of his or her life, and on this basis to make the best estimate of risk. This is true in all clinical settings. (pp. 237–238)

The primacy of the clinician in the process of assessment cannot be overstated. Violence risk factors and research are supplemental to the analytical process orchestrated by the person conducting the assessment. Now that we have reviewed in great detail the core threat concepts and violence risk factors found in the literature, we focus on the process of understanding violence risk in a structured and organized manner.

1. Gather Information

Gathering information might seem obvious, but there is no more important step in threat assessment. We are limited in our risk assessment by the information we have at hand. There is certainly a great deal we can learn from the clinical interview, but that should not be the limit of our inquiry. It is essential to gather data from past treatment, criminal records, student conduct violations, class attendance and participation, work performance, social interaction, and family of origin. Imagine how Stacie's case formulation would change if we learned she had a similar issue with another professor in her undergraduate class and she had followed him home and lied to his wife about an affair they had. What if Dustin had prior assault convictions with past relationships that paralleled his current situation with the girl in his class?

Gathering all the information available to the clinician increases the accuracy of the clinical formulation. Without good data, it becomes impossible to fully conceptualize the individual's potential risk for violence. The information gathered should have a depth and breadth to it to ensure a full understanding. Although it is always preferable to have an in-person interview, there are times when that is not possible. The same is true with past records and a review of past behaviors. Ideally, we would like to gather all information that is available, but we must also understand that this is not always possible.

2. Determine the Presence of Risk Factors

The HCR-20 version 3.0 developed by Hart provides a good starting place to understand the historical, clinical, and current risk factors that correlate with potential violence. Chapters 4–6 of this book review numerous risk factors that should be understood by clinicians who are completing a threat assessment.

In the case of Dustin, several risk factors come to light in the brief narrative. We understand that Dustin has a past history of impulsive violence. He is described as a "loose cannon" capable of almost anything. He has a pattern of objectifying women and lacks insight into his actions when held accountable for threatening another student in class. He fails to follow his professor's request to leave class, and the police become involved. He has access to weapons and military training on how to use them.

In Stacie's narrative, we see her determination to complete her academic program and the forces that stand against her reaching that goal. She has a history of depression and some question of suicidality. There is an impulsive threat made to the professor with little evidence of her having the ability to carry the threat out to completion. She has some friends and family, but these social supports offer questionable solace in the face of her problems. She has a past romantic relationship that ended badly and caused her profound distress.

Both cases have risk factors present that should be fully explored. As the clinician masters violence risk factors in the literature and from previous attacks, it becomes easier to detect them during a clinical interview. Those working in a college setting might find it helpful to keep a written checklist of the risk factors outlined in the SIVRA-35 (Appendix C) when conducting interviews.

3. Determine the Relevance of Risk Factors

When the risk factors have been identified and understood, the next step is to sort through those that are germane. A risk factor may be present, but it may not be relevant to the case at hand. This concept is one that I found novel in the structured professional judgment approach—the clinician is encouraged to think outside of a standard checklist and ascertain if a particular risk factor is applicable for a given case.

For example, Dustin has served in the military. This may or may not increase the risk of violence in his case narrative. Although he has access to weapons and the knowledge base to kill, the nature of the main concern in the case does not seem to involve weapons or a desire to hurt someone in a tactical or predatory manner. Dustin's problems seem to center on personal interactions and an unsavory tendency to objectify and depersonalize women. These traits might relate to his military service, or they might not. Each risk factor must be identified, and its relevance to the current situation must be weighed and considered.

Similarly, Stacie has a history of depression and a relationship that ended badly. Both of these are considered risk factors for violence. The relevance of these risk factors in this current case, however, may be called into question because her depression is not currently related to her threat. It may be a concern in the future if she is removed from the class or her academic program, but the depression does not appear to be a risk factor that is relevant in understanding her current potential for violence.

Stacie's past relationship that ended poorly also may or may not be related to her potential for future violence. It could be that this relationship is part of a normal, developmental disappointment that most college students experience. It could be that the ending of the past relationship mimics some of the same cruelty and power differential that is present with Professor Galloway. In the end, the clinician must use skill to determine during the interview which hypothesis fits better.

4. Develop a Good Formulation of Risk

This step addresses the question "Why might the person commit violence? What is his or her motivation?" Hart and Logan (2011) described the process of gathering and integrating diverse information to develop a concise account of the nature and etiology of the problems affecting a person's mental health to guide decision making. In other words, can we find a way to "get into the person's head" and develop a theory that explains why he or she might commit violence?

During the training, I was surprised that Hart encouraged a more artistic exploration of the individual's motivation here rather than returning to probabilities and a more objective, quantitative checklist. What he encouraged, and I would echo, is the importance of understanding the idea that all violence is goal directed. If you don't understand the goal, you don't understand why the person engaged in violence. In other words, how does the person make decisions about violence; how does he or she weigh the acceptable costs and benefits to violence and ultimately come to a moment of commitment? How does he or she wrestle with the question of feasibility? Is this something he or she could do and get away with? Is surviving the attack irrelevant to the person?

To this end, Hart offered three areas to consider when developing a formulation of risk: motivators, disinhibitors, and destabilizers. These become important in understanding why an individual commits a violent action and are weighed when an assessor writes a threat evaluation.

Motivators

The following sections describe motivators, the factors that drive an individual forward in a potentially violent attack. One or more of these motivating factors might be at play. They are common inspirations for those who commit violence.

Justice/Honor
Individuals might commit acts of violence because they seek justice for a past wrong or frustration or believe that a matter of honor is at stake (Barnes, 2011). On April 7, 2011, Wellington Menezes de Oliveira shot 32 students in Tasso da Silveira School, killing 12, before committing suicide. In a video explaining his attacks posted days before the shooting, he said:

> The struggle for which many brothers died in the past, and for which I will die, is not solely because of what is known as bullying. Our fight is against cruel people, cowards, who take advantage of the kindness, the weakness of people unable to defend themselves. (Van Brunt, 2012, p. 19)

Gain/Profit
A person might commit violence in the process of seeking profit (e.g., a bank robber or thief, for whom violence is secondary to the desire to gain or profit).

Status/Esteem
Some violent individuals are motivated to achieve a status or place in the world. This motivation is a growing concern with the increase in

school and college shootings in the United States that may be related to a desire for the shooters to "one-up" one another. Reports from the Newtown shooting indicate Lanza had studied previous shooters such as Anders Breivik in Norway and Stephen Kazmierczak at Northern Illinois prior to his attack (Weizel, 2013).

On November 12, 1966, Robert Smith took seven people hostage at Rose-Mar College of Beauty, a school for training beauticians. His plan was to bind the women, tie plastic bags over their heads, and watch them while they suffocated. The bags turned out to be too small. Smith instead ordered the hostages to lie down on the floor in a circle. He then proceeded to shoot them in the head with a .22-caliber pistol. Four women and a 3-year-old girl died; one woman and a baby were injured but survived. Police arrested Smith after the massacre. Smith had reportedly admired Richard Speck (killer of eight women in 1966) and Charles Whitman (the clock tower gunman in Texas). Smith announced, "I wanted to get known, just wanted to get myself a name" (Van Brunt, 2012, p. 20). During his childhood he was teased in school for his lack of coordination and developed an interest in serial killers and mass murders. He was sentenced to two 99-year sentences and four life sentences for the murder.

Arousal/Activity

For some individuals, the desire to be violent is related to the increased adrenaline rush and social activity; this might be the motivator for those involved in bar fights or mixed martial arts.

Proximity/Affiliation

Violence is motivated by an affiliation and connection to a certain group and often occurs as part of a mob (e.g., European Union football matches).

Release/Expression

There are times when the motivation for violence is a final release or expression of pain. The person committing violence communicates, "See! See what you have done!" and the violence perpetrated is a release from pain and the build-up of emotional trauma.

On March 25, 1994, Brian Head shot and killed himself during his high school economics class at Etowah High School (Headley, 1994). Head had been a longtime target for bullies because of his weight and thick glasses. His father subsequently successfully lobbied for a law that criminalized bullying and required schools to alert parents of bullied children.

Control/Change

The motivation for violence might be to alter the current circumstance and shake up the status quo.

Dylan Klebold and Eric Harris, the Columbine shooters, are prime examples of individuals motivated by a desire to spread a larger message of change. The unreleased footage of Klebold and Harris talking for hours about their desire to inspire other school shootings has been kept from public view (Gibbs & Roche, 1999).

Defense/Distance

Violence can be preemptive, part of a larger plan to protect the ideology of the person planning the attack. Violence here is driven by a desire to create distance between the person and the targets so he or she can protect himself or herself from future harm.

Anders Behring Breivik (2011) set off a bomb killing eight people in Oslo, Norway, before continuing onto Utøya and gunning down 69 youths at a labor party camp in July 2011. He claimed these events were marketing for his 1,500-page manifesto outlining a coming war against the Muslims. The manifesto also included detailed plans on how to make bombs and obtain weapons and a journal account of the months leading up to the shooting. Breivik's attack could be described as being motivated by his view of himself as a modern day Knight Templar upholding his religious purity against an attack from the Muslim faith.

A student who has been bullied or teased who attacks his oppressors to prevent future teasing or bullying could be said to be acting defensively.

Disinhibitors

Disinhibitors are the characteristics present that increase the likelihood of violent action. An inhibitor might be something like a positive self-image or stable and supportive peer groups. Disinhibitors are the traits and qualities that encourage and provide increased momentum for those considering an attack. I see these as the "devil on the shoulder" items that push the person closer to violent action.

Negative Attitudes

A violent person might use reinforcing negative messages in a way that makes the world seem bleaker. This could be described as a bit of an "Eeyore complex" where the world around is seen as a hostile and negative place.

Clay Duke, who took a Florida school board hostage in a 2010 attack in Panama City, saw the world as a negative place and talked about revenge after his wife was fired. After firing two shots at a member of the school board, he shot himself as the SWAT team moved in. The entire shooting was caught on tape. It is reported that he created a Facebook page that included the following statement:

> My Testament: Some people (the government sponsored media) will say I was evil, a monster (V) . . . no . . . I was just born poor in a country where the Wealthy manipulate, use, abuse, and economically enslave 95% of the population. Rich Republicans, Rich Democrats . . . same-same . . . rich . . . they take turns fleecing us . . . our few dollars . . . pyramiding

the wealth for themselves. The 95% . . . the us, in US of A, are the neo slaves of the Global South. Our Masters, the Wealthy, do, as they like to us . . . . (Owens, 2010, p. 1)

Negative Self-Concept

Some individuals regard themselves as worthless and hopeless, a negative self-concept that may be reinforced by teasing and bullying at school or be related to mental illness. The negative worldview increases the likelihood that the person moves forward with a violent attack. A more positive viewpoint would help mitigate the risk.

In February 1996, Barry Loukaitis killed three and injured one person at Frontier Middle School in Moose Lake, Washington. Loukaitis was severely bullied at school; he had his head shoved into toilets and was urinated on. He held a strong negative self-concept and saw his only chance at redemption through killing (Vaughan, 1998).

Lack of Integration

Individuals who are poorly connected socially to their peers lack social integration, which removes the opportunity for friendships and positive social interactions that would help move the student off the pathway to violence. Without social support, individuals become further isolated and find themselves without much in the way of positive support in times of crisis.

Asa Coon shot four students before committing suicide in October 2007 at Success Tech Academy in Ohio. The shooting started after another student punched Coon in the face after bumping into him. Other students and teachers reported that Coon had been bullied for his Gothic-style appearance and eccentric behavior. Such treatment by his peers probably fed his desire to exact revenge and to feel in control.

Nihilism

The nihilistic individual suffers from an utter lack of faith in humanity and desires nothing but dark emptiness. A nihilistic view of human action and thought rejects any shred of hope.

Sixteen-year-old Brenda Spencer fired shots out of a window in her home, randomly shooting at students across the street outside of the Cleveland Elementary School in San Diego on January 29, 1979. She killed two and injured nine. The prior Christmas her father had given her a semi-automatic .22 rifle. During the attack, a reporter called her house trying to interview neighbors who might know something. She told him she was the shooter and said, "I just did it for the fun of it. I don't like Mondays. This livens up the day. I have to go now. I shot a pig [policeman] I think and I want to shoot more. I'm having too much fun [to surrender]" (Jones, 1998, p. 118). She also said, "I had no reason for it, and it was just a lot of fun," "It was just like shooting ducks in a pond," and "[The children] looked like a herd of cows standing around; it was really easy pickings" (Jones, 1998, p. 118). After firing

30 rounds, she barricaded herself in the house for 7 hours before surrendering. According to reports, she had mentioned the possibility of the attacks months earlier: "One of these mornings, you're gonna look for me," "no one understands me," "you don't have to wait very long to see what is going on with me." She had previously broken windows in the school with her BB gun (Jones, 1998, p. 118).

Lack of Anxiety

Anxiety and fear serve as two very useful inhibitors for potential violence. When anxiety about the future ramifications of a violent attack is not present for an individual, this lack of anxiety serves to encourage potentially violent action rather than prevent it.

On November 5, 2009, Major Nidal Hasan lowered his head for a few minutes in the cafeteria and then began shooting. A total of 214 rounds were fired from 20- and 30-round pistol magazines (he did not use the .357). He had an additional 177 rounds of unfired ammunition in his pockets. A local police officer shot Hassan five times and placed him in handcuffs. Hasan was a psychiatrist and often talked about Islam. Fellow students and faculty described Hasan as disconnected, aloof, paranoid, belligerent, and schizoid. Hasan displayed little anxiety about his attack and saw his actions as justified given the nature of the unjust military action in Afghanistan (Owens, 2009). He shouted, "Allahu Akbar!" (God is greatest) prior to the shooting. He was said to be in contact with Islamic extremist Anwar al-Awlaki, who preaches in his sermons, "I pray that Allah destroys America and all its allies" (Van Brunt, 2012, p. 17).

Lack of Guilt

Individuals who lack a sense of guilt or remorse for their actions might have more potential for future negative action. The idea that one might be held accountable for her or his thoughts or actions serves as an inhibitor for potential violence; one might think "While I may want to commit violence, I'm not sure I could live with myself afterwards." Those who lack guilt are unencumbered by this stabilizing factor.

Robert Poulin raped and killed a fellow classmate in his home and subsequently burned his own house to the ground. He then arrived at St. Pius X High School in Ottawa and killed one and injured five others with a shotgun (Cobb & Avery, 1977). Poulin was born with a chest deformity and eyesight problems that prevented him from becoming a pilot. During his childhood, he was shy and had difficulty socially. It is reported he had an addiction to pornography, often experienced depression, and was suicidal. He trained in a Canadian militia and learned combat skills.

He kept a diary outlining his plans to burn down his parents' home and make them suffer. He also wrote, "I don't want to die before I have had the pleasure of fucking some girl" (Cobb & Avery, 1977, p. 160). During the rape and subsequent stabbing and murder of his classmate, he had gone upstairs from his basement bedroom and had a peanut butter sandwich with his mother.

Destabilizers

Destabilizers tear away at the fabric of support for individuals and increase the potential risk for violence. Imagine a well-set table with china and fine crystal. Glasses are filled to the very rim with champagne. Now imagine a herd of dogs running through the restaurant like the Bumpus's dogs in the movie *A Christmas Story* when they steal the Christmas turkey. The table shakes and items on it become unstable. Destabilizers are external factors that increase the risk of violence by creating upheaval in the individual in question.

Many of the destabilizing factors in the list that follows are related to mental illness. This accounts for some of the popular media hype that suggests mental illness is always a causal factor in violent behavior. In reality, mental health problems do not directly cause the violence but certainly could increase the likelihood of violence because they have a destabilizing effect.

Disturbed Attention
Those with a disturbed sense of attention have difficulty staying on task and have trouble following through with plans. They become easily distracted by slights and frustrations and have difficulty focusing in a linear manner on their predicament.

Disturbed Perception
An individual who becomes overwhelmed by alternative-reality delusions and paranoia and has difficulty parsing reality from fantasy experiences an increased vulnerability to commit violence.

Latina Williams purchased a .357 magnum handgun and a box of ammunition at a New Orleans pawnshop on February 7, 2008, and concealed it in her handbag before entering a classroom the next day. She shot two other female students and witnesses report she said, "Don't worry, I'm not mad at y'all" before shooting herself (Dyer, 2008, p. 4). There is some evidence that an anonymous caller contacted the counseling center the day before, saying she was going to take her own life. Williams had no reported residence and was living out of her car. She reportedly had a history of paranoia and schizophrenia (Dyer, 2008).

Impaired Memory
The inability to recall information and attribute meaning to a linear set of experiences and circumstances is a destabilizer. People with impaired memory have difficulty remembering what happened and may attribute blame or responsibility incorrectly because they have difficulty remembering the facts and past experiences related to their violence threat.

Inability to Reason

Individuals with severe mental health concerns might be unable to remain rational and reasonable. This is a destabilizing factor in their risk for future violence.

Douglas Pennington had been treated for mental illness. On September 2, 2006, he arrived at Shepherd University and (with a .38-caliber handgun he had bought 2 days earlier) shot and killed his two sons who were students there in the Thatcher Hall parking lot. He left behind notes in the car he drove to school and in a notebook at his home. He talked about his internal battles, his love for his family, and the feelings of guilt and pain that surrounded his life. "I see what I've done and I see what's coming for my family and I can't let that happen to them," he wrote in the notebook. "I lose anyway I turn, and so do they" (Van Brunt, 2012, p. 253). He mentioned paranoid thoughts of his children being tortured and killed. Family members had previously attempted to have him hospitalized.

Obsessive Thinking

People with obsessive thinking misattribute blame, develop a sense of tunnel vision, and cannot think logically and rationally about their circumstances.

Racing Thinking

Individuals might be unable to consider reasonable avenues of thought and logic because they are overwhelmed with one set of facts or have thoughts that jump quickly from place to place. They have trouble maintaining focus and their racing thoughts may lead to incorrect conclusions that are frustrating and potentially paranoid.

Peter Odighizuwa was a nontraditional Nigerian former student who had failed out of law school. On January 16, 2002, he opened fire with a handgun, killing three and injuring three. Two students subdued Odighizuwa outside the school. After the shooting, Odighizuwa said, "I really don't know what happened, I feel like I'm God sometimes, and I was running demons out of the school. It was like an exorcism" (Jerome & Foster, 2002, p. 95).

Clinical Formulation

After the motivators, disinhibitors, and destabilizers are assessed and explored by the clinician, the next step to the formulation of risk is to take this constellation of descriptive facts and use them to begin to speculate about the potential for future violence. Let me pause here and acknowledge this concept, because it was difficult for me to fully appreciate the first time I heard it. What structured professional judgment suggests here is a speculation about potential future violence. The clinician is encouraged to put forth a hypothesis regarding the individual's likelihood of committing an act of violence. The risk factors and motivators, disinhibitors, and destabilizers inform the hypothesis, a starting place to better understand an individual's potential for violence.

The clinician's formulation should have the following key characteristics.

Individualized

Each case formulation should be tied to the particular case at hand and the unique risk factors and specific motivators, disinhibitors, and destabilizers of the individual in question.

In Stacie's case, there might be a temptation to see her as yet another overworked, stressed-out graduate student unable to deal with a professor's criticism. In fact, Stacie seems to be more of the victim of an instructor's unchecked cruelty hiding in the guise of artistic critique. Her explosive outburst, while unwise, becomes more understandable in this narrative. The threat assessment professional may be in the position of creating a report that encourages the school administration to explore Professor Galloway's arrogant teaching approach in addition to taking corrective actions with Stacie.

Stacie's potential violence may be understood through her motivation for release or expression. In the future, predatory or targeted violence may be considered under a motivation of justice or honor. Her negative self-concept from her past relationship and concerns over her work not being good enough may serve as disinhibitors for violence. Obsessive thoughts or racing thinking may act as destabilizing factors for her in the future.

Narrative

A good formulation of risk is narrative in nature and unfolds over time. It is a story about why and how the person may commit violence. The story contains facts and risk factors that are tied together in a plot.

In Dustin's case, a risk formulation may center on his impulsive actions (bar fight, yelling at student in class, refusal to comply with professor) in the context of his objectified and misogynistic outlook. A story about his potential for violence would include an understanding of how he sees women (the girl he threatens in class, in particular) as not deserving of his empathy or understanding. This tendency is further exacerbated by his feelings that she is not entitled to challenge him and that she gets whatever she deserves after she made the decision to sleep with him. Violence, in Dustin's case, may erupt from these motivations of arousal/activity or control/change. He may become further destabilized by his lack of attention and disinhibited by his lack of anxiety and lack of guilt.

Diachronic

The risk formulation unfolds over time. The story is not static but is laid out over time to capture the interactive nature of the individual being assessed and his or her environment.

In Dustin's narrative, one could create a story of him becoming motivated to commit violence during the conduct interview in an attempt to control or change the outcome of his case. The story doesn't stop with his threat in class but carries forward as we imagine his reaction to being held accountable by the school's judicial system and facing potential separation from the class or academic program. One could imagine Dustin becoming increasingly enraged at the potential threat to his off-campus emergency medical technician job because of his behavior in the classroom. Clinical risk formulations should be organic and always have a "what next?" quality to their naturalistic exploration of the potential for violence.

Testable

Good stories, like good hypothees, are testable. If the story stands up to our testing and critiques, then it may be useful and allow us to make some predictions. We are then able to tell ourselves, "If I'm right, then these kind of treatments should work." This is an active and ongoing process of testing and prediction. The experiential feedback helps us then update our risk formulation.

In Stacie's case, it might be interesting to explore the frustration she faced in her past relationship in comparison to her current difficulties with Professor Galloway. It would be easy to imagine a story where Stacie's difficulty with Professor Galloway is largely tied to her unresolved issues arising from the trauma of her past relationship where her boyfriend was overly critical and abusive. In other words, is it Stacie's past experience that keeps her from adopting the stance most students take with Professor Galloway? Is that why she cannot accept his arrogance and narcissism as part of the hoop-jumping process of graduate school?

This theory is an interesting one, and it has to be tested against the reality of Stacie's past experience. In essence, there are no bad first theories, but they do need to be tested and confirmed before moving forward. In this case, there needs to be further questioning on the clinician's part regarding her past relationships and how the most recent one ended.

Amplitive and Fertile

A good risk formulation is more than just taking a list of facts and stringing them together in a predictable way. Instead, the risk formulation should help tie the information together in a way that produces new lines of thinking and provides potential areas of insight. Good formulations of risk highlight multiple facets of a person's worldview and life.

In Dustin's case, it would be interesting to think about what might happen next if he were returned to the classroom with the same female student. How might the professor react to his return? Are there ways to mitigate the professor's adjustment to having Dustin return to the class? For that matter, how might the entire class react to Dustin returning after being escorted out of class by the police?

If the risk formulation for Dustin suggests that he overreacted but has no real potential for violence and that he will choose to avoid future outbursts and comply with his professor's requests (given the perceived hassle—threat assessment process, conduct hearing, potential for off-campus job impact), then what might be some potential scenarios that would trigger or exacerbate a violent reaction? A risk formulation, like a good story, creates new avenues of thinking and exploration.

5. Develop Scenarios of Violence

The clinician continues the imaginative process of creating a story of violence by expanding the concept and composing several potential stories. Given the primary hazards and risk factors that have been identified, the following questions can be formulated into stories: If the person in question were to commit violence, what would he do? Who would he hurt? What kinds of things would make any of this more likely?

Scenario planning is the process by which multiple positive and negative scenarios are imagined by the clinician in order to better conceptualize the potential risk. This method has been used in public safety, health, engineering, and military planning to be better prepared for all potential outcomes while attempting to account for complexity and uncertainty. Building from the clinical risk formulation, one can develop possible scenarios that might occur.

The process of scenario invention is a useful one for several reasons. It helps the clinician avoid tunnel vision and avoid putting forth only a single hypothesis rather than conceptualizing the full range of potential outcomes. It allows the clinician to strive for the desired outcome and avoid undesired outcomes. Exhibit 7.1 presents the qualities common to robust scenarios.

Potential scenarios should explore four different archetypes.

- *Repeat:* Stories that are a replication of past violence
- *Twist:* Similar story with a change in motivation (a different target or location)
- *Escalation:* Increase in lethality of the attack or a "worst case" scenario
- *Improvement:* Stories that involve a positive change and reduction of threat

Table 7.1 uses the case studies from Chapter 3 and explores what potential repeat, twist, escalation, and improvement scenarios might be for Stacie and Dustin. A particularly important twist scenario that should be explored by the clinician conducting Dustin's assessment involves Dustin expanding his potential veiled, direct, or contingent threats to the professor who involved law enforcement. Although it was not explicitly stated in the transcript, it is reasonable to assume that this female authority figure may also draw Dustin's attention.

Exhibit 7.1 | Qualities of Good Scenarios

Externally coherent. Every story has facts. Every case has pieces of information that need to be explained. A formulation of risk should be derived from those facts. If a scenario is not consistent with the facts, then it isn't a very good scenario. Think of a movie whose plot lines are left unexplained when the movie ends—an occurrence that would make most viewers unhappy. A good scenario matches the facts of the formulation. There should be no major facts that are left unexplained.

Factually coherent. There should be a good number of facts used to develop the scenario. Imagine a book or movie that is too short and leaves things unexplained. It's hard to have the plot make sense. Having only a few bits of information incorporated into the scenario makes it harder to develop a plot. On the other hand, don't overload it with details.

Internally coherent. The scenario must make sense to us. There cannot be big contradictions. The scenario should be a nice, simple, straightforward story. Don't create a scenario based on a formulation that leaves the reader asking, "If this is the plot, then how did that happen?"

Accepted. Would other clinicians and referral sources who know about the case accept this scenario as credible and as a good story?

Reliable. Is the scenario accurate and valid? Would others come up with a similar scenario, or is the story something drawn from left field? If the scenario is tested out, would it produce results?

Generative. Does the scenario provide possible predictions and information that is useable to address the potential for violence? Is the story helpful, and will it assist us in preventing future violence?

Plausible. Is the information in the scenario relevant, comprehensive, and credible?

Useful. Does the scenario guide the development of specific risk management plans?

Consensual. Are different people able to come up with similar scenarios based on the risk formulation?

6. Develop a Case Management Plan Based on Scenarios

One of the differences between other approaches to threat assessment and Hart's structured professional judgment approach is the intertwining of assessment with treatment. The assessment naturally raises questions about the interventions that reduce the potential risk of violence and the exacerbating factors that could make it worse.

Table 7.1 | Potential Scenarios

Scenario	Dustin	Stacie
Repeat	Dustin returns to class and gets into another altercation with the girl. He yells at her again and the professor asks him to leave.	Stacie is able to return to class and Professor Galloway makes a joke about her getting all "PMS" crazy and trying to kill him again. The class laughs.
Twist	Dustin gets into an argument with a staff member in financial aid and berates her; the police have to respond.	Stacie begins to have problems in her other classes in keeping up with the workload and catching up with assignments. She yells at a professor in another class.
Escalation	Dustin begins to see the professor as the problem in this case and threatens her with a firearm in the parking lot.	Stacie creates an online blog titled "Let's Kill Galloway" and begins to solicit the best ways to get away with killing him from other students.
Improvement	Dustin responds well to the threat assessment and conduct action; he realizes the seriousness of getting kicked out of the program. He avoids future outbursts in class.	Stacie is able to return to the class and completes her assignment. Galloway leaves her alone and she continues with her program.

Hart suggested that a good case management plan should include a discussion of strategies, tactics, and logistics. Strategies involve thinking about the goals and objectives of the overall case management plan. Tactics are related to how we are going to accomplish the goals and objectives. Logistics address how we support the tactics.

The same approach applies here when developing a strategy to reduce the risk of violence. This overall strategy is developed from the case formulation and resulting scenarios. The tactics involve putting treatment in place and adjusting environmental factors (such as having the student Dustin threatened sit far away from him in the classroom). Logistics involve case management meetings with Dustin and the professor or dean to ensure the tactics are addressing the strategy's goals and objectives.

A strategy for working with Stacie may focus on getting her to either be able to return to class or obtain the credit in another manner. The tactics in Stacie's case involve narrowing down the focus on the most likely course of action for Stacie to gain credit for her courses, either working with the professor and academic affairs or seeking an alternative route through the department head. The logistics are about ensuring that Stacie attends case management and academic support meetings that help her support her approach to getting credit in the course.

Another way to put this is to see the plan as the strategy, the specific goals of the plan as the tactics, and the actions we take to make sure the specific goals of the plan are accomplished as the logistics. All three parts are needed to ensure the overall plan is accomplished for the student.

7. Develop Conclusory Opinions About Violence Risk

The threat assessment pulls together the clinical formulation for risk along with the scenarios and ends with a statement of the assessor's opinion about the individual's violence risk. The assessment is communicated to the referral source by letter, a phone call, or a formalized report.

Summary

In this chapter, I outlined the use of Hart's structured professional judgment model through the use of two case examples described in Chapter 3. Structured professional judgment offers a way to bring together in a structured and organized process threat and risk assessment as well as treatment recommendations. Chapter 3 also includes sample letters that summarize the results of the risk assessment of the two cases in that chapter; the remaining chapters of the book focus on treatment.

Questions for Further Discussion

1. What are some of the challenges of predictive models as they attempt to address uncertainty inherent in the risk assessment process? How does the structured professional judgment process approach assessment differently?
2. Discuss some of the challenges to gathering information prior to the risk assessment in noncontrolled settings (such as those outside inpatient hospitals, schools, and colleges).
3. Van Brunt reviews the various motivations for violence. Discuss how these can be determined from the threat assessment interview.
4. Discuss how case management and assessment are tied together. Why is it important to have case management and treatment decisions based on the assessment?

PART 2
Treatment of Dangerousness

Introduction

The individual has been assessed through a structured formal assessment, or concerns have been raised through (less structured) observation by a clinician. Police have been involved if there was a threat of a crime. Parents are notified. The school and administration are concerned. Additional interventions have been taken within the school or workplace to help mitigate the risk of violence. Everyone looks to the treating therapist to now take the at-risk individual into treatment and fix the problem.

What Now?

First, there should be an encouragement to explore additional interventions beyond the treatment suggestions found in this book. Some suggestions from E. Deisinger et al. (2014) when considering managing an at-risk college student include the following:

- Maintaining communication and engagement
- Involving a trusted ally (family member, peer)
- Assist[ing] with problem solving and access to support

- On-going mental health treatment
- Confronting subject and establishing expectations for behavior (p. 111)

This section is based on my years of clinical practice, teaching graduate students, and training new therapists and psychologists. I have brought together the theories and techniques I have found most useful in managing risk and helping my clients better understand where and how their irrational and troubling thoughts have pulled them away from society.

Like the new generation of clinicians leaving graduate school, I see myself as a technical eclectic, adapting and making use of various therapeutic theories and techniques to help my patients better reintegrate into society and find some degree of meaning and happiness in their lives. My core foundations are drawn from the work of psychologist Carl Rogers and psychiatrist Irvin Yalom. I see these two philosophies—humanistic theory and existentialism, respectively—as my twin pillars of treatment. In my work with clients, I look to build rapport, create a relationship, convey understanding, and engage my clients by caring and holding them accountable for their actions. That being said, I've also seen power in addressing cognitive distortions and irrational thoughts, early trauma, birth order, family conflict, and the importance of finding spirituality and meaning in the pain and suffering native to human existence.

For me, the problem of selecting a treatment goes back to Gordon Paul's (1967) iconic question: What treatment, by whom, is most effective for this individual with that specific problem, and under which set of circumstances? It isn't feasible to create evidence-based treatment research on each of the (dozen or so) theories and techniques I review; to do so would fill several books and require decades of scholarship. Nor is it possible to rely exclusively on case studies of rampage violence—thankfully, these dark events don't occur frequently enough to allow us to draw statistically significant conclusions.

So, this leaves us simply with my experience and advice in working with hundreds of children, teenagers, and college students who considered harming others or harbored thoughts of violence against society. I share with you the clinical theories I have found most influential in my scholarship and in teaching graduate students to become counselors. I use case studies to highlight the utility of the theories in practice and create an accessible and practical series of chapters to inspire you, the clinician, to assess and explore the efficiency and effectiveness of these approaches with your own clients.

As is always necessary in these kinds of psychological theory and practice books, it is necessary to remind counselors, psychologists, social workers, pastoral counselors, and couples and family therapists to always provide treatment within your state licensure regulations and within your scope of practice and training. I would recommend these following chapters as starting places to explore additional reading for discussion in clinical supervision and general directions rather than as specific treatment advice.

A final warning for clinical staff who are in a position to conduct the forensic threat assessment and might be struggling with the temptation to continue ongoing treatment with the individual with whom he or she has completed an assessment. Changing one's role from assessor to therapist is a difficult and often unwise approach. This blurs the lines between therapist and client and has the potential to create blind spots for future violence. The role of a clinician conducting a threat assessment is balancing the needs of two distinct clients, the person being assessed and the third party requiring the assessment. The therapist providing treatment often has a more focused definition of who the client is and the goals of the intervention.

Likewise, therapists should always avoid conducting an assessment on a current or past client to whom they have provided treatment. This same potential for blind spots and bias occurs here in an even more pronounced way. The roles of the clinician performing the forensic threat assessment and the one performing treatment should be distinct and, ideally, separate.

Managing the potential for violence should be thought of this way: "Management is the process of acting to gain or maintain control of a situation. There is a clear link between management and assessment: assessment precedes and guides management, and management may alter subsequent assessment" (Meloy, Hart, et al., 2014, p. 4).

Chapter 8

Learning to
LISTEN

Chapter Highlights

1. This chapter offers insight into treatment through the work of Carl Rogers (1961) and his person-centered approach to therapy. This approach stresses empathy, congruence, genuineness, and authenticity.
2. The case study of Paul (angry and alone) is introduced to help the reader have a reference point to explore the concepts of person-centered therapy. Paul is a 400-pound, depressed high school student who has been teased and bullied. Paul writes a disturbing story about a school shooting.
3. Active listening skills are explored as a useful starting place for the therapist to engage with Paul. The therapist conveys his or her ability to listen in a nonjudgmental manner and allows the client to tell his or her story without defensiveness and hesitation.
4. Forming connections to others allows for increased exposure to social norms that, in turn, may help defuse negative behaviors and help break antisocial habits. The therapist does this by assisting Paul in building from existing strengths and encourages him to overcome obstacles to growth.
5. Learning to be heard helps Paul express himself and the things that upset him while also learning to listen to others and pay attention to how they see the world. This also helps address the potential for objectification of others.

I believe that this treatment chapter is the most important of the remaining chapters. I've been a therapist for 19 years and have treated thousands of clients for dozens of different mental health problems. I can tell you that most of what I did during this time was focus, *really* focus, on what they were trying to tell me. If this sounds overly simplistic, I'd suggest you find other long-time therapists and ask them what they found most effective in their practices. I'd be willing to wager that the answer is similar. I am willing to bet that any therapist you ask will make some reference to listening, caring about the person, understanding things from the client's perspective, and providing a sense of hope for a better future.

Those not familiar with the process of psychotherapy will read this with some trepidation. There is of course more to the art and science of therapy that simply learning how to listen. My graduate training in research methods and various treatment theories and techniques have indeed been helpful in working with patients, referring them for additional group and medication support, and offering homework and examples of exercises and meditations they could do to improve their mental health. But if you were to ask me if any of these was more important than learning to listen and care for another person while offering him or her hope for a better tomorrow, I'd say no. These are the most important concepts, personally battle-worn and time-tested with a variety of my own clients.

Carl Rogers (1961), whom I reference throughout this chapter, offers the following: ". . . when someone understands how it feels and seems to be me, without wanting to analyze me or judge me, then I can blossom and grow in that climate" (p. 62). Empathy and congruence are the essential qualities for a therapist seeking to encourage change in his or her clients. Empathy means seeing the world from their eyes, understanding from their perspective. Congruence is about the therapist conveying a sense of genuineness and authenticity to the client. We tend to trust those whom we can understand and who seem honest and direct about their goals.

This chapter highlights the seminal concepts drawn from Rogers's humanistic approach to treatment. I apply these concepts to tell the story of Paul, who experiences anger and isolation. The importance of developing active listening skills as well as assisting Paul form more lasting social connections to others is explored. Paul's use of objectifying language is addressed, as is helping him better understand how to share with others and be heard.

Case Study: Paul, a Teenager Who Is Angry and Alone

Paul was a very large 17-year-old Latino, easily topping 400 pounds. Whenever he walked down the halls in high school, other students would frequently tease and talk about him behind his back. For solace and distraction, Paul took up writing and spent much time writing stories.

Paul struggled with depression and low self-worth but had never sought out therapy. He was an only child and lived at home with his mother and father. Paul's family was against the use of alcohol, and he often would share his beliefs at school about how stupid it was to drink and to let alcohol control your perspective. One day during class, he got into an argument with another student in class and he lost his temper. He stormed out of class and slammed the door loudly. He was sent to the vice principal's office and given an in-school suspension for his behavior.

Paul had a few friends who worked in the theatre department with whom he hung out during rehearsals and productions. He helped with set construction on some of the plays and went out with them late at night after the rehearsals were done. He had not yet started a dating relationship with anyone. While Paul had some friends, he remained frustrated at how easy it was for others to get along with one another.

Paul's writing often emulated the horror and science fiction authors he enjoyed reading. He also liked movies that had the same kind of themes like the *Saw* films, *The Matrix* trilogy (Wachowski & Wachowski, 1999), *Star Wars* (Lucas, 1977), *Kill Bill* (Tarantino, 2003), *Pulp Fiction* (Tarantino, 1994), *A Nightmare on Elm Street* (Craven, 1984), *Halloween* (Carpenter, 1978), and *Friday the 13th* (Cunningham, 1980). Paul escaped into these movies and found himself increasingly angry with everyone around him who seemed to be living the "good life." He even began to avoid his few friends involved in theatre.

Paul wrote a story about a school shooting for his creative writing class. An excerpt from it is included here:

> Titus opened his eyes slowly as though he had just come out of a coma. He blinked several times and looked at his new surroundings. They weren't what he had been expecting. Titus saw a room, a large room with cafeteria tables lined neatly in rows, though several of the tables closest to him were crooked. He then saw the reason why they were crooked. Draped across the tables were the bodies of several dead teenagers with gunshot wounds in their chests, backs and heads. My God, he thought in a disgusted manner, this is not what I had expected to be on the other side.
>
> The smell of blood came to him as he realized something wrong with his situation. He couldn't move any of his arms or legs. He couldn't even move his head. His eyes were the only things that moved and the range of what he saw was limited. He felt as though he was looking through a pair of binoculars. Titus could hear heavy breathing coming from him, but he was not the one doing the breathing. He was scared. For the first time in his life, something was scaring him.
>
> His gaze turned sharply to the right as more and more dead teenagers came into sight. Titus wanted to close his eyes but found that he couldn't. He seemed to no longer have control over his eyelids. They

moved up and down by themselves, almost as though they were controlled by someone else. The same one doing the breathing? he wondered. His gaze stopped when he saw a young boy of maybe 16 curled up against a corner of a painted cinderblock wall with a bloodied bulletin board to his right. He moved closer to the boy, not moving his legs but still moving them. From the corner of his eye he saw a hand lifting and pointing a Glock at the boy.

"P-p-p-please! Don't shoot me too!" pleaded the boy with a frightened stutter.

"Oh!" came a harsh voice from the one who was breathing. "Now look who the stuttering freak is!"

"C'mon Ben, I n-n-never teased you about that," the boy pleaded more.

Ben? Titus thought. Why would he call me that?

"Yeah, but what else did you taunt me about, fuck ass!" shouted the angry voice. It sounded deep but it also sounded young. "Oh let me think . . . oh right! My last name! You forget about that already, shit face? You wanna try living with my last name?"

"B-b-b-but that was last year man!" the boy jittered. "B-b-besides, 'Doom – os' isn't that hard to say when—"

"Then what the fuck was the deal with taunting me about it!" the voice bellowed. But my name's not . . . Titus began to think. Then a combination of realization and philosophy began to overwhelm him. My lord, he thought, I am this person. But how?

Just then, he felt his mind begin to flow. It seemed to break apart and fuse with the young boy who owned the angry voice. He found that his words were also becoming the words of the boy's. "Well!" Titus heard himself shout. "I'm waiting! You'd better give me a good reason or this Glock's next bullet's going straight through your mouth!"

"L-l-look, I was younger and immature," said the jittering boy. "I admit, I w-w-was—"

"Sorry asshole, not good enough," Titus Yorick (formerly Benjamin Dumas) said quietly as he pulled the trigger.

Paul was mandated to complete a threat assessment with the school psychologists after he wrote the story. His parents were also called to discuss Paul's depression and difficulty connecting socially with others. Paul denied any desire to hurt anyone and reluctantly agreed to enter therapy at the pressure of his parents to address these potential concerns.

Developing Active Listening Skills

I recently changed jobs and no longer practice therapy full time. One of the side effects of this change was the realization of how many times a day I had the opportunity to connect intimately with another person. One of the amazing things about training for decades to become a therapist is the ability to stop and patiently listen and understand things from another person's perspective. While I imagine some therapist and psychologists were able to make it through their master's and doctoral programs without developing this skill set, most of us enjoy the ability to put our own needs aside for a time and truly focus on another person's perspective with the expressed desire of trying to understand and help.

In Paul's case, this ability to actively place oneself in the cockpit of his worldview should be the starting place for treatment. I develop multiple hypotheses as I sit down with Paul and as I hear more of his story; I find myself able to test and accept or refute the educated guesses I have made in order to understand how he sees the world. It all starts with a willingness to put your needs as a person aside and focus instead on how clients view those around them. When we do this for our clients, we teach this to our clients. As Rogers (1961) put it, "An empathetic way of being can be learned from empathetic persons" (p. 150).

For instance, I may assume that Paul's height and weight may contribute to his feelings of isolation and separation. He may have trouble fitting in with others because of this difference and may end up beginning to distance himself from those around him in a defensive action to keep his own feelings safe and free from injury or insult. It may also be possible that he accepts his weight and height and that they do not influence the way he sees the world. Like any good hypothesis, ours is tested against his story and explored without fixed assumptions about how we would feel if we were in Paul's shoes.

Another point of inquiry should be around Paul's reluctance to enter therapy. His defensiveness here should be reasonable given that he may have trouble seeing that he did anything that necessitates a threat assessment or subsequent therapy. The initial stance of the therapist as sympathetic to his mandated sessions would help Paul begin to appreciate the therapist's ability to understand.

At the heart of active listening, the ability to understand is the underlying message communicated from therapist to client. The therapist conveys an ability to listen in a nonjudgmental manner and allows the client to tell his or her story free of defensiveness and hesitation. When training therapists, I use the example of a normal household glass. I have them imagine the client coming in with a gallon's worth of liquid and seeing that you have only a normal household glass. The client refrains from sharing because he knows you won't be able to handle the volume of information he needs to share. When a therapist adopts an open, nonjudgmental, active listening–based stance, it is as if he or she brings a gallon jug to the session. It conveys to clients a willingness to receive as much information as they are willing to share.

As the client becomes more comfortable with the therapist's ability to listen, he then increases the trust between the two and further lowers his defenses. In Paul's example, it would be wiser for the therapist to begin with a nonthreatening exploration of Paul's love of creative writing, movies, TV shows, and horror/science fiction than to begin immediately with his own short story.

I have found that people are more comfortable sharing parts of their lives where they are passionate and feel sure of themselves. One potential opening that could work to build trust and allow the therapist to learn more about Paul would be to ask about his feelings around alcohol abuse. This would be a particularly interesting area to explore because he had very little opportunity to share these views in his everyday life and even fewer moments where they were thoughtfully received and accepted. When a therapist provides a safe and nurturing environment for Paul to share his views on this topic, it allows for the potential for Paul to feel more comfortable sharing his more protected and less well-defined views on other subjects.

Carl Rogers summed up these ideals best in his book *A Way of Being* (1980):

> [Empathetic listening] means the therapist senses accurately the feelings and personal meanings that the client is experiencing and communicates this understanding to the client. When functioning best, the therapist is so much inside the private world of the other that he or she can clarify not only the meaning of which the client is aware but even those just below the level of awareness. This kind of sensitive, active listing is exceedingly rare in our lives. We think we listen, but rarely do we listen with real understanding, true empathy. Yet listening, of this very special kind, is one of the most potent forces for change that I know. (p. 116)

Too often, therapy from the outside is seen as a practice full of analysis, hidden semantics, and difficult German terminology. Yet more often than not, successful therapy is about what Rogers mentions here. It is a caring, empathic listening, an intimacy, a sharing. It is this that becomes the condition, the environment in which lasting change occurs.

Forming Connection to Others

A key treatment concern for a client like Paul is his ability to form relationships with others. As was demonstrated in the first half of the book, social isolation and objectified images of others are two factors that can exacerbate the risk for violence. Increased social connection allows for increased exposure to social norms that, in turn, may help defuse negative behaviors and help break antisocial habits. There is also the opportunity to address some of Paul's depression and feelings of isolation through conversation about developing a wider social network.

The added value of a positive client–therapist relationship is the potential for the client to believe that he or she will be able to form these kinds of positive relationships with others as well. The active listening and support offered by an experienced therapist serves to create a training ground for clients in order to improve their own social skills and increase their chances of success when they attempt to form connections on their own. Rogers (1961) wrote, "If I can provide a certain type of relationship, the other person will discover within himself the capacity to use that relationship for growth, and change and personal development will occur" (p. 33).

When encouraging connection to others, the therapist may also seem to adopt the approach used by social workers and case managers in order to help direct the client toward more positive choices and overcome obstacles. In Paul's case, the therapist might encourage involvement in a book or movie club, writers group, or science fiction club. Paul could be encouraged to look for friends who share his interests through convention trips such as Comic-Con or HorrorFest fan events. There could be an opportunity to meet new students through a weekly article written in the school paper or a review of new horror movies for the school's television station. The therapist should encourage Paul to seek out others with similar interests in order to help him better appreciate the lesson that all adults have come to understand: There is always someone who shares your point of view.

Building from existing strengths is one way to develop better connections to others. Another way is for the therapist to help encourage Paul to overcome the obstacles and reluctance he might experience when his efforts do not go as he plans. This approach could help Paul to reconnect to his theatre friends (perhaps encouraging Paul to explore theatre himself) as well as assist him in developing additional ideas for making friends and dealing with disappointment when his plans don't work out.

Learning to Share and Being Heard

Paul needs to find ways to express himself when he is frustrated with others who are unwilling or unable to hear his point of view (see also Chapter 10). Paul's outburst in class and the resulting door slamming should be an additional area of exploration in therapy. The therapist could assist him in developing better frustration tolerance skills as well as increasing his ability to engage in empathic listening.

Paul is well attuned to his own feelings of separation and frustration with those around him. A clinical area of focus here would be to help him express himself and the things that upset him while also learning to listen to others and pay attention to how they see the world. This is possible in the here-and-now of therapy and may be possible with his friends in theatre or with his family. This process of turn taking in conversation and repeating back what the other says and is feeling should be an area of focus for therapy.

Paul should also focus on how to regulate his frustrations when sharing them with others. For example, sharing his views on alcohol consumption with an audience of teenagers who likely have the exact opposite view requires a bit more finesse than Paul previously used. Likewise, making choices about whom to share information with should be done in a more regulated manner. For Paul to share the deep, painful existential crisis with a friend right before class isn't the best way to share these ideas. A skillful therapist will appreciate the catch-22 nature of Paul's frustrations—he wants to share himself with others yet he finds those around him unable to fully hear and understand what he wants to share. The therapist now becomes the surrogate, encouraging Paul to practice sharing his thoughts in an appropriate way with someone who not only can handle what he has to say but can understand it in an empathetic manner.

Avoiding Objectification

The objectification and depersonalization of others is one of the central risk factors discussed in Part I. Without exception, every incident of mass casualty violence I have studied has an attacker who fundamentally sees himself or herself as disconnected from others—often better than, and sometimes worse than, but always separate.

Objectification language is commonly experienced in everyday life. Many can recognize the hurtful comments made about "those people" who are a different ethnicity or from a different culture. Misogynistic language is evident through the use of terms like *bitch*, *whore*, or *slut* to refer to women; also disturbing is describing women in ways that place them on a pedestal (e.g., *saintly*, *innocent*, and *motherly*). When a person describes an individual through a behavior or similarly limited characteristic instead of the individual's humanity, there has been objectification.

Another area of objectification is what I call the *dark knight phenomenon*, evident in many school shootings. Violent offenders sometimes view themselves apart from society and as all-powerful vigilantes taking revenge on those who cause harm. I give examples of this kind of thinking in Chapter 4 (e.g., Kipland Kinkel's writings about people who believe in God as "sheep" and "weak" whereas he is strong).

Revenge can be a strong motivator. Luke Woodham was 16 years old when he stabbed and beat his sleeping mother before taking her car and driving to Pearl High School wearing an orange jumpsuit and a trench coat and carrying a .30-caliber rifle. He fatally shot his former girlfriend and one of her friends and injured the nearby band instructor. He wounded seven others and had planned to go to the Pearl Junior High School to continue shooting when the assistant principal subdued him with a .45 from his car. The assistant principal asked, "Why did you shoot my kids?" He responded, "Life wronged me, sir" (Chua-Eoan & Monroe, 1997, p. 54; Hewitt & Harmes, 1997).

Woodham planned the shooting with six other friends who were in a satanic cult called "the Kroth." In his manifesto, he wrote:

> I am not insane! I am angry. This world has shit on me for the final time. I am not spoiled or lazy, for murder is not weak and slow-witted, murder is gutsy and daring. I killed because people like me are mistreated every day. I did this to show society "push us and we will push back!" I suffered all my life. No one ever truly loved me. No one ever truly cared about me. (Chua-Eoan & Monroe, 1997, p. 54)

Woodham left several journal entries that demonstrate his anger and objectification of others:

> . . . I am the hatred in every man's heart! I am the epitomy [sic] of all Evil! I have no mercy for humanity, for they created me, they tortured me until I snapped and became what I am today! My advice to any man who has been tortured by humanity is this: Let these words ring through our heart, mind, and soul! Hate humanity! Hate humanities! . . . Hate what humanity has made you! Hate what you have become! Most of all, hate the accurssed [sic] god of Christianity. Hate him for making humanity Hate him for making you! Hate him for flinging you into a monsterous [sic] life you did not ask for nor deserve! Fill your heart, mind, and soul with hatred; until it's all you know. ("A community and its shooter," 2008, p. 1)

In Paul's case, it may be helpful to explore his feelings toward others. They are unlikely to be as extreme as those comments made by Woodham, but still the problem lies in seeing oneself as separate from others. Paul may be starting to think of himself as a punisher of sorts; the school shooting paper he wrote supports this hypothesis. The paper could be seen as a fantasy rehearsal of sorts, trying out in writing what he might be curious about in real life. This is not to say that Paul's paper indicates that he is going to be the next school shooter or is planning an attack; it is merely an assertion that this shocking sort of subject matter is a passion for him and worthy of future exploration.

To be practical, the focus of therapy to reduce objectification of others starts with the process of assisting Paul in understanding that he is not unlike the people he objectifies. Through increased active listening and building social connections with those around him, Paul has the opportunity to better understand the motivation and thinking of others.

It is important to help Paul not become frustrated or disheartened by his interactions with others. If these attempts at connection and understanding go badly, Paul could have his belief system of separation and objectification reinforced. A therapist can help him stay focused on the positive aspects of spending time with others in order to help him reframe his negative beliefs about others.

Summary

In this chapter, I explored several treatment concepts, including active listening skills, empathy, sharing with others, improving social connectivity, and reducing objectification. In the next chapter, I introduce another case study and explore the importance of a focus on the client's story through the approach of narrative therapy.

Questions for Further Discussion

1. What are some ways a therapist can engage a student like Paul who has difficulty forming connections with others? How might you use Paul's writing to encourage more direct and open communication in treatment?
2. What are some ways to teach active listening skills to Paul through the therapeutic alliance?
3. Discuss how a therapist might be able to help Paul engage in more social activities to form better connections with those around him. What might be some of the obstacles Paul will likely have to overcome to be successful at forming new relationships?
4. What are some ways to address Paul's difficulty in empathizing with others? How does the objectified language Paul uses relate to this?
5. What are some of the hurdles a therapist may encounter when trying to bring about change in Paul's life?

Chapter 9

Understanding Their STORY

Chapter Highlights

1. The concept of narrative therapy, created by Michael White and David Epston (1990), is used to demonstrate how to address potential violence. Narrative therapy suggests people organize and give meaning to their experiences through the stories they tell. Individuals construct the meaning of life through stories that can be reshaped to address anger and violence.
2. The case study of Dan (abused and broken) is introduced to assist the reader in applying the narrative therapy concepts introduced in the chapter. Dan is a gay college student who has been the victim of extreme teasing. His father has been abusive, and he has access to weapons. He makes a threat to kill other students in his residence hall.
3. *Externalizing the story* is a technique used in narrative therapy that encourages persons to objectify, and at times to personify, the problems that they experience as oppressive. When Dan begins to experience a level of comfort sharing his stories, he can externalize them in order to allow the narrative to be more deeply explored.
4. When the stories themselves are identified and given detailed characteristics, the influence the problem has on the client can then be mapped. This mapping process examines how the problem influences the client, his significant others, and his environment. For Dan, the influence of teasing on his life has been rather significant and would be a focus of mapping.

5. Kopp (1995) stressed the importance of engaging in client's story through attending to the importance of language and metaphor as therapeutic tools. Kopp suggested that therapists attend specifically to a client's metaphors and analogies that are used within sessions. A six-step approach is reviewed and discussed: 1. Notice metaphors. 2. Explore the metaphor using the client's own language. 3. Broaden the exploration through questioning. 4. Assess feelings and emotions associated with the image. 5. Use the metaphor as an agent of change. 6. Bring the metaphor back to the presenting life problems.

Everyone has a story. When I first began studying rampage violence, it was hard to understand what kind of motivations the attackers had that could justify their extreme violence. As I continued, I found myself captivated by the sadness of their lives. I don't mean this to be anything like an apology for destructive and heinous acts; I just want to acknowledge that the people who do horrific things are not monsters, but rather lost souls surrounded by pain and disillusion. They become separated from those around them and escape into the fantasy that their attack will gain them some kind of meaning, some kind of infamy that will create a purpose for their suffering.

The methods for preventing this kind of violence often include high-definition video cameras in hallways, early-alert text warning systems, gun-free school zones, and more highly trained police forces, but the most effective solution to rampage violence is early, easy, and frequent access to care for potential perpetrators. They need access to someone who can better understand their stories and then help shape them to move in another direction; to act as mentor, life coach, big brother/big sister, and guide to inspire hope and provide alternatives to their violent, empty fantasies.

In this chapter, I introduce the case of Dan and offer a therapeutic approach to working with him based on the narrative and metaphor approaches to treatment. I see these treatments as building on the concepts introduced in Chapter 8.

Case Study: Dan, an Abused and Broken College Freshman

Dan was not having the best of times in high school. He was picked on and teased because of his effeminate appearance and manner. Dan was gay, other students knew it, and he was frustrated by the way people treated him. Dan experienced intense anxiety when going to school and spent his time at home locked in his room reading. Dan hoped that college would be different.

Dan's family consisted of two older brothers who excelled in sports during high school. His father left the family when Dan was in elementary school; his mother worked double shifts as a nurse in order to keep the family finances in order. Dan's father was abusive to all three boys. He drank frequently and would hit the boys whenever the mood struck him. Dan's teacher noticed that he had bruises and reported him to social services, which investigated; Dan's father left as a consequence. After her husband left, Dan's mother purchased a handgun and learned how to shoot for home protection. There were several handguns and long rifles in the house. Dan's mother thought it was important that the entire family learn how to use them.

Dan's first semester away at college proved to be just as bad as high school. It was difficult for him to make friends, and his roommate was always out at parties and did not spend any time with him. Other students teased Dan in his residence hall. They shoved pennies in the door to prevent it from opening. They set up a trashcan filled with water that fell into Dan's room when he opened the door. They started to call him "Dan the man" and put gay pornography around the walls of the dorm with Dan's picture Photoshopped onto one of the models.

After weeks of teasing Dan shouted, "I'm going to execute every last one of you!" He then slammed his door closed.

Dan was required to complete a threat assessment with the school's counseling center. Residential life staff met with Dan's floor mates to address the teasing that had been going on. Dan agreed to be relocated to another residence hall, and he was able to stay in school under the condition that he continue to meet with a therapist in the counseling center office. Dan agreed.

Learning Their Stories

The term *narrative therapy* was used by Australian family therapists Michael White and David Epston (1990) to define the way we all use stories to relate to our experiences. They suggested that people organize and give meaning to their experiences through the stories they tell. Individuals construct the meaning of life through stories and then treat these stories as the "truth" (Corey, 2001). Furthermore, "With every performance, persons are re-authoring their lives. The evolution of lives is akin to the process of re-authoring, the process of persons entering into stories, taking them over and making them their own" (Van Brunt, 2007, pp. 27–28; see M. White & Epston, 1990). Through the process of helping patients examine their lives through the stories they tell, M. White and Epston found it possible to help those they worked with revise the telling of their stories in a manner that gave the patient more ownership and ability to gain dominion over negative past experiences. Narrative therapy helps patients separate themselves from negative, unhelpful stories and gain an ownership of their life beyond subjugation. Narrative therapy encourages patients to adopt stories that free them from culture's oppression and live out their alternative chosen stories (Besley, 2002).

M. White and Epston (1990) viewed stories as creations between the client and the therapist. Their book *Narrative Means to Therapeutic Ends* has many examples of tasks that bring the therapist and client together in a joined process. Contracts are created with younger children against particular fears, anxieties, and behavioral symptoms in order to invest them in the cure. M. White and Epston also used letters to connect with clients in between sessions and as a preventive measure prior to an anticipated difficult meeting, such as confronting a hostile family member.

The therapist who works with Dan should seek to elicit stories related to his past experiences in order to better understand his point of view. This exploration would involve Dan discussing his early trauma experiences, what it was like to grow up with two brothers, his relationship with his mother, his hopes that college would be different than high school, and what has recently happened with his threat and relocation on campus. The simple telling of these stories gives Dan an opportunity to reflect and eventually uncover meaning.

Externalizing the Story

The process of externalizing the story is an essential aspect of the narrative approach to therapy. M. White (1988–1989) wrote, "Externalizing is an approach to therapy that encourages persons to objectify, and at times, to personify, the problems that they experience as oppressive" (p. 5). M. White and Epston (1990) suggested that behavior, fears, and worries must be first separated from the client prior to any attempt to reconstruct them. An analogy would be that a transmission must be removed from a car prior to rebuilding it. They wrote, "As persons become separated from their stories, they are able to experience a sense of personal agency; as they break from their performance of their stories, they experience a capacity to intervene in their own lives and relationships" (p. 16). This allows clients to explore unique outcomes to their stories and obtain some freedom from the stories that previously restricted their options. This process of "storying" their experiences—adding description, sensation, and detail to their creations—gives clues to the meaning they ascribe to their own life problems and experiences.

When Dan becomes comfortable sharing his stories, he can externalize them. By being helped to take a step back from the stories of his experience, Dan can tolerate greater exploration and alterations during these stories. The therapist can then further explore his stories of abuse by his father, teasing in high school, and the more recent events that culminated with his threat in the residence hall.

Mapping the Story

When the stories themselves are identified and given detailed characteristics, the influence the problem has on the client can then be mapped. This mapping process examines how the problem influences the client, his significant others, and his environment. For Dan, the influence of teasing on his life has been rather significant. It started at home with his father's abuse and continued through high school and now college through persistent teasing from classmates.

In "The Case of the Night Watchman," Epston (1992) described the treatment of a child who became nervous at night and had developed a number of rituals that were becoming increasingly difficult for his mother to manage. Through the mapping of the influence of these behaviors, Epston was able to understand the source of the child's fear and how it was also affecting his mother, who had separated from the boy's father. Epston crafted a narrative contract with the boy, giving him a list of "night watchman" duties that he was sworn to conduct; the result was a reduction in the behaviors. Although the effectiveness of the treatment is essentially a cognitive–behavioral task of exaggeration or paradox (Gurman & Messer, 1995), the approach succeeded because therapist, client, and the client's family mapped the influence in the story and crafted a joint narrative; the treatment joined the patient and family in a collaborative, constructive way. The formalization of a checklist for the night watchman's duties creates an imaginary narrative in which the child and mother become invested and that can be repeated and replayed outside of the treatment room.

Imagine that Dan has learned over time that he is unattractive and has little in the way of anything special to offer anyone in a relationship. Stories that support these ideas are collected as he develops: I'm someone who cannot do anything right; no one would like to date me; I have nothing to offer anyone. These stories become stifling and overwhelming. They remove options, restrict possibilities, and steer his life toward a self-fulfilling prophecy. The task of the narrative therapist is to help the client separate himself from these stories. The stories must be relieved of their power before the process of reconstruction can begin. The therapist helps the client set aside his negative stories through confrontation, charisma, and enlisting him in the creation of metaphors and imagery. Perhaps the therapist and client create an imaginary box where the negative stories can be temporarily laid down for the length of their sessions together. This jointly created metaphor should use descriptive terms and attempt to create a memorable, realistic image. The box could be strong and made of old wood, sturdy, and strapped with weathered iron bands. The therapist could encourage the client to create a key or talisman that would open the box, allowing its dark interior to accept the weight of his stories. The box could then be locked with a metallic turning click. With the stories safely locked away for a time, the therapist and client are free to dream of other stories that put the client in a more positive, advantageous light. This process of imagination, freedom, and creation creates the tapestry of narrative therapy.

There is a strong power inherent in understanding, shaping, and then reconstructing others' thoughts and stories. Although thought shaping has been essential to the commission of some of the greatest atrocities of our age, the shaping of thoughts and stories for good can be equally powerful.

Using stories for good is the bedrock on which M. White and Epston founded their concepts of narrative therapy. They sought to harness patients' sense of self through the stories that make up their lives. Through this method, language becomes a constructive, powerful creative force in the reauthoring of patients' lives. Foucault (1965) wrote, "There is no madness but that which is in every man, since it is man who constitutes madness in the attachment he bears for himself and by the illusions he entertains" (p. 26). Man is only limited in his madness by the truth he perceives. By collaboratively reauthoring the stories that become the roadmap to a patient's behavior, self-image, and way of being, the therapist taps into the powerful forces of social control and reinforcement. The patient's new view of self through the newly authored stories helps her or him to overcome the status quo, to fully question what a person is, how problems can be defined, and under which conditions change occurs (Zimmerman & Beaudoin, 2002).

Engaging in Their Story

Kopp (1995) expanded some of the narrative therapy approach and suggested the importance of language and metaphor as therapeutic tools. Kopp suggested that therapists attend specifically to the metaphors and analogies that clients use within sessions. These narrative pieces offer a crucial connection to the client's inner worldview. Raymond Corsini, encyclopedist and lexicographer in the field of psychology, wrote in the Foreword to Kopp's (1995) text:

> The client and therapist, acting like detectives, look for clues to understanding the essence of the mystery by exploring and transforming the client's metaphoric language, hoping to find something that has little significance either to the client or to anyone who does not know the secret of the metaphor, but which, when the secret is revealed, becomes the key that opens the lock of the door that has stood between the person and freedom. (pp. ix–x)

It is precisely these little clues that provide both the insight and framework toward solving the presenting problem.

Kopp (1995) wrote of a patient who described her husband's lack of caring, coming and going from the house as he pleased and not look-

ing for a job, with the metaphor "he barges into the house like a loco-
motive" (p. xiv). He then used this clue as an opportunity to create a
dialogue about the situation. He questioned the client, "If he is a loco-
motive, what are you?" The patient clarified what the therapist asked
and then replied, "A tunnel" (p. xiv). Kopp then asked, "What if you
could change the image so that it would be better for you, how would
you change it?" The patient thought and then suddenly exclaimed,
"I'd be the derailer!" (p. xv). This self-as-derailer metaphor then became a shared construct between the therapist and patient. It served as
a focal point for the patient to shift from a passive model, as the tunnel,
to an active model, as the derailer, and allowed the patient to visualize
the potential of new, unique outcomes.

In Dan's case, the clues to his inner narrative appeared in the metaphors he used: "I'm all alone like a bird that broke its wing and was
left behind as the other birds flew for warmer climates." Dan viewed
himself as defective and broken, unable to keep up and continue the
journey. Dan and the therapist could then explore what he would need
in order to fix his wing and continue with the journey. Or they could
explore how important it really is to Dan to keep up with the other
birds. The narrative provides fodder for the metaphor. The metaphor
provides some clinical distance for Dan to make changes to the story
and find new ways to move forward.

One way might be for Dan to look for ways to fit in more at college
and avoid being seen as an object of teasing. He may work on his dress
or conversation skills or practice altruistic giving to bridge connections
with the flock that has left him behind. Alternatively, Dan might decide that fitting in with the flock isn't truly the most important thing
for him. He may come to realize that his problems come more from
a lack of acceptance of his current conditions (broken wing), and he
could work more on accepting where he is now. This might lead to
Dan seeking out other individuals on campus who also have a "broken
wing" and learn to make his friendships there.

Kopp (1995) offered a six-stage model of how to assist therapists
new to the approach on how to use metaphors in practice:

1) noticing metaphors, 2) exploring the metaphor using the client's own
language, 3) broadening the exploration through questioning, 4) assessing feelings and emotions associated with the image, 5) using the
metaphor as an agent of change, 6) bringing the metaphor back to the
presenting life problems. (pp. 5–12)

Let's assume that Dan often feels alone and frustrated with social contact. Dan may describe the behavior as, "I feel like an alley cat, independent and alone. No one will come close because they don't know when
my claws may come out." The Kopp (1995) model would have the
therapist first notice the use of metaphor and the language attached to

it. The metaphor could be explored: What type of alley would you live in? What are the claws like? When do they come out? The metaphor then is accepted by both therapist and client and may be expanded upon: What kind of people does the alley cat encounter? What type of experience makes the claws come out? Does the cat ever get hungry? Would hunger change its behavior? The fourth step would involve the therapist questioning: What must it feel like to be the alley cat? How would it feel to be attacked? The fifth step would have the therapist exploring other ways the alley cat could respond: What if someone spent the time to feed and care for the alley cat? Could the alley cat ever be a house cat in the right situation? The final step would connect the symbolism of the client to the alley cat and explore the possible new ways of looking at his life and interaction with others: When have you felt like this alley cat with others in your life?

Let's address Dan's potential for violence rather than focusing on the trauma of abuse. Dan may share, "I want to burn away everyone that hurt me. I'd be a small boy throwing sticks into the fire. I'd watch the flames gather around and consume them and then there would be nothing left to hurt me."

- *Notice the metaphor.* The therapist catches the client's use of metaphor around the fire and makes a treatment decision to stay here and use the metaphor to address Dan's desire to harm others.
- *Explore the metaphor.* What kind of fire is it? How many sticks are there around waiting to be thrown in the fire? What motivates the boy to throw the sticks into the fire? Are there ever any sticks that might not get thrown into the fire? These questions use Dan's language and encourage Dan to talk more about the image he has and to expand on it.
- *Expand the metaphor.* Where do the sticks come from? What would happen if the sticks weren't thrown into the fire? Would they accumulate? Can the boy move or must he sit there? These questions expand the metaphor beyond what Dan originally thought and encourage him to broaden the concept and further flesh out his ideas.
- *Assess feelings and emotions.* How does the boy feel about his situation? Do the sticks have feelings as well? How did the boy come to be here? Is he trapped or free to leave? How does he feel when he throws the sticks in the fire? The questions are designed to help Dan begin to explore the obvious connection between himself and the boy. Because the therapist is only talking about the metaphor, Dan is likely to respond freely. The alternative would be to ask direct questions that would increase his defensiveness, like "How do you feel when you are being teased?" The boy in the story serves as a surrogate to allow Dan to project his feelings and share more directly with the therapist.

- *Metaphor as agent of change.* Are there other things the boy could do instead of throwing the sticks on the fire? What might these be? Could the boy walk away from the sticks and fire altogether? Could the sticks be shaped into something more useful? The questions here help connect Dan to the idea of alternative options available to him. As mentioned above about problems with direct questions, this approach allows Dan to explore the options in a more distant, creative manner that is more detached from the emotions he would feel if asked, "Can you just ignore or walk away from those who bully you?" On that level, Dan would likely be overwhelmed by emotions and anger. When using the metaphor of the boy and the sticks, there is an emotional distance that allows Dan to explore his options as an agent of change.
- *Apply the metaphor.* The therapist might ask Dan: How does the boy give you insight into your situation? What are some other options you have besides burning those who hurt you? Is it worth trying to find a way to connect with those around you (like the sticks) or better to avoid contact? The opportunities for the questions become endless as we explore ways Dan connects the boy, the sticks, and the fire to his own life. The metaphor develops a life of its own and may come up again down the line in therapy as Dan explores ideas and options about his life.

If a client like Dan has trouble coming up with metaphors, the therapist can help by offering stories and ideas that may inspire the client to think more about his life in terms of options. Close (1998) advocated that the therapist use stories, symbolism, and metaphor as treatment examples. The author, who described himself as a pastoral counselor, advocated for a Christ-like method of using parables and examples through teaching. Close described his work with a female patient "to transcend the effects of [a] rather harsh and deprived childhood" (p. 59). She was rapidly becoming a recognized musician with a promising career, which was abruptly halted when she was involved in a plane crash and lost use of her left hand, keeping her from playing the cello. Close told his patient a long story involving a rare and beautiful tree that had to overcome many difficulties; it was planted under a rock and a strong storm uprooted the tree. Through these experiences, the tree learned to grow again and became a nesting place for songbirds.

The story weaves in the importance of uniqueness, overcoming environmental traumas, and the importance of loving others and being loved. Close's (1998) method connected with the heart of the client, an area beyond simply connecting with the mind. He gave the example of the difference between looking at sheet music and actually hearing a beautiful aria. The use of metaphor in psychotherapy is a similar concept. The stories connect with the client's heart, becoming long-lasting touchstones for her or his journey through life.

In reviewing Dan's life, there are numerous examples of how the therapist could introduce metaphor and story into his treatment. Exhibit 9.1 provides several examples.

Summary

Narrative and story have always been part of the human condition. The purpose of their use in therapy is to help the counselor learn to better help clients own their story and understand it in the environmental context of their development. With clients who are socially isolated, harboring violent thoughts against others and caught up living stories full of fantasized violence and committing horrific acts, the utility of narrative therapy can be found in its ability to help the client reauthor his or her story and gain a more positive sense of self. This provides the client with the opportunity to engage more fully with others and have the needed self-esteem and hope that his or her life may be amenable to change.

Many times, the stories told by clients offer a useful key to understanding how they see the world. If the client's world is a dark and lonely place, narrative therapy provides a key to unlock another way of thinking about his or her potential in the world. In the next chapter, I illustrate how to apply various cognitive behavior therapy techniques when working with clients who are potentially violent.

Exhibit 9.1 | **Metaphors Used in Dan's Case Study**

Metaphor: A boy who was meant to be king is separated from his family and is left to fend for himself. He must fight many battles to get back to his rightful place.

Rationale: This story could be useful to describe the various traumas and frustrations Dan has faced in his life. It has the added element that Dan has the hidden power to be amazing, as long as he finds his way back to claim his birthright.

Metaphor: A man has a lockbox full of all the wisdom in the world. The box is secured by a set of seven spinning dials, each with the letters of the alphabet. The man would be at peace if he could only figure out the combination.

Rationale: This story focuses on the secret life Dan feels as a result of not being connected to and known by others. The combination gives him the opportunity to unlock his destiny. The combination could be something such as the word *abusers, blessed, helping,* or *outcast.* The individual letters could even have some larger meaning; maybe they each represent another word, like an acrostic poem, that is tied back to Dan's life ("a" is for agonizing, "b" is for banished, etc.).

Metaphor: A man lost something very important to him. A crowd that swarmed around him stole it and hit him on the head. He no longer can remember what it is he is looking for but knows that he must find it.

Rationale: This story helps Dan focus on the meaning of his life and trying to find out what is important to him above all else. He can name the people in the crowd who have stolen from him and try to see who took the thing that was so important in his life.

Questions for Further Discussion

1. Think about how stories have been formative in your own development. Discuss how the stories you tell yourself create meaning in your life.

2. What are some of the ways Dan could be encouraged to externalize the stories he has of being teased in high school and college? How might the therapist help Dan talk about his stories given the sensitive nature of their content?

3. Would talking to Dan more directly about his sexual orientation be helpful in the treatment process? In what ways could this help Dan address his problems? In what ways might this line of inquiry be either difficult or intrusive for Dan?

4. Think of some metaphors in your own life you have used to explain past life problems. Guided by Kopp's (1995) five-stage model, walk through your metaphor and discuss whether the process was a helpful one for you.

Chapter 10

Learning to Think
DIFFERENTLY

Chapter Highlights

1. This chapter outlines the usefulness of cognitive behavior therapy approaches (Ellis, 2007; Glasser, 1975, 2001) for helping clients think differently about stress events, frustrations, and unfair experiences.
2. The case of Matt (a paranoid and anxious) is introduced to illustrate how a therapist can bring about a change in a client's view of the world. Matt becomes overwhelmed with the idea of paying back his student loans and engages in odd (knuckle biting) and threatening behavior.
3. The ideas of identifying potential triggers and catching irrational thoughts are introduced. This builds on Ellis's (2007) work on identifying activating events, beliefs, and consequences. The importance of developing alternative explanations is demonstrated for the clinician.
4. Dr. Nay's (2004) work on identifying and addressing anger intensifiers such as sleep, stress, substances, sustenance, and sickness is explored as it relates to Matt's case.
5. The concept of making a plan and sticking to it is introduced based on the cognitive behavior therapy approach. Goal setting, mental rehearsal, arousal control and self-talk are offered as suggestions to create more successful plans.

Many of the therapists and psychologists who went to school in the 1990s to practice psychotherapy became exposed to the work of Rogers (1961,

1980) and humanistic psychotherapy. This approach values emotional connection with the client, offers unconditional positive regard, and encourages a nonhierarchical view of the doctor–patient relationship. In this context, cognitive behavior therapy (Ellis, 2007; Glasser, 1975, 2001) became the popular methodology with a focus on empirically validated treatment and helping those who come to therapy to think differently about stress events, frustrations, and unfair experiences, a perspective shift that is critical to bringing about lasting change. The cognitive behavior therapy approach offers the tools and techniques needed to make that happen.

This chapter uses the story of Matt to help illustrate how a therapist can work to bring about a change in a client's view of the world around him. The case is an interesting one given the introduction of several powerful medications and a hospital stay at the outset of treatment. As the crisis behaviors are addressed, the therapist is now challenged with the scenario many of us are tasked with in the field, namely: Now that the crisis has passed, work with the client and make sure things don't get bad again.

Case Study: Matt, a Paranoid and Anxious Young Man

Matt struggled with anxiety that increased dramatically over the course of his sophomore year at college. He worried about his classes and his grades and how he would pay for the semester. He talked constantly to his professors about the syllabus and assignments, trying to understand exactly what was required. In his intense scrutiny, he was usually so specific in trying to meet the course requirements that he left large segments of the classwork incomplete. For example, he would stay up all night making sure that his worksheets were correct for his accounting class but then oversleep and miss the exam. He was in danger of failing many of his classes this semester.

Matt blamed much of this on his overcritical father growing up. He could never do anything right in his eyes and would worry about everything from how his room was kept to his grades in high school. He worried about what music he listened to, how to make friends, and whether he would ever find a girlfriend. He lived in terror that his father would punish him for not living up to his expectations. Matt's mother was distant and his two younger sisters didn't seem to draw the same attention from their father's critical gaze.

Matt's behavior worsened at college when he began to perseverate and worry about how he would pay his tuition. He calculated that he needed $47,000 to pay back his college loans and began to talk about this amount with multiple people around campus. He showed up at the registrar and made appointments to talk through how he would get this money to pay for school. They patiently walked him through the student loan process and how it would be paid over time. He asked, "But what if I don't do well enough at my job? How will I pay that back? What will happen then?" He continued to talk through his worries with his resident advisor, roommate, staff and administrators in financial aid, health services, and the Dean of Student Affairs office.

Matt started to bite his knuckles and pace back and forth in various offices on campus. He became agitated when he was told that he had to wait for an appointment or that there wasn't anyone available to talk to him. He left blood traces from his bitten knuckles on the waiting room furniture. Matt called his roommate's mother to ask her for $47,000 to pay for school. Staff and faculty were concerned about Matt's behavior, and he was referred for a threat assessment after the college behavioral intervention team reviewed his case.

Matt became belligerent and extremely agitated during the threat assessment. He was taken to the local hospital and admitted for 2 weeks at the state hospital. Matt was started on a combination of mood stabilizing medications as well as some antipsychotic and tranquilizing medications. He became less agitated about returning to school and seemed more capable of keeping his anxiety and paranoia about the future to himself.

Identifying and Managing Triggers

The therapist working with Matt should help him identify how his body is experiencing biological changes as he becomes increasingly upset and frustrated. The trigger events are the environmental stimuli that elicit a biological reaction. These could be another student yelling at the client, a lost cell phone, or a bounced check returned from the bank causing the client to have a negative checking balance. When that happens, his heart rate increases, his breathing becomes faster, adrenaline is produced, and his capacity for creative and rational thought is diminished. Dr. Nay (2004) also highlighted how the stomach and gastrointestinal systems empty of blood as digestion slows or holds to free up blood for the brain and muscles. This may cause shallow breathing, chest heaviness, and feelings of suffocation. Senses may become more sensitive and magnified; movements toward you may seem more threatening. Muscles begin to tighten, particularly around the shoulders, neck, forehead, and jaw.

As Matt finds himself in a stress-inducing situation, he would benefit from using the process of "cycle breathing" to reduce the biological changes that begin to escalate as he becomes upset (Byrnes, 2002). The process of cycle breathing involves breathing in to a slow count of 4, holding the breath for a slow count of 2, breathing out for a slow count of 4, holding the breath for a slow count of 2, and then repeating. This process lowers blood pressure and heart rate, allowing the individual to regain calm and move down the escalation phase rather than up it.

As with many concepts in this chapter, the initial explanation and description of what to do differently is the easy part. The challenge for the therapist working with Matt is to encourage and to practice techniques like cycle breathing until they become second nature for him. In Matt's case, it is unlikely that the medication and inpatient hospital stay are going to permanently fix all of the problems he has experienced. This is particularly true as he returns to campus after a 2-week absence from classes. The techniques demonstrated in this chapter must be practiced and encouraged throughout treatment in order for them to be incorporated into Matt's daily life.

Catching Irrational Thoughts

Rational emotive behavior therapy was developed by Albert Ellis (2007) and can help individuals identify irrational thoughts that are reactions to activating events. This treatment approach can be described in terms of ABCs: activating events, beliefs about these events, and the consequences of these beliefs.

Assisting clients to see their irrational thoughts is the first step to helping them find alternative ways to process the world around them. One way to do this is to see the upsetting things that they find themselves thinking about as "activating events."

Activating events can happen in a variety of settings. These could occur through daily hassles that the individual encounters in the environment (daily work stress, financial worries, self-esteem), life changes (graduation worries, family divorce or conflict, being away from home the first time), environmental stresses (construction noises outside the dorm, heating or cooling problems in the residence hall, frustration from living in close quarters with other college students), chronic pain (from past surgery, illness, or injury), or acculturation stress (moving from another country or geographic region, living in a religiously different area).

In Matt's case, the upsetting events for him are specific: He is worried about his finances and about his ability to pass his classes. Following the hospitalization, these worries could likely include fear of a readmission to the unit or changes in his medication or paranoia around how others see him now that he has come back to school. They could also be seen as specific events like being told that no one is available to talk to him at the financial aid office or receiving a failing grade on an assignment because he did not complete it correctly.

The therapist should help Matt identify some of these stressful activating events, which can be anything from arguing with an important other, getting cut off in traffic, spilling coffee on a favorite shirt, or experiencing a computer crash. These events cannot be prevented; they occur throughout our lives. When the stressful activating events are identified, the therapist can then focus on applying techniques (e.g., cycle breathing) to improve the client's ability to cope and reduce further escalation.

After the stressful events have been identified, Matt should be encouraged to explore his "beliefs" about the activating events that led to aggressive actions and negative consequences. Although he cannot change the activating events that occur in his daily life, he can change the beliefs about the activating events and the resulting consequences of the behavior.

I use several examples to highlight how Matt might approach this ABC process. Positive and negative examples are provided in Table 10.1.

In therapy, Matt can be helped to identify beliefs about activating events that end up increasing his panic and paranoia about the future. He can be encouraged to appreciate that there will always be upsetting activating events that he will have little control over and that he should instead focus his energy and effort on finding alternative ways to think about the activating event in order to increase the likelihood of positive consequences.

Finding Alternative Explanations

The ability to empathize (i.e., see things from another perspective) is a step toward moving away from aggressive behavior. For example, we are less likely to be aggressive toward the driver of a car that cuts us off when we understand that the other driver may be rushing his pregnant wife to the hospital. Our aggression is dissipated because we acknowledge that we might act in the same manner if we faced a comparable situation. A student who is frustrated by a professor for receiving a failing grade on an exam is likely to be less aggressive if the reason for the grade is clear and the student can acknowledge that the quality of work merits the grade that was given.

The therapist should encourage clients to see the "why" behind behavior and better understand the motives of their behavior. This

Table 10.1 | **Responses of a Paranoid and Anxious Client to Triggering Events Before and After Rational Emotive Behavior Therapy**

Activating Event	Positive Response	Negative Response
Matt gets a poor grade on one of his class assignments.	He takes his time to review the expectations for the assignment to identify any mistakes he might have made. Matt schedules a time to sit down with the professor to see what he missed.	He thinks he must address this immediately and is upset because he tried very hard to do well on the assignment. Matt interrupts the professor to argue about his grade.
Matt receives a financial aid notice in his mail that says he owes $47,000 upon graduation.	Matt sees this letter as going out to everyone on campus—not just him—and writes down his concerns. Matt practices cycle breathing to stay calm, brings his concerns to the financial aid advisor, and talks to his therapist to keep things in perspective.	He becomes overwhelmed by the amount and panics about being able to pay that back. Matt goes to the financial aid office 2 hours before they open and paces in the office waiting to talk to someone.

process could be cognitive and academic through exploring different possibilities to various scenarios:

- Imagine you are late for class and someone is taking too long in the only shower that is working in the bathroom. You find yourself stressed and tense, frustrated that there is only one working shower and mad that this other inconsiderate student is keeping you from getting to class. What are some ways you could empathize with the person in the shower? How about with the building maintenance staff?
- Imagine you are interested in a girl in geography class. You spend 3 days working on a poem for her and buy a special locket charm with money you saved from working a summer job. When you give her these things after class one day, she laughs uncomfortably and says, "I can't take these—thanks anyway. Why might she have reacted this way? What are some other ways this situation could be addressed? How else could you have handled your interest in this girl?

In some cases, this process can almost become a game played back and forth between therapist and client. Matt could be encouraged to find alternative ways to think about his overwhelming worries about his financial aid, such as normalizing the amount he owes compared to other students who owe similar amounts, or reducing the worry of paying back the money he borrowed by talking to alumni who have successfully paid back their student loans.

Managing Anger

Therapists can assist their clients in understanding the five intensifiers toward anger and aggressive behavior outlined by Nay (2004):

- *Sleep.* Students in high school and college are notorious for not getting enough sleep. This lack of sleep makes them more irritable and reduces their ability to be flexible and positively focused when approaching negative stress or activating events. The therapist should assist the client in discussing his underlying difficulties with sleep (lack of exercise, inconsistent sleep schedule, and substance abuse) and how these lead to difficulty in getting enough rest.
- *Stress.* The body feels stress when reacting to change and frustrating situations. High stress levels lead to higher irritability and difficulty in responding flexibly and positively when dealing with activating events. Stress is cumulative and builds up to dangerous levels, setting the stage for the next activating event; eventually it might lead to an explosion. When college or high school

students engage in too many tasks, struggle to balance competing deadlines, and are surprised by life events like problems at home or relationships ending, they are at risk for intensifying their aggressive responses.

- *Substances.* Alcohol and caffeine can dramatically intensify our emotions. College students are surrounded by these substances offered at parties and advertised through energy drinks and study aids. Substances increase irritability, and they decrease impulse control and frustration tolerance, both of which can affect how stressful events can be perceived. They can be overused in an attempt to reduce stress and ultimately make the situation worse.

- *Sustenance.* Students often struggle to eat a healthy diet and maintain proper exercise. When trying to balance class work, relationships, social life, athletics, club memberships, and family, it is easy to see how good nutrition and exercise quickly fall by the wayside. Too much sugar and junk food may also increase mood swings and intensify aggressive behaviors.

- *Sickness.* When students become ill, their ability to cope with stress is reduced. Pain and discomfort increase their arousal and irritability and decrease their ability to think clearly. Poor nutrition, lack of exercise, and increased stress leads to a weaker immune system and a higher potential for sickness.

Addressing Matt's overall wellness, sleep, eating, stress, and substance use all have the potential to help reduce his existing problems. In the same way a gardener ensures the right soil, sunlight, water, and nutrients for plants, addressing anger intensifiers can be useful to support other cognitive behavior therapy efforts.

Making a Plan and Sticking to It

During their "hell" week training, Navy SEALs are taught four key stress control techniques that help them better cope with stress and stay focused on their goals (Blair, 2008).

Goal Setting

Goal setting is the process of encouraging clients to have a clear picture of their goals and creating a way to see progress toward them. This can be done through journaling about progress or creating a chart of successful times they coped with activating events or were able to reduce their escalation phase. The client should be encouraged to focus on an immediate, measurable goal.

A SEAL trainee might focus on "I need to make it to the next hill on the beach" or "I just need to stay under for another 5 seconds . . . I can do another 5 seconds." A client may need to focus on getting through a class without arguing with the professor or "making it through a disagreement by finding a way to step out of the situation and not get upset." For Matt, this would mean looking over all of his assignments and setting up a plan to attend to each one in turn for a set period of time. In this way he stays focused on the task at hand and avoids worrying about becoming overwhelmed by the next assignment on the horizon.

Mental Rehearsal

Clients are encouraged to mentally imagine themselves being successful at a particular interaction that in the past caused problems. It is easy to imagine Navy SEAL trainees visualizing successful missions or accomplishing a goal. Sports psychologists teach this technique for basketball players to improve their foul shots. Students can complete the following steps:

1. Clearly visualize a conflict where you could become aggressive or continue to escalate.
2. Visualize responding calmly and avoiding an escalation or allowing frustrations to develop. Focus on the best possible response, such as "Well, that is certainly one way to see it. I don't see it the same way, though."
3. Imagine obstacles to a successful interaction. Possibly imagine another student pushing or yelling back. Visualize the best possible response.
4. Repeat this process several times a week until you begin to see results.

Matt could be encouraged to look for ways to address his knuckle-biting behavior and to work with his therapist to brainstorm different responses when feeling overwhelmed and stressed to the point of biting his hands. The repetition of these events would help Matt experience more success in applying these changes.

Self-Talk

Positive self-talk will assist clients in developing an internal "cheerleading team" that can help push them during difficult times. The client should identify a supportive person in his or her life—a cheerleader—and then imagine that person mentally accompanying him or her during a conflict. While the conflict is going on, the client can imagine the cheerleader saying, "You got this one. No way are they going to push your buttons. Calm and cool. The more they push, the more you relax."

As Matt works to his reduce his anxiety and improve his studies, he imagines a supportive group encouraging his positive changes and offering forbearance during more difficult times. This positive self-talk could be used to reduce his worry about financial aid, stay focused on his classes, and limit the number of people he talks to about his concerns over paying back his student loans.

Arousal Control

By taking slow, deep breaths with controlled exhalations, individuals communicate to their bodies that they are not in a panic situation (fight/flight) and that they must maintain control. This process is similar to what expectant mothers, Navy SEAL snipers, and meditating monks use to control their biological functions. As with any technique, practice and repetition are key.

Summary

In this chapter, I have briefly reviewed some cognitive–behavioral approaches to working with a student who displayed some potentially threatening and concerning behavior to others. This treatment approach should not be used in isolation from the humanistic approach (Chapter 8), motivational interview/change theory concepts (Chapter 11), or existential therapy concepts (Chapter 12). Instead, these theoretical and technical examples illustrate to the clinician how to apply theoretical concepts as part of an overall treatment plan with an at-risk client.

In the following chapter, the client has more impulsive anger problems leading to violent outbursts; I describe how the techniques of motivational interviewing could be used to engage and work with the client toward lasting change.

Questions for Further Discussion

1. What are some of the concerns that come up for you given the case study of Matt? How would you address the behavior occurring around campus?
2. In the chapter, Van Brunt introduces the concept of identifying and managing triggers. How might you assist clients in mastering this process when the majority of the time they experience the triggers outside of the therapeutic hour?
3. Think of an activating event that occurred in your life. Talk about the irrational beliefs and rational beliefs that corresponded to the activating event. How did each impact the consequences that followed?
4. Discuss ways to address irrational thoughts that come up during the course of treatment with a client. What are some approaches that both value the individual's thoughts while challenging him or her to think more productively in the future?

5. Discuss how the cognitive behavior therapy approach can be combined with Rogers's humanistic theory and the narrative therapy approach. Are these mutually exclusive? What are the benefits and limitations in adopting an eclectic approach to treatment?

Chapter 11

Taking It
STEP by STEP

Chapter Highlights

1. The dual approaches of motivational interviewing (Miller & Rollnick, 1991) and transtheoretical change theory (Prochaska, Norcross, & DiClemente, 1994) are introduced as practical approaches to working with those who are unwilling to change their behavior.

2. The case of Kelly (impulsive and violent) is introduced to illustrate the challenge of working with an individual who is unwilling to engage in treatment. She has a tendency toward impulsive behavior and threatens a teacher at school after being challenged for her behavior in class.

3. Motivational interviewing (Miller & Rollnick, 1991) is reviewed as an approach to working with difficult and resistant clients. The core concepts of expressing empathy, avoiding argumentation, rolling with resistance, developing discrepancy, and supporting self-efficacy are explained and demonstrated through examples.

4. Transtheoretical change theory, developed by Prochaska et al. (1994), provides the clinician with insight into how clients may become stuck in certain stages before becoming ready to act. The theory identifies five stages: precontemplation, contemplation, preparation for action, action, and maintenance and relapse prevention.

5. Practicing patience is useful for those who experience impulse control or anger problems because it helps them increase their frustration tolerance and become more mindful of their sur-

roundings. The technique of guided imagery is taught here as a practical example. Redefining failure helps address the internalized negative messages about the client's worth, quality of his or her abilities, physical features, or place in the world.

Not all violent behavior ends in a school shooting and becomes front-page news. There are times when violence is more limited to impulsive interpersonal arguments, fistfights, and general fit throwing. In these cases, the challenge is to help individuals become aware of their triggers and find new ways to approach upsetting events. These trigger events are the everyday life experiences that elicit negative response behaviors. Some examples of how to do this were outlined in Chapter 10: helping the client understand activating events, use cycle breathing, and look for ways to remain calm in the face of upsetting events.

In this chapter, I introduce you to Kelly, who experiences frequent trigger events and is highly reluctant to complete treatment. Dustin, introduced in Chapter 3, presents similar difficulties in terms of engagement in therapy. The person-centered approach to therapy defined by Rogers (1961, 1980) offers some techniques to reduce defensiveness and form connection with others, but the client may not be ready to engage with the therapist. To this end, I explore two approaches to therapy that are useful when working with clients like Kelly and Dustin who have numerous problems, difficulty engaging in the therapeutic process, and little hope or willingness to work toward positive change. These clients will not magically engage in treatment, but the persuasive techniques found in motivational interviewing (Miller & Rollnick, 1991) coupled with the underlying theory of how people change (Prochaska et al., 1994) help tremendously in redirecting their reluctance to engage in treatment.

Case Study: Kelly, an Impulsive and Violent Teenager

Kelly's history of getting into fights reaches back to elementary school. In high school, her explosive outbursts have increased. She gets angry at having to rush from class to class, always feeling behind and trying to get to class on time. Already 2 weeks into her junior year, she has had one in-school suspension for getting into a fistfight with another student in the hallway over a disagreement about a pack of cigarettes.

Kelly argued with her teachers about not having assignments in on time, and she was doing poorly on most of her exams and reports. When she was asked to talk to guidance counselors about her behavior and attitude toward work, she was negative and disrespectful. She had not been involved in mental health counseling, nor had she ever been hospitalized or started on medication.

Knowing that she had a short fuse, her peers at school tried to get her angry to see what she would do. Someone might purposefully bump into her in order to watch her explode with a "You fucking whore!" and then get sent to detention by a teacher. People drew on her locker, whispered about her in class, and looked for ways to push her buttons.

Kelly had a few friends who share her life outlook. They spent time loitering in the hallways between classes and talking about sex and drinking and selecting the house they would hang out at on the weekend. Kelly came from a large family and was the fifth of seven children. Her parents worked long hours and she got little attention at home. Both of her parents drank, and she was expected to help take care of her two younger siblings.

During a chemistry class, Kelly was talking with one of her friends and the teacher stopped the lecture and asked, "Am I interrupting your conversation?" in a sarcastic tone. Other students laughed around her and Kelly felt embarrassed. She barked back to the teacher, "No, dickhead. We were just talking about how to make a bomb to blow up this whole worthless shitpile of a school."

Kelly was expelled for her threat and was required to complete an assessment off campus with a forensic psychologist before enrolling in another school. The assessment revealed a low likelihood of Kelly actually putting together a bomb to blow up the school. The psychologist did express concern about her anger management and impulse-control problems and recommended ongoing treatment to address these problems if she were to be allowed to return to school.

Motivational Interviewing

Motivational interviewing (or motivational enhancement therapy; MET) was developed by Miller and Rollnick (1991) and used primarily with mandated alcohol treatment to help people change addictive behavior. I've used their approach and find it helpful in working with mandated students in ongoing treatment and connecting with those who are initially unwilling to explore a change in the way they behave. It is a proactive approach to working with those who don't yet see they have a problem or aren't yet ready to tackle it or head in a new direction. The heart of Miller and Rollnick's approach centers on five key concepts that can be applied well to working with students who are mandated to treatment.

Expression of Empathy

Expression of empathy involves a conversation with the client that attempts to both understand the client's perspective (empathy) and communicate an understanding of that perspective (expression of empathy). This expression of empathy respects the client's point of view, freedom of choice, and ability to determine his or her own self-direction. Suggestions from the therapist for change are subtle, and the ultimate change is left in the hands of the client.

In Kelly's case, one of the easiest places to begin developing a connection is to synch with her feelings and frustrations with school. It is likely that she feels treated unfairly after being expelled for her remarks. She has never been very interested in school and seems to only enjoy spending time with her friends. She likes drinking and may also enjoy certain music, TV shows, or clothing. Connecting with Kelly around these experiences and preferences helps build a connection between her and the therapist. This may be an easy process of centering the conversation on topics she is willing to discuss, such as her feelings of being targeted or things she likes to do outside of school. It may be more difficult (as demonstrated with Dustin in Chapter 3) and she may see through these attempts to connect as part of a plan to be nice in order to gain her trust.

I find myself having an easier time expressing empathy when I am congruent with a client like Kelly and I am able to be genuine in my conversation and reflections. I may share a brief story from my own life where I felt I had been treated unfairly. I might avoid taking the bait when she challenges my profession or my thoughts/feelings and instead stay focused on building connection. (I give some more examples of this in the *Rolling With Resistance* section.) The five techniques of motivational interviewing are not applied in any particular order but rather organically as the therapist builds an alliance with the client.

Avoidance of Argumentation

This is probably the easiest technique to understand but the most difficult to put into practice. Therapists and clinicians would do well to remember my EMT instructor's famous admonition to my class when dealing with the unruly patient: "If it feels good to say the thing you are about to say, don't." When you argue with the client who is arguing with you, neither of you is listening.

Kelly engages in many thoughts and actions that would provide opportunities for argument—her underage drinking, potentially risky sexual decisions, lack of career focus, and fighting and arguing with other students and teachers. Although there may be opportunities later in therapy to help Kelly explore and potentially modify these behaviors, a key mistake would be to engage these points early in treatment, prior to the development of a trusting relationship.

Most therapists have had the experience of watching clients who cease to pay attention to what they are saying. They tune out; they look down and away; they fidget or roll their eyes. The argument might not be a verbal one, but instead it is communicated more subtly through a slow distancing of the client from the therapist. In some ways, this can be even more destructive to the change process. The client becomes disillusioned with the process, disengages, and loses faith in the therapist and his or her ability to understand and relate.

Being agreeable with the client, at least at the outset of treatment, is one of the best ways to build rapport and establish a connection. As treatment progresses, the therapist typically has established some credibility and trust, which allows the therapist to challenge the client's established, harmful thoughts or behaviors. Direct argumentation rarely addresses any underlying change but rather becomes caught up in the process of exchanging opinions back and forth without any kind of empathic consideration.

Rolling With Resistance

Clinicians are encouraged to avoid meeting a client's resistance to change head on. Instead, they should try to engage the client in new ways of thinking about the situation, perhaps trying to evoke from the client new solutions to the conflict. Lack of motivation or an unwillingness to change and be positive are understood as normal developmental responses, and interventions are designed to avoid becoming mired down in the client's lack of developmental growth and personal responsibility for change.

Kelly may have difficulty seeing the teacher's point of view in this scenario because the teacher embarrassed Kelly, and this (in Kelly's schema) justifies a defensive response. A rational observer can see that the teacher's intervention was not an ideal approach to classroom management and could not lead to corrective action for Kelly or her classmate, but it would also be fair to suggest that Kelly's rude crosstalk behavior invites a similar discourteous intervention. Pointing this out to Kelly, however, while she is ranting about "what a bitch the teacher is for talking some smart-ass shit" about her is likely to induce a defensive response.

Instead, the therapist would be better served to ask more open-ended questions designed to expand the conversation and encourage more thoughtful reflection. Responses such as "What would you have liked the teacher to do when she was distracted by your talking?" or "Have you ever experienced a time when you were talking and someone was ignoring you? How did you handle that?" might encourage a less defensive response from Kelly.

Development of Discrepancy

Development of discrepancy is the process by which the therapist helps clients understand that the current behavior won't help them achieve the desired goal. The therapist explores the consequences of the client's actions in a neutral manner, avoiding sarcasm or a condescending tone. The client then becomes aware of his or her choices and starts to explore the advantages to choosing a different way to behave.

This skill is better applied when some trust is already established with the client. A common mistake is attempting to develop discrepancy with a client early on; the client then sees the therapist as over-intellectualizing the problem and becomes upset with the therapist for ignoring the emotional component of her frustrations. Kelly would be a good candidate for a development of discrepancy after she has vented her emotional frustrations and feels the therapist better understands the problem from her point of view.

Imagine Kelly saying with an exasperated sigh, "I just don't know what I'm supposed to do anymore. I feel lost. Every time I try to find something I'm interested in at school I end up not liking it or finding that it is too hard for me." Here, the exchange might look like this:

Therapist: Kelly, tell me what kind of things you've tried to explore?

Kelly: I don't know, science and stuff.

Therapist: What kind of science?

Kelly: When we were studying a chapter in biology. Stuff with fish and the ocean. I liked that. But then it got all technical and everything went to shit. I'm no good at any of this stuff. My mom says I should just get a job at the factory like her.

Therapist: What part exactly was hard for you?

Kelly: I don't know. The reading in the chapter, I guess. Like every other word was something I didn't recognize. It's like I'd have to have some kind of dictionary in my brain to know all of that biology stuff.

Therapist: Biology is certainly full of some tough vocabulary. I know some of my friends who studied biology and they had the same problems when they started out. They did say that it got easier as time went along. It was particularly hard in the beginning.

Kelly: Yeah, I guess I could see that.

Therapist: Have you thought about doing some more research and reading in the area of marine biology? Maybe looking at a club at school or talking to your teacher about other resources that might not have so much technical writing? Maybe like a blog of a marine biologist or some kind of photojournalism project?

Kelly: No, I didn't think of that.

Therapist: I'm not 100% sure it would work, but for me, that's what I did when I was first interested in psychology. I read some of the easier stories and articles that got me more interested. I put off some of that harder research methods and graduate school stuff until I was sure I really wanted to do this as a career.

Kelly: That makes sense.

Support for Self-Efficacy

Supporting self-efficacy involves helping the client understand that change is possible and that the future can be better than the present. The therapist does this by encouraging and nurturing growth in clients, finding times and opportunities to "catch them doing well," and praising this behavior with hopes of shaping future positive behavior.

For Kelly, this would involve praising her for positive behaviors and thoughts with the goal being to shape repeat examples of these behaviors. If Kelly were to follow up with her teacher about marine biology, the therapist should make sure to praise her for that positive choice to reinforce the likelihood of more follow-up behavior. Supporting self-efficacy can be easily overlooked in therapy where there is a focus on movement forward and focus on addressing new behaviors. I have found it helpful to remind myself each session to mentally scroll through the client's thoughts and actions and make sure that I support and reinforce those positive decisions to better ensure replication in the future.

Change Theory

Miller and Rollnick (1991) offered a useful set of practical techniques when working with unmotivated or defensive clients; I have found it helpful to ground their technical work within the philosophical framework of transtheoretical change theory developed by Prochaska et al. (1994). Their powerful book *Changing for Good* is one that I often consult when I'm struggling with a client who seems to be stuck, incapable of changing his or her behavior. The concepts are universally helpful when looking to answer the question "Why is it so hard for students to change their behavior?"

The authors outlined how people move through various stages before achieving lasting change in their lives. They offered a unique perspective on clients who repeat difficult or frustrating behaviors. When explaining these concepts to colleagues, I ask them to pause and consider a behavior they have tried to change in their life. This can either be something they are currently struggling with (smoking, watching too much TV, not getting enough exercise) or something they have tried to change in the past. As I review the five stages of change, keep in mind a behavior you have tried to change before in your life.

Precontemplation

At this stage, the client is unaware that there is a problem and hasn't thought much about change. The therapist's goal is to help the client gain increased awareness of the need for change. This is done primarily through nonjudgmental, nondirective open discussion. The therapist helps the client understand how his behaviors may be affecting his life.

To ignore that Kelly is likely in the precontemplative stage could be a crucial error in the treatment process. Any advice, from behaving differently in class to exploring career options for future employment, falls on deaf ears because she has no desire to change. In her mind, she doesn't have a problem or a behavior that needs to be changed. Until Kelly develops a desire to change her behavior in order to avoid negative consequences, any advice or positive suggestions will be ignored. The therapist's challenge is to engage and explore, helping her to understand that what she is currently doing is causing enough problems to necessitate a behavior change.

Contemplation

This is the most common stage of change for a client. The client has thought about change and is getting ready for movement in the near future. He or she realizes that current behavior is not productive but is not yet ready to begin a plan to change. The client isn't happy about the current state and wants things to be different but has not yet explored how to do things differently or take action to make change in his life.

In this stage, the therapist continues to motivate the client and encourage him or her to think in more detail about the negative impact of a specific behavior on the client's life. Together they should explore ways the client might plan for change and what resources could be helpful in implementing change.

Kelly comes into session aware that things are not going well in her life. She is unhappy and frustrated that she has been expelled from school. She is worried about her future and experiencing a good deal of anxiety about what she needs to do in order to get back into school. She has likely not experienced a true understanding of how her behavior is immature and working against her positive future goals but is more likely uncomfortable enough now to want to get better, perhaps even just a return to a status quo.

The therapist's role here is to continue to explore and push the client closer to a plan for action. The focus here is less on the specifics of how this plan would be implemented, but instead a further exploration of why she wants to behave differently. Kelly may state, "This really sucks, I feel like my life just crashed into fence. I'm spinning my wheels and anything I do keeps me stuck at home with my parents. Something needs to give." The therapist's response acknowledges what Kelly feels and pushes it forward, urging her to think more about what direction she wants to be headed: "It sounds like you are unhappy and can't seem to find a foothold on what you should do next to get unstuck. If you weren't stuck like this, what kind of things would you like to be doing? What would your life look like if it was unstuck?"

Preparation for Action

In this stage, clients are aware of a problem and are ready to actively create goals to address the problem behavior in their life. Plans and goals should be focused, short term, and designed to be modified as needed to ensure client success. Plans should be measureable and easy to monitor to see if they are moving forward, staying in place, or moving backward. The therapist can help the client brainstorm and update plans to ensure a better chance of success.

Here, Kelly is ready to go. Her response to the therapist's question above "What would your life look like if it was unstuck?" would be "I know exactly what it would look like. I want to do something to get there now. I'm ready to make some changes. What do I do?" The therapist can help Kelly establish a plan that has a high likelihood of success.

Glasser (1975, 2001) founded a therapeutic system called reality therapy that emphasizes the importance of creating plans with clients that are achievable. To this end, he argued that plans should be focused and short term. A plan like "Kelly will do better in her classes and go to college" is too broad and difficult for her to monitor and put into action. The goal is so big it would be hard for her to make adjustments to the plan or know if she is moving forward, standing still, or falling behind. A better plan would address what she would need to do in each of her classes to achieve a specific grade needed to raise her grade point average, which would, in turn, improve her chances of getting into college. The plan would then include scheduling discussions with her guidance counselor to talk about college possibilities, perhaps even scheduling career aptitude testing to help her explore possibilities. The plan would explore financial aid options and discussion of community or technical colleges as an intermediate step to a 4-year college.

Glasser (1975, 2001) outlined a process of change based on understanding of and assessing the client's WDEP: **W**ants and needs, **D**irection and what they are doing, an **E**valuation of his or her behavior, and **P**lanning and commitment to change. Glasser advised therapists who are reviewing plans with clients to make sure that the plans are simple, attainable, measureable, immediate, consistent, controlled by the client, committed to by the client, and timely. Appendix E contains a worksheet that can be used to help clients working individually or with their therapists to develop WDEPs.

Action

In the action stage of change, clients put their plans into action in order to change behavior. They attempt to alter their negative behaviors and develop new positive behaviors to replace them. The therapist can support clients as they try out these action steps and encourage them to persist despite setbacks.

Kelly's reintegration into the high school is not likely to be a smooth one. The therapist must balance a mixture of optimism and hope with the reality that Kelly is going back into a new school setting with few friends and will likely be behind in much of her work. These challenges are not insurmountable, but they present a challenge for her to achieve her goals. The therapist becomes the cheerleader, mentor, life coach, and advisor to her success.

Maintenance and Relapse Prevention

The goal of the maintenance and relapse prevention stage is to continue successful plans and repeat those action steps that work and adjust things that don't. The client has experienced change and a reduction in problem behavior and now needs to maintain the successful change and reduce the risk of falling back into bad habits. The therapist can help bolster the client's success and develop awareness of potential obstacles that could lead to relapse.

Kelly is likely to be successful with some of her endeavors and to encounter trouble with others. The therapist should support Kelly in maintaining her successes while identifying obstacles and working with her to avoid relapse of previous negative behaviors. If relapse prevention is not achievable, then the therapist can help Kelly get back on track quickly without becoming mired in negative thinking.

Practicing Patience

I was giving a presentation to the faculty at a Catholic college in the Midwest. My host was directing me to the lecture hall and we talked about the school's stunning architecture as we walked down one of the many stone corridors. Becoming lost in our conversation, I initially had not noticed a nontraditional-age student walking behind us. I turned to her and apologized for blocking her path and offered to let her pass by. She smiled back and said in a genuine manner, "No thank you. I'm practicing my patience."

Years later, I still think about that student's response and how it affected me. I thought about her comment and considered how some of the virtues we hold dear only improve when practiced and meditated upon. There is no book on patience or set of steps one can follow to achieve a sense of patience. Yet this student seemed to stumble upon an interesting concept—how to actively practice the development of patience.

Developing increased patience is useful for those who experience impulse control or anger problems because it helps them increase their frustration tolerance and become more mindful of their surroundings. With this increased attention, the hope is that the client will have a better opportunity to choose from a range of options rather than being forced into a reactive stance. For Kelly, for example, it is possible that if she had more patience and a higher frustration tolerance, her threatening response might have been modified.

The cycle breathing approach mentioned in Chapter 10 is one that can help the client gain better control over emotional and biological responses in the face of escalation. Another approach that can be practiced prior to conflict is *guided imagery*, the process of creating a relaxing image for the student in order to visualize a peaceful, calming scenario (such as relaxing on the beach, sitting quietly in a favorite spot, or lying in bed). The clinician talks while the client imagines this scenario. Some excellent examples that are available for use are located at www.innerhealthstudio.com.

Redefining Failure

In relation to developing patience, how clients define failure in their lives can have an effect on how easily they are able to let go. Having a grounding in preventive practices such as guided imagery and in-the-moment techniques like cycle breathing will help improve frustration tolerance and increase mindfulness, but it is important to challenge the underlying thoughts and emotions that clients experience in their environment.

Kelly might see her teacher labeling her as someone in need of instruction and, therefore, a poor student. An underlying assumption for Kelly might be her internalization of the negative beliefs that she is a poor student, has nothing to offer, and is worthless. Others might see a teacher's redirection of a negative behavior as simply part of what it means to be a student. A therapist may challenge Kelly and help her appreciate that when an authority figure challenges her, this does not automatically reinforce her belief that she is a poor student.

Clients often internalize negative messages about their worth, the quality of their abilities, their physical features, or their place in the world. When they see these as absolute failures rather than temporary obstacles, they overemphasize the importance of the event and become reactive rather than thoughtful about their response.

People who are successful in their ventures have a rather open and flexible view of success. They see achievement as more of a marathon than a sprint. They see obstacles to their success as temporary setbacks rather than permanent roadblocks. Helping a client like Kelly goes beyond teaching her skills to handle frustrations and impulse control; it has to include addressing the core issue of her struggles in high school. To put it bluntly, someone in her life should share the message that few of us know what we want to do in high school. Many successful people, from *Harry Potter* series author J.K. Rowling to Abraham Lincoln, have faced considerable adversity and setbacks prior to achieving their goals. Part of the treatment for a student like Kelly must be a reinstallation of hope in her ability to achieve her goals and be successful even in the face of doubt, indecisiveness, and hesitation about what she wants to become when she is older. Her behavior to her teacher, while certainly ill advised and replete with natural consequences, should not be allowed to define who she is to become.

Summary

In this chapter, I reviewed an important philosophy of change as well as a set of techniques useful for developing connection and overcoming resistance with difficult clients. In the next chapter, I address an even more challenging case with higher treatment resistance and larger implications for rampage violence.

Questions for Further Discussion

1. What are some of the challenges you have encountered when working with clients who are resistant to treatment? How have you worked to overcome these obstacles? What has been effective? What has made the situation more difficult?
2. Which approaches outlined in motivational interviewing (expressing empathy, avoiding argumentation, rolling with resistance, developing discrepancy, and supporting self-efficacy) have been helpful in your work with treatment-resistant clients?
3. Think about a time you were looking to change a bad habit or behavior in your life. This could be something you were successful at or had difficulty with overcoming. Discuss the attempt at change from the perspective of precontemplation, contemplation, preparation for action, action, and maintenance and relapse prevention.
4. What are some ways you have looked at success and failures in your life? How does redefining failure as delayed success help to encourage a more positive, solution-focused outlook?

Chapter 12

Searching for
MEANING

Chapter Highlights

1. Existential psychology (Yalom, 1980) offers a unique insight into the loneliness and isolation that often are experienced by those who contemplate violence. These individuals become isolated from society, fearful of their own death, and overwhelmed with the freedom of choice, and they are unable to find any greater purpose or meaning in life.

2. Caleb (lone wolf) is introduced as a case study to help illustrate the treatment concepts provided by existentialism. Caleb is isolated and alone, suffers from depression, and harbors thoughts of violence to others. He is in a sadomasochist relationship and has recently been studying school shootings.

3. Yalom's (1980) work in existential psychotherapy is discussed in terms of helping the client feel empowered and addresses the themes of freedom, death, isolation, and meaninglessness.

4. May (1983) encouraged clients to take responsibility for their life choices. He warned of the danger when therapists focus too much on symptom relief and not enough on the true underpinnings or the purpose behind the symptoms.

5. Perls (1947, 1951, 1969) offered insight through his work in gestalt therapy. The goal of gestalt therapy is awareness, to assist clients in gaining moment-to-moment awareness and greater choice. Core concepts such as the *empty chair, internal dialogue, exaggeration*, and *staying with the feeling* are given as practical treatment examples.

> "Nihilists! Fuck me! I mean, say what you want about the tenets of
> National Socialism, Dude, at least it's an ethos."
> —Walter Sobchak, *The Big Lebowski*

Cinema and literature provide myriad examples of characters who experience existential nothingness: Examples include the nihilists chasing the Dude around with a pair of scissors in *The Big Lebowski* (Coen & Coen, 1998) or Meursault killing the Arab on the beach for no reason in *The Stranger* (Camus, 1989). In these examples, existential nothingness comes with the allure of committing violence given the absurdity of life.

We all struggle to find a purpose in life, a meaning in the suffering of existence. Life is duality, pregnant with its own death. There is an absurdity in living that requires some form of resolution in regards to the anxiety that comes with fear of death, the challenges and paradoxes of freedom, wrestling with our own ultimate isolation, and uncovering the meaning in our existence.

Some clients become trapped and isolated from others. In this disconnection, they find some cold comfort in the fantasy rehearsal of planning violence against others. This happens as they lose touch with the hope for a better future. They become lost in their pain and fail to find any meaning in the suffering they endure in the forms of isolation, bullying, or teasing. Some may feel that they are not being cared about or understood; an example is provided by Ally Sheedy's character in *The Breakfast Club* (Hughes, 1985), who asks, "What do they do to you? They ignore me." Whatever the reason, these people remain lost and looking for purpose.

Existentialism offers insight into how some clients struggle with their lives. They become isolated from society, fearful of their own death, overwhelmed with the freedom of choice, and unable to find any greater purpose or meaning in their lives. Although these conditions can provide potential motivations and destabilizing contributing factors for future violence, there is also an opportunity to address and explore these problems through the existential approach to psychotherapy.

In a rare overlap between literature, philosophy, and psychology, Irvin Yalom's (1980) *Existential Psychotherapy* brings together great thinkers and writers like Rollo May, Jean-Paul Sartre, Viktor Frankl, Friedrich Nietzsche, and Franz Kafka to explore and challenge clients to come through their despair and find a greater sense of purpose beyond the siren song that rampage violence offers. The existential therapist stresses individual responsibility, personal freedom in choices, and the importance of finding meaning in life.

In this chapter I describe Caleb, a client who struggles with finding a purpose and meaning in his life.

Case Study: Caleb, a Lone Wolf

Caleb slid into the chair across from the counselor and regarded him with inquisitive and intelligent eyes. He spoke quickly and shared that he had been treated for depression and loneliness for most of his life. He entered therapy now because he was "not happy with my current progress in my studies." His voice had a matter-of-fact quality that lacked an emotional layer. He told the counselor that he lived off campus at his father's house and did not get along very well with him. His father was an alcoholic and they had very little in common. Caleb's mother left the family when he was only 8 years old because of the father's drinking. Caleb described himself as "a ghost in the walls."

He told his counselor that he enjoyed speaking with someone who would "not freak out" about the kind of thoughts he had. He talked of his love of guns and firearms and referred to them as the "tools of the trade." His father owned several weapons that were kept unsecured in the home. Caleb talked about the weapons with a knowledge and understanding of how to use them.

Caleb talked about his emotions and said, "I often feel like Dexter in that HBO show. Are you familiar?" The counselor nodded. Caleb continued, "I see. Well, he doesn't feel things and that is the same way I am. I know I am supposed to feel things, I just don't."

Caleb explained that he was dating a girl named Sarah who lived on campus. They were both first-year students. As Caleb told more about himself and their relationship, he paused thoughtfully. He borrowed a pen and a piece of paper. He drew a symbol and asked, "Are you familiar?"

The counselor nodded: "It represents bondage, domination, sadism and masochism (BDSM), right?" Caleb smiled for the first time in the session and said, "Yes, that's what we like." He went on to explain that he often bit her and found the taste of blood "erotic." He became sexually aroused at the idea of hurting others and watching them in pain. He said they had sex frequently (several times a day) and shared that his girlfriend also has had depression.

His counselor talked to him about his sadistic thoughts of hurting others outside of his consensual BDSM relationship. Caleb replied, "If you ask me that now, I will tell you this isn't something I would ever do. There are times, however, I do have darker thoughts. That dark space comes and I have thoughts that I know are best kept to myself."

He continued, "Sometimes, I feel explosive. Like a shepherd in charge of a flock who realizes the entire flock relies on his will, his purpose, his desires. That shepherd can have a moment of clarity where he comes to the realization that they are his to control, to care for or to destroy. I have moments like this shepherd. I have moments of darkness."

The counselor talked more in depth about when these times occur (every few days), what he did when he felt that way (mostly wrote and kept to himself, or became more hurtful and aggressive in his sexual play with his partner), and what helped him get out of the mood (the feeling eventually faded with time).

They spent some time talking about more practical issues of his studies, his relationship with Sarah, and any changes that had occurred between him and his father. Caleb shared that he was doing slightly better with going to class and had been interested in World War II studies in his history class. He said that Sarah had been more distant and sad lately and he found himself frustrated that she was not giving him the attention he felt he deserved. Caleb said that his father showed very little interest in his life. He said, "To him, I am nothing. Not even a sheep to be watched over. I am a blank shadow; an obstacle to be passed when he walks to the fridge for another beer."

Caleb talked to his counselor about spending time on the Internet studying campus shootings like those perpetrated by Holmes, Loughner, Cho, and Kazmierczak. He admitted, "I admire their determination and willingness to take the ultimate stand for their beliefs. There is a purity in that, I think."

One of Caleb's professors is concerned about his writing for class. The professor said that they were discussing World War II and Nazi Germany and Caleb asked detailed questions about the torture and persecution of those in the concentration camps. Caleb wrote a paper that praised "seeking perfection and the power of superiority and control over others." The professor was concerned and subsequently shared this with the behavioral intervention team (BIT).

The chair of the BIT met with Caleb and required him to complete a threat assessment with an off-campus evaluator. The person conducting the threat assessment was concerned about Caleb and recommended ongoing treatment to address his thoughts of harming others and the sadistic aspects of his dating relationship. Caleb agreed and wished to continue with the counselor he had been seeing at the counseling center.

Wrestling With Freedom, Death, Isolation, and Meaninglessness

In his book *Existential Psychotherapy* (1980), Irvin Yalom maintained that all people confront four ultimate concerns in life: the vastness of the freedom of our choices, the anxiety that exists when contemplating death, what it means to be connected with others yet ultimately alone, and coming to terms with an ultimate meaning in our existence. Yalom acknowledged the overlap in these complex themes and separated them only to explore each in more depth.

Freedom

In the immortal words of Janis Joplin (1971), "Freedom's just another word for nothing left to lose." Yalom (1980) encouraged us to look at the other side of freedom: How do we all cope with the freedom we have? What do we see when we stare into the abyss? How does someone like Caleb look at his infinite options for life and choose a path that he can feel confident about? Yalom wrote: "'Freedom' in this sense, has a terrifying implication: it means that beneath us there is no ground—nothing, a void, an abyss. The key conflict is how a patient struggles between groundlessness and our wish for ground and structure" (p. 9).

In other words, one of Caleb's struggles may not just be what to do with his life. Instead, so overwhelmed with the vast majority of choices, he becomes invested in a sort of anarchistic philosophy railing against structure, order, and, in the end, life itself. In my practice, as I attend to this potential underlying sickness in the client, I address the mindset as casual to the fantasy of violence rather than simply addressing the shallow, verbal layer. Successful treatment for a student like Caleb is found not in reducing the number of times he talks about violence with others in a classroom setting, but instead making active choices about what path to go down in life. Like Sylvia Plath's (1971/2005) protagonist Esther in *The Bell Jar*, Caleb risks becoming so overwhelmed with the choices in front of him that he chooses nothing rather than wrestle with the loss inherent in making one choice at the expense of others. Caleb's suicidal thoughts are certainly prominent in any treatment strategy.

Death

We exist now, but one day we will cease to exist. Death will come for all of us and there is no escape from it. The famous Dutch philosopher Benedict de Spinoza (1901/2010) wrote: "Everything endeavors to persist in its own being" (p. 136). With this idea in mind, it becomes important for the therapist to help the client resolve "the awareness of the inevitability of death and the wish to continue to be" (Yalom, 1980, p. 8). For Caleb, the awareness of his own death and potential nonexistence may be a motivating factor driving his sadistic and ultimately nihilist thoughts and potential actions. In other words, to avoid thinking deeply about his own death, he may explore death through the fantasy of killing or harming others; the fantasy becomes a pleasurable, masturbatory distraction from the true fear inherent in facing his personal mortality.

Yalom (1980) described this phenomenon as it occurs with patients facing terminal disease and coping with a "myth of specialness" (e.g., feeling as if medications won't work on you because you are unique or that death comes for everyone except for you). Whereas it is common for some clients to increase their sexual activity or promiscuity when faced with death, a client like Caleb may embrace the fantasies of violence against others in an attempt to dominate death itself.

With a client like Caleb, finding a place of equanimity in his thoughts may first require that he face some difficult and challenging conversations about his own mortality. The stoic philosopher Lucretius offers a calming statement: "Where I am, death is not; where death is, I am not. Therefore death is nothing to me" (Yalom, 1980, p. 45). Yalom (1980) offered something of a therapeutic approach to address these challenging conversations; I refer to these moments as an *existential exercise*.

The existential exercise is one suggested by Yalom (1980) in *Existential Psychotherapy*. The core idea is for clients to wrestle with how they define themselves. They make a list of five key roles or traits they possess on five index cards. Over time, they are encouraged to imagine themselves without these roles or traits and search for the deeper meaning and finding a place in the world. An example script I have used with clients is included in Appendix F. Clinicians will find it helpful to review Yalom's full text and consult with a clinical supervisor before using the script as part of their clinical practice.

Isolation

No matter how close each of us becomes to another, there always remains this final, unbridgeable gap. We are individuals in a collective community. How do we cope with the idea that each of us enters existence alone and must depart from it in the same manner? We struggle to exist, caught between our awareness of our absolute isolation and our desire for contact, our need for protection and wish to be part of a larger whole, the knowledge that we are alone and ultimately can depend only on ourselves.

Yalom (1980) made a powerful observation in his discussions of existential isolation. He wrote:

> I believe that if we are able to acknowledge our isolated situations in existence and to confront them with resoluteness, we will be able to turn lovingly to others. If, on the other hand, we are overcome with dread before the abyss of loneliness, we will not reach toward others but instead will flail at them in order not to drown in the sea of existence. (p. 363)

As a teenager, I taught swimming classes. Children who could put the fear of the water behind them, who held their breath and went under, confident that they would not drown, were the ones who then mastered the water and were able to move on and experience the many joys of swimming, diving, Marco Polo, and the like. No child can learn to swim without first overcoming the fear of the water. When children let this go, they glide through the water and play in it. The water loses its ability to evoke fear. Only by letting go of our fears can we truly enjoy our life. Yalom (1980) quoted Tolstoy early in the book saying, "He is dying badly because he has lived badly" (p. 33).

Regarding Caleb, it may be that his desire to harm others, through either his sadistic thoughts or BDSM relationship, may come from his feelings of disconnection and isolation from the rest of humanity. The therapist here may encourage a connection back with the larger college community. In fact, the relationship between Caleb and the therapist itself addresses Caleb's feelings of isolation and helps connect him to the larger whole.

Meaninglessness

If we must die, if we constitute our own world, if each is ultimately alone in an indifferent universe, then what meaning does life have? The dilemma for most is the conflict faced by a meaning-seeking creature who is thrown into a universe that has no meaning. This may be the most likely contributing motivator for Caleb's thoughts and fantasy of harming others. What do his actions matter if nothing matters? If we all must die, then why should we restrain our darker thoughts?

Many of us have pushed off this conflict by finding religion, a hope that an afterlife exists that will create meaning for our earthly experiences. Others choose to pursue a career or create great art or literature to define their lives. Some lose themselves in the loving of another—a wife, husband, partner, child, or friend. This love then becomes defining for them and staves off feelings and thoughts of meaninglessness. Yalom (1980) suggested we create ways of protecting ourselves from the inevitability of death by looking at our specialness, altruism, and compulsive behaviors and by finding an ultimate rescuer.

Caleb's search for meaning in his life becomes a way to address the symptoms of sadism and thoughts of harming others. A therapist could challenge Caleb to wrestle more directly with finding a purpose in his life. Viktor Frankl, founder of logotherapy, talks about the importance of finding meaning even in the suffering. *Logotherapy* is derived from Greek word *logos* or "meaning." Frankl's own work was strongly influenced by the time he spent in the concentration camps of World War II Germany. Frankl (1965) wrote, "Clients must find a purpose to their existence and pursue it. The therapist must help them achieve the highest possible activation" (p. 54).

Empowering the Client

With a client like Caleb, it is important that he take responsibility for his life and his choices. The idea that Caleb has no other choice but to immerse himself in fantasy about death because he doesn't have a career path must be rejected. Things don't just happen to Caleb; Caleb makes things happen for himself. The therapist serves as an agent of change for this metamorphosis of personal accountability.

A central theme in Rollo May's (1983) book *The Discovery of Being* is the focus on the immediacy of the moment, the inherent power in the individual's choice, and freedom from the deterministic view of past experience and the specter of the unconscious influencing the present. To this end, Caleb is encouraged to take responsibility for his thoughts and actions. He begins the work of finding his meaning and place in the world rather than feeding his obsession with violence and dominance. Resistance to these changes could be addressed with techniques found in Chapter 11.

May emphasized the concept of *Dasein*, a German word meaning "being there," and the importance of the real encounter between client and therapist. This echoes Rogers's focus on genuineness and congruence in the therapeutic contact. May (1983) explained the client in terms of *potenia*, or "being" as a source of potentiality. He wrote: "'Being' is the potentiality by which the acorn becomes the oak or each of us becomes what he truly is" (p. 97). He preferred to ask "Where are you?" as opposed to "How are you?" May urged therapists to be concerned with the patient's direction and potential as opposed to being distracted by the chief complaint or mere symptoms. The therapist should see what Caleb can become, not just his current state.

In practical application, May encouraged us to focus on the direction, or "becoming," of the client rather than on the specifics of what the client presents.

May's strength lies in presenting a theory that goes beyond the simple techniques of practice; it looks instead to the direction or movement of the client–therapist interaction. How do each of us exist as true entities, true *Dasein*, willing to connect and experience each other's humanness first, before any technical skills are introduced?

Caleb is challenged for his beliefs and asked what he wants to become. He is encouraged to think about his fantasies and how they feed the likelihood of what he might become in the future. He is held accountable and responsible for his study of violence and comments about Nazi atrocities not because they are morally right or wrong or against some kind of decency or student conduct code, but instead because his current actions shape the kind of man he will become. The therapist holds hope for Caleb and his future, encourages connection with humanity, and aids him in his struggle to find meaning in his life.

According to May (1983),

> Knowing another human being, like loving him, involves a kind of union, a dialectical participation with the other. This Binswanger calls the "dual mode." One must have at least a readiness to love the other person, broadly speaking, if one is to be able to understand him. (p. 93)

Thus the relationship, much like Rogers (1961, 1980) suggested, is more important than advice, information, or solutions. May (1983) quoted the noted German psychiatrist and contemporary of Sigmund Freud Frieda Fromm-Reichmann: "The patient needs an experience, not an explanation" (p. 158).

In May's (1983) view, anxiety is "the loss in the range of possibility" (p. 45) and the battle is half won when "the patient [can] focus on some point in the future when he will be outside his anxiety or depression" (p. 135). The client's anxiety can be seen as an ontological focus on the fear of nonbeing and hypersensitivity to the here-and-now functions of the anxiety. Treatment focus moves away from mere symptom relief to helping the patient face her fear and place it in the appropriate context. Pathological anxiety can never be explained away. Time and time again, I nod across from an anxious client and say, "You are right. Death is terrifying. There are too many choices. We are out of control." The healing comes from gaining power and comfort over life choices and finding solace in the revelation that we are all in this together.

May also wrote about the danger of therapists focusing too much on symptom relief and not enough on the true underpinnings or the purpose behind the symptoms. May (1983) used a metaphor to explain the dangers of attending too much to the presenting mechanisms rather than the client's *potenia*: You are "teaching a farmer irrigation while damming up his streams of water" (p. 164). This temptation is often encouraged by well-meaning administrators and school officials looking to quantify and demonstrate a reduction in at-risk behavior or speech. In Caleb's case, a therapist might erroneously assume that a reduction of sharing concerning ideas in class correlates to a reduction in the overall risk. This kind of direct connection is overly simplistic. It could be that Caleb has simply learned to keep his enthusiasm about violence to himself if he wishes to stay enrolled. The underlying fascination with the morbid and macabre remains.

Stringer (1999) offered a brief story that further elucidates this phenomenon:

> The story goes that a man rescued a number of people from drowning in a river. Eventually, he tired of dragging one after the other from the river and walked upstream, where he observed a bully pushing people into the water. He struggled with the bully, who was eventually arrested and taken away. The problem of the drowning people was solved by his "upstream" work. (p. 140)

This, to me, is the heart of existential psychotherapy—attending to the true problem, not simply squelching the symptoms.

We need the law, police, and school communities to pay attention to the victims of the bully, just as we need to attend to Caleb's potential leakage in the classroom around his fascination with Nazi war atrocities. We must be cautious, however, to not confuse addressing the symptoms with curing the disease. As Polish American philosopher Alfred Korzybski wrote, "The map is not the territory" (Kendig, 1990, p. 299).

Practical Application

So far in this chapter, I have explored the rather challenging subjects of the primary existential dilemmas as well as some ideas about engaging clients at these core points to address the underlying difficulties, frustrations, and anger they may be experiencing. In this section, I discuss gestalt therapy and some common treatment exercises used in the practice to address existential issues in clients such as Caleb.

Fritz Perls (1947, 1951, 1969), the German-born psychiatrist and psychotherapist, founded a system of treatment called gestalt therapy. The word *gestalt* comes from the German word *gestalten* (which means "form," "to make a form," and "a comprehensive one"). Perls argued that a person is capable of, and has a desire for, movement toward homeostasis, an internal balance of the physical and the mental organism. Clients are encouraged to experiment with new behavior, seen as striving toward wholeness, the full gestalt.

The goal of gestalt therapy is to assist clients in gaining moment-to-moment awareness and greater choice. The therapist helps the client become aware of his or her own awareness processes so that he or she can be more responsible and can make better choices. The therapist seeks to challenge the client to accept responsibility for internal support and not external support. The therapist hopes to see the client gain the ability to seek help from others and offer help to them, as well as acquire skills to be able to satisfy needs without violating the rights of others.

A summary of gestalt therapy's figure/ground dynamic, the polarities, body movement and congruity, and the more detailed philosophy of human nature is beyond the scope of this work. However, gestalt therapy does offer a series of interesting techniques that are used to challenge and help the client explore the existential issues raised throughout this chapter; a few of these techniques are described here. As with any therapeutic techniques, they should be practiced after a review of the theorist's writings, under clinical supervision and within the limits of state licensure requirements.

The Empty Chair

The therapist asks the client to address the chair as if the person he or she is discussing or even an object is sitting in it. This could be used with Caleb to help him explore his dominant attitude toward sexual partners or his feelings toward his father, mother, mass killers such as Eric Harris or Dylan Klebold, or some of the victims of such attacks. One of the desired outcomes for Caleb would be a focus on the here and now of the emotional experience and a movement away from the fantasy activities he currently engages in.

Internal Dialogue

This promotes a higher level of integration between the polarities and the conflicts that everyone experiences. Perls suggested that each aspect of behavior moves between two opposite polarities (Perls, 1951, 1969). For example, although a person may crave the intimacy and closeness of human contact, he or she also may cherish the separation and quiet of existing in solitude. A client like Caleb may be experiencing others as distant and unfeeling inferiors who are not worthy of his consideration yet might also desire closeness and interconnection with others. While he may voice one view very clearly, the other (polar opposite) view remains silent and out of balance. Internal dialogue exercises would offer Caleb the opportunity to give voice to the desire in himself for personal connection and memories of feeling close to others in a nondominating, caring manner.

Exaggeration

Used as a technique, exaggeration involves overtly increasing one's physical reactions to an idea, sometimes in conflict (e.g., clenching the fist while saying "I'm calm"). Caleb would be encouraged to become aware of how his body experiences the emotions he channels during session. The therapist would challenge and point out the disconnection between Caleb's fantasy speech about killing or hurting others and his overly calm and in-control demeanor. Caleb could be encouraged to stand and shout and yell as he experiences the desire to hurt others, bringing the emotions and actions into a more direct equilibrium. As mentioned earlier, some concepts from gestalt therapy can be controversial and should only be used with supervision and a fuller understanding of the goals of the exercise.

Staying With the Feeling

This is an invitation to have the client go further and explore his feelings and emotions. Caleb may find himself tentative about expressing an emotion and may move away from it quickly in session. The therapist encourages the client to stay with the feeling despite the uncomfortable nature of the emotion he or she is experiencing.

Summary

In this chapter, I reviewed the existential dilemmas that underlie some of the frustration, anxiety, and anger present in those who contemplate violence. I reviewed how to apply these treatment concepts through the case of Caleb and offered some examples of how to address not only the outward symptoms of violence but the underlying contributing thoughts.

The final chapter expands on some treatment recommendations I would have if I continued to work with Stacie and Dustin, the assessment case studies described in Chapter 3.

Questions for Further Discussion

1. What concerns do you have when working with a client like Caleb? How do you handle the disturbing content of his therapy session regarding his thoughts on hurting others, weapons access, and school shootings?
2. In considering Yalom's four main themes (freedom, death, isolation, and meaninglessness), which stands out as most important when working with Caleb? How would you address each of these areas with him in treatment?
3. What are your thoughts on personal responsibility for an individual's choices as they relate to rampage violence? How does society have an impact on these decisions?
4. Discuss some ways you might apply Perls's techniques outlined in the chapter in working with an individual like Caleb.

Chapter 13

Case Studies
Treatment
SUMMARY

Chapter Highlights

1. This chapter outlines some specific treatment guidance related to the two case studies (Stacie and Dustin) described in Chapter 3. Issues of diversity and legal risk are also discussed.

2. Stacie is cooperative, has less lethality attached to her threatening statements, has access to supports, and displays a willingness to work with the process. Her treatment goals include addressing her impulsivity, strengthening her confidence in her choice of career, and ongoing monitoring of her previous suicidal thoughts.

3. Dustin's treatment will involve addressing his defensiveness and seeming inability to form trust. Building rapport and a treatment alliance will be a difficult task given his weapon access, substance abuse, objectified and misogynistic language, impulsivity, anger, and incongruence of his hostility toward others. The exploration of the professor as a secondary target is also a central concern.

4. In terms of assessment, liability is mitigated when the clinician builds his or her clinical judgment on the firm foundation of existing research and evidence. Other ways to reduce liability include not overpromising or overselling your ability as a clinician to predict the future outcome of unpredictable action and basing assessment and treatment decisions on accepted practice and research.

5. The clinician performing the assessment and therapist offering the treatment must take into account the unique perspective and experiences of the client. The clinician must acknowledge that he or she will be subjected to occasional *microaggressions*, those unintentional slights that are triggered by group membership.

In Chapter 3, I introduced the cases of Stacie and Dustin to primarily provide examples useful for clinicians conducting threat assessments. As I came to the close of the book, I realized that most readers would be left with some unanswered questions about what exactly should be done with Stacie and Dustin in treatment after the assessment has been completed. A traditional treatment plan might be very appropriate for Stacie, but Dustin certainly raises concerns (e.g., "How does a therapist avoid getting stabbed at the end of each session?") that always arise when working with a client with so much anger, animosity, and resistance toward self-reflection and change.

In this final chapter, I walk you through some of my thoughts about treating Stacie and Dustin if they were to engage in treatment following the threat assessment included in Chapter 3.

Stacie's Treatment

Stacie's case was certainly more straightforward than Dustin's. She was cooperative, had little if any lethality attached to her threatening statements, had access to supports, and was willing to work with the process. Some kind of arrangement could be worked out by the college to allow her to complete the class; Stacie's willingness to engage in therapy would likely help the process to happen smoothly.

The main goals for treatment with Stacie would involve addressing her potential for impulsive behavior when feeling embarrassed or threatened by others. I would likely focus on some cognitive therapy techniques outlined in Chapter 10. This would center on helping Stacie identify triggering events and find alternative behaviors when frustrated, such as reporting a professor's behavior to the department head, journaling about the frustration in the moment, and using self-calming exercises such as cycle breathing and guided imagery.

An additional goal of therapy would be to help Stacie as she works on her transition from being a student to a professional in the field. One approach is to help her develop a thicker skin around potential criticism of her work, but it may be even more helpful for Stacie to examine her choices when it comes to selecting those she looks up to in the field. It is very reasonable to want a successful mentor who is talented as well as kind and encouraging toward students and those in training. Professor Galloway's comments may or may not be justified, but his hostile and embarrassing delivery was a contributing factor to Stacie's outburst. In the assessment, she admitted, "He's a horrible person, but he's amazing." It is important for Stacie to realize that someone can be very good at what he does and not be a very good teacher.

Stacie mentions that her family is not overly supportive of her choice to become a photojournalist. Exploration of this area might involve using some of the techniques mentioned in Chapter 12 centering on Stacie's sense of meaning in life and how she is making the transition from daughter to an independent woman making her own decisions. Her ability to engage in dating relationships and live in an apartment with other students indicates that she is well on her way to establishing herself apart from her family of origin.

Stacie's therapist would do well to attend to her desire to communicate her feelings through writing in her online journal. This provides useful insight into her thinking and an opportunity to further explore thoughts, ideations, emotions, and concerns that may not naturally come up during the course of treatment.

Finally, I would make sure to continue to monitor and address Stacie's potential for suicide and depression. She has not had a positive experience with medications in the past and admits to entertaining ideas of self-harm. During crisis events like these, there is an opportunity to review past traumas and crisis events to ensure that Stacie has some perspective on what happened and how she can prevent similar emotions from overwhelming her in the future. This awareness of her story and choices may be successfully encouraged by the narrative therapy approach discussed in Chapter 9.

Dustin's Treatment

Dustin presents more of a challenge to engage. Dustin will not willingly get into treatment. He is defensive, suspicious, and has many strongly held thoughts and feelings about what he is entitled to and how he should treat women that will make treatment tenuous, if not impossible at times. With a student like Dustin, I am reminded of the old Hemingway quote from "The Gambler, The Nun, and The Radio" (1987): "Continue, slowly, and wait for luck to change" (p. 51). Dustin is a case study in harm reduction.

In Dustin's case, the key feature to address in treatment is his defensiveness and seeming inability to form trust. It may be that this is an artifact of the assessment process alone, but more likely this is a difficulty Dustin experiences in most of his relationships and daily activities. Based on the assessment transcripts, it would be reasonable to conclude that Dustin has trouble feeling vulnerable or expressing emotions or thoughts that put him in an exposed setting. On several occasions, Dustin reacts to moments where he is caught allowing minimal trust with a quick 180-degree turn. He believes the evaluator is "buttering him up" or trying to get him to share information he does not want to share.

The challenge for most therapists with a client like Dustin will be slowly developing a sense of trust. The creation of this rapport and relationship will likely be rocky and tumultuous given Dustin's defensive thoughts and his belief that he is correct in his behavior despite the clear antisocial elements. In fact, one of my major challenges as a therapist with a client like Dustin would be in maintaining a sense of equanimity in his offensive, inflexible, and frequent expressions of contempt and anger toward others.

This incongruence of his feelings toward others juxtaposed against his commitment to work in helping professions such as being an emergency medical technician (EMT) and nurse is an area in need of further exploration. The existence of these two varying poles of extremes might lend themselves well to Perls's (1951) gestalt therapy. Caution and slow discussion of these ideas will always be required given his general lack of insight and defensiveness.

This leads to the central treatment concept of addressing his objectified and dehumanizing language reflecting his separation from those around them. He frequently uses misogynistic language to describe the females around him (*whore, cunt, bitch*) along with some concerning entitlements such as, "I've seen her naked, okay? I fucked her. I know what it's like. I can call her what I want." In his meeting, Dustin also insults and objectifies the obese, bureaucrats, professors, and the staff at the Veterans Administration. Given his guarded nature and contrary arguments on other topics, it will take time to address why he sees other people this way and how he might be able to learn to empathize and see himself more in others.

Dustin's original veiled, conditional threat was made to a woman he had slept with who was sitting behind him in class, but a secondary potential target to be considered would be the professor who set the limit with him and involved law enforcement. While no direct threat is present, this should be an area of exploration in future treatment and monitoring. It would be helpful, additionally, to reach out to the professor and further explore her concerns and seek information about potential contact and leakage indicating a more direct potential threat. O'Toole and Smith (2014) described the importance of monitoring such behavior:

> A priority for threat assessment teams must include outreach plans to monitor individuals once they have left, voluntarily or involuntarily, the workplace or educational institution. These activities help to determine if there is a deterioration in their thinking and behavior and whether the likelihood of their acting out has increased. (p. 275)

It is unlikely that Dustin will initially be comfortable with the ideas focused on cognitive behavior therapy in Chapter 10. The therapist will probably draw heavily on the motivational interviewing techniques discussed in Chapter 11 in order to avoid argumentation, express empathy, and develop discrepancy. It is important that the therapist understand that Dustin is firmly in the precontemplative state of change (see Chapter 11); in other words, he is not committed to therapy.

Dustin's impulsivity, anger, and substance abuse are also areas of concern for the therapist to address. All of these will likely be uphill battles and will only be effectively addressed after the therapeutic alliance, rapport, and trust is established. With a client like Dustin, I would find myself drawing frequently on the narrative therapy approach outlined in Chapter 9 in order to better understand his story and why he has come to think about the world in the way he does. Several theories may include mistreatment at the hands of an authoritative female figure, his military and EMT experience and/or trauma, or a deep mistrust of others' motives. Each theory should be explored tentatively and carefully to avoid Dustin feeling as if the therapist is trying to "get something by him."

On a hopeful note, for all of Dustin's bravado during the course of the assessment, he does show moments of desire to stay connected to the clinician for future sessions. The "stick" of being separated from the college and his dreams may be enough to keep him connected to a therapist long enough to bring about some lasting change. In addition, this mandated treatment provides some connection and potential experience in improving his communications with others, perhaps even to begin to empathize with a perspective other than his own.

Thoughts on Liability for Assessment and Treatment of Violence

The question of legal liability for the clinician assessing and treating clients such as Stacie and Dustin is often at the forefront for clinical supervisors, program administrators, counseling directors, and the clinicians themselves. In our society, an individual may be sued for just about anything. In terms of assessment, the liability is mitigated when the clinician builds his or her clinical judgment on the firm foundation of existing research and evidence. In the area of threat and violence risk assessment, this research is often drawn from the fields of law enforcement, psychology, and workplace violence.

During a recent staff meeting, one of the partners in our law firm introduced me to the concept of "belt and suspenders." This common legal saying implies that while a belt may be sufficient to hold your pants up, you are in a better place if you use both a belt and suspenders to be extra sure your pants stay up. In the world of violence threat assessment and treatment, the belt and suspenders are (a) not overpromising or overselling your ability as a clinician to predict the future outcome of unpredictable action and (b) basing assessment and treatment decisions on accepted practice and research. A clinician should be cautious to not oversell his or her ability to predict future violence and should base any conclusions on the research available in the fields of psychology, law enforcement, and workplace violence.

Predicting violence is an exceedingly difficult if not impossible task. The structured professional judgment approach reviewed in Chapter 7 helps address this issue through the use of a structured judgment model to identify risk factors, develop potential scenarios for violence, and enact case management and treatment strategies to reduce the risk of potential violence and increase the positive social and therapeutic factors to help the individual move away from his or her pathway of violence.

The difficulty of this task, however, should not preclude clinicians from attempting to understand the motivations and risk factors of those who are referred for assessment. Consider the following analogy: There is a general understanding that factors such as lack of exercise, poor diet, smoking, and having a high body mass index increase the risk of a cardiovascular event. The ability to identify and address the risk factors provides an opportunity to mitigate the risk of the event. To be sure, this approach does not always work, but it is the best one can do to reduce the risk.

Similarly, in the world of threat and violence risk assessments, the identification of well-understood and accepted risk factors such as focus and fixation on a target, action and time imperative, organized rather than disorganized threat, social isolation, weapon access, and fantasizing and planning for an attack all provide us with an elevated risk profile for the individual being assessed and subsequently seeking treatment.

Another issue critical to threat and violence risk assessment is gathering information from supplementary referral sources to confirm or refute possible motives and potential for violence. An assessment is only as good as the quality and depth of information that goes into it; a thorough assessment (which requires accurate, thorough, and well-organized documentation and supplemental information from third parties) will give interested parties a good understanding of the full context of the threat, behavior, and motivations of the individual being assessed. Clinical documentation should avoid subjective comments or speculation. It should be supported by the literature and research (if not directly through citation in the writing then implicitly through the assessment and narrative).

Clinicians should also be familiar with the specific rules regarding duty to warn others in the event of immediate risk that apply in the state. Each state has a slightly varied definition, and requirements direct when a clinician should, ought, and must notify authorities quickly if there is an acute risk for violence by a client in assessment or treatment. Similarly, clinicians should be aware of state commitment laws and procedures that are applicable to clients who pose a potential harm to themselves or others.

When addressing the issue of treatment for those with numerous violence risk factors, one cannot sufficiently stress the benefits of connection, empathetic listening, developing alternative ways to find meaning in suffering, and engaging the individual around his or her irrational thoughts. While empirically validated treatment is essential to efficacious and efficient care, clinicians cannot walk away from high-risk clients simply because there are no guarantees the treatment will reduce the risk of violence.

I am reminded of this when I review Eric Harris's writing describing the anger management counseling he received after he and Dylan Klebold broke into a van to steal electronics equipment on January 30, 1998. Harris wrote exactly the kind of insightful and reflective summary of his experiences that any clinician would like to see from someone completing mandated treatment:

> I believe the most valuable part of this class was thinking of ideas for ways to control anger and for ways to release anger in a non-violent manner. Things such as writing, taking a walk, talking, lifting weights, listening to different music, and exercising are all good ways to vent anger. (Langman, 2008, p. 65)

Harris completed the diversion program in early February 1999. The diversion officer described him this way: "Good prognosis. Eric is a very bright young man who is likely to succeed in life. He is intelligent enough to achieve lofty goals as long as he stays on task and remains motivated" (Langman, 2008, p. 65). Less than 3 months later, his high school was the scene of a mass shooting.

Harris's glowing assessment by a mental health officer provides a terrible reminder of the nightmarish complexity of treating those referred for violent acts and the impossibility of predicting their behavior. Yet clinicians who work with them must remain committed to maintaining an ongoing connection with these individuals, monitoring their progress and steering them from violent paths.

As with assessment, it is essential that documentation of treatment be thorough and accurate. Treatment notes should be consistent and include, at minimum, three components: (a) the presenting issue(s) being addressed in the current session, (b) the interventions applied by the clinician to address said treatment issues, and (c) a clear action plan for the future. As a director of counseling at two university counseling centers, I often encouraged new clinicians and psychologists to attend to the concept of ensuring that any door they opened in a treatment note was closed by the end of the note. For example, if the clinician noted the patient was suicidal, this always required a corresponding action plan to address the suicidality in the same treatment note. If a patient mentioned weapons access, a plan to harm another, or excessive substance use, the clinician had to ensure the treatment note included a recommendation to address these risks. If a door is opened in a treatment note, address it before ending the note.

So how does one accomplish these goals without getting sued when things go awry? As many of my lawyer colleagues and friends tell me, there is nothing to prevent one person from suing another. This is just the nature of the society we live in. To that end, the best defense is ensuring that treatment is focused on reducing the violence risk factors as well as avoiding predicting a positive outcome once treatment is completed. Clinicians should consult with others, work within the scope of his or her practice and training, and ensure proper connection and follow-up care once the initial treatment is complete. In addition, clinicians doing this kind of work need to familiarize themselves with the research in the field through ongoing reading of journal articles and books and seeking additional training. (See Appendix C.) This not only serves to keep clinical treatment fresh and applicable, but it also demonstrates a commitment to improving clinical skills and collaborating with leaders in the field. This is a key part of practicing defensively.

Additionally, clinicians should follow their ethics codes in regards to treatment and assessment, attending specifically to cautions regarding dual relationships (such as assessing or treating colleagues, friends, or relatives), declining the assessment of someone who is already in treatment with them because of the potential for bias in the assessment, using psychological tests and measures that are supported by literature and designed to assess the individual in question, and basing assessments on a detailed and concise review and validation of facts gathered from multiple sources (such as law enforcement, school officials, employment history, family, and peers).

And while it should go without saying, simply reading this book is not sufficient training in order to do clinical threat assessment or treat those who are referred for mandated treatment. Instead, this book serves as one of many designed to help augment a clinician's skill set to cultivate a better understanding of risk factors, assessment techniques, and treatment approaches that have served this author well in his clinical work over the past two decades.

Returning to Issues of Diversity and Rapport

An essential theme mentioned early in the book (Chapter 2) is the importance of assessing the individual with an understanding of the factors that contributed to his or her worldview and past experience. This includes growing up around limited access to health care or education, learning to cope with a physical or mental disability, discussing sexual identity in a community where tolerance and acceptance are lacking, or coming from a culture or ethnicity that has historically been discriminated against or the victim of hate crimes. The clinician performing the assessment and therapist offering the treatment must take into account the unique perspective and experiences of the client.

To be successful at this task, clinicians must first acknowledge that they are subject to committing occasional *microaggressions*, those unintentional slights that send denigrating messages to others because of their group membership. Adopting humility and a willingness to explore the potential for unintended offense to the client helps the clinician model a desire to avoid offense and quickly and effectively resolve a barrier to rapport. While simply being aware is not sufficient to address the potential for microaggressions, awareness is a necessary starting place.

Summary

When reviewing the differences between the two central case studies of Dustin and Stacie offered in Chapter 3, it should be obvious that Stacie presents a lower risk of violence and a higher likelihood of engaging in treatment that will further reduce the risk of violence. She shows remorse and a willingness to find a collaborative solution to her problem with her professor. She exudes reasonableness and would likely be an easy client to build a working therapeutic alliance with in treatment; even if she refuses treatment, the likelihood that she would commit violence is minimal.

Dustin, on the other hand, presents a much higher risk of potential violence and a much lower probability of engaging consistently in treatment. He has numerous risk factors that raise his potential impulsiveness and lethality upon action. He is defensive, rude, arrogant, and difficult to connect with during the assessment. It is often the most difficult individuals, slow to share information, that pose the highest risk. Dustin is difficult to engage with, and it can be assumed from his assessment that even if he connected with a therapist in treatment, the risk of violence would still be elevated. Additionally, the treatment alliance would likely experience turbulence over the course of time and stretch the abilities of the clinician to remain connected and offer assistance.

Those most in need of accurate assessment and productive and effective treatment are the hardest to connect to these services. It requires not only a clinician willing to build a connection with a difficult client but a therapist willing to sustain a rocky, tumultuous relationship in order to bring about any small modicum of risk mitigation. The task remains an arduous, but vital, journey.

Questions for Further Discussion

1. What approach to treatment would you find most efficacious with a client such as Stacie? Discuss the benefits and limitations to working with Stacie from a single framework as opposed to a model that blends various approaches mentioned in the second half of this book.

2. What are some techniques you would use to help lower Dustin's defensiveness in treatment? Discuss the balance between building a relationship versus the challenge of addressing pressing issues such as weapon access, threats, and substance abuse.
3. What are the greatest concerns you have related to liability when conducting a threat assessment or providing treatment to individuals such as Stacie and Dustin? Does the assessment or treatment create a larger risk in your mind?
4. Discuss some obstacles related to developing awareness of microaggressions during treatment. A common phrase used by Sue (2010) in his discussion of microaggression is the importance of making the invisible visible. What does he mean by this? How might you approach this prospect?

Appendix A

On-Campus Risk Assessment Informed Consent

The college works to assist students who have been considered potential risks to themselves or the community. Our department provides qualified, local, reasonably priced assessments, evaluations, and treatment. After the initial evaluation is completed, treatment plans can be developed to meet the individual's specific on- or off-campus needs (often determined in conjunction with campus student conduct or the Behavioral Intervention Team [BIT]). Our services are offered to students to make the process easier and less expensive than off-campus alternatives. In some cases, our department may need to refer an individual to an off-campus setting. This could happen if the situation is deemed beyond our scope of practice or our department is unable to devote resources away from its primary role of counseling, education, and wellness.

Eligibility

Risk assessments are available to students referred by the student conduct office or the campus BIT. There is no cost to students.

Initial Interview

All students are scheduled for an initial intake interview with an evaluator. The purpose of the initial interview is to gather information

Note. Reprinted from "Off-Campus Provider Questions" by B. Van Brunt, 2014. Copyright 2014 by The NCHERM Group. Reprinted with permission.

about the current incident, the student's concerns, background information, pressures that may impact current problems, and to explain the risk assessment process.

Meeting

The initial meeting may last from 30-90 minutes with a follow-up meeting scheduled as needed. Follow-up meetings are often scheduled to complete testing, gather more information, and clarify information given during the first interview

Confidentiality

The evaluator will release information from the meetings to outside parties only at the request of the client. Records are confidential and will not leave the department unless there is an emergency situation. We will not answer questions about any student from parents, family, friends, significant others, professors, employers, or anyone else outside of the office conducting the risk assessment without expressed permission of the student.

We are committed to providing the best possible risk assessment to our clients. The person conducting the risk assessment is bound by confidentiality, which means that what is said during the meetings remains confidential. There are a few exceptions to this rule:

1. Plans to harm self or specific others
2. Permission provided by the client
3. Abuse of a child, adult, or elderly person

You are encouraged to ask any questions about the informed consent or risk assessment process during the initial meeting and as you review this document.

The risk assessment process requires the student to allow the evaluator to share information with the referral source when the evaluation is complete. Information is first reviewed and shared with the student prior to the information being shared with the referral source (BIT, student conduct, police). *By signing this document, you give permission for this information to be shared with the office or person making the referral.*

Record Storage

Records and individual documents are maintained electronically. They are password protected and accessible by the person completing the risk assessment. Records will be kept for *at least* seven (7) years after the date of the last contact with our department.

Testing Data

Raw data, such as answer sheets and test booklets, are protected by copyright and may only be released to trained clinicians. Assessment and testing data are provided in summary form and explained during the follow-up session.

Email

Email communication with the person conducting the risk assessment should be used in scheduling appointments only. We recognize the importance of email, but, because it is not a secure medium of communication and our staff does not maintain 24-hour access to their email, it will not be used to discuss ongoing treatment issues.

Student Rights and Responsibilities

- ❏ I understand I have the right to review credentials of staff members, including but not limited to education, experience, and professional counseling certification and licensure(s).
- ❏ I understand I can terminate the relationship at any time (though this termination will be shared with the referral source).
- ❏ I will arrive on time for my meetings.
- ❏ If unable to keep an appointment, I will call the office to cancel at least 24 hours in advance.
- ❏ I will actively participate in the process by asking questions and staying involved.

I, _____, a student at the university, agree to make every effort to keep all of my scheduled appointments. If I have missed appointments, I am aware that limits may be imposed on services available and this will be shared with the referral source. I have read and understand the above information, and I have had the opportunity to ask questions about it.

_____   _____
Student Signature   Date

_____   _____
Witness Signature   Date

Appendix B

Off-Campus
Provider Questions

The following is a list of questions we would recommend asking to an off-campus professional in order to "get out ahead" of any problems as a college develops a relationship with an off-campus provider.

1. What kind of training do you have in the areas of threat assessment, workplace violence assessment, and psychological evaluation?
2. How much experience do you have conducting these types of assessments in your professional career?
3. Have you worked with college students before? What are some of the unique challenges and opportunities in working with this population?
4. What are some of the reasons an assessment would require additional time or cost?
5. What is the typical time it takes to conduct an assessment on a student?
6. How much will the assessment cost?
7. How quickly can the student be seen for an appointment (e.g., 24 hours, a few days, 1 week, several weeks out)?
8. How many times do you meet with the student?
9. Realizing context is important, what additional information or interviews would you conduct to ensure a full picture of the student's functioning?
10. Do you talk to parents?

Note. Reprinted from "Off-Campus Provider Questions" by B. Van Brunt, 2014. Copyright 2014 by The NCHERM Group. Reprinted with permission.

11. Do you review criminal background checks?
12. Do you look at work history or grade point average?
13. Do you discuss cases with prior therapists or review past in-patient hospitalizations records?
14. What kind of information do you share back with us as the referral source? Is this a phone call, letter, or assessment report?
15. How long after the assessment does it typically take to generate this report?
16. Does the student also receive the report or review the results with you?
17. Do you discuss cases with prior therapists or review past inpatient hospitalization records?
18. How do you handle sharing information with us as a referral source if the student no-shows an appointment?
19. What kind of paperwork do you require the student to fill out?
20. What kind of psychological tests or assessment measures do you typically use in these kinds of assessments? Are there additional costs for these tests or are they included in the original fee?

Appendix C

The Structured Interview for Violence Risk Assessment (SIVRA-35)

The SIVRA-35 is an informal, structured set of items useful for those staff and faculty who work in higher education to use with individuals who may pose a risk or threat to the community. The SIVRA-35 is not designed as a psychological test, and it is not designed to assess suicidal students. It is a guided structured interview useful for classifying risk into low, moderate, and high categories.

Risk and Threat Assessment

The ideal approach to violence risk assessment is found in utilizing an individual trained and experienced in violence risk assessment to interview the subject. The SIVRA-35 serves as a starting place for behavioral intervention team members to conduct a more standardized, research-based violence risk assessment with individuals determined to be at an increased risk.

While risk and threat assessment cannot be predictive, multiple agencies (Federal Bureau of Investigation, Secret Service, Department of Education, U.S. Post Office, ASIS International, the Society for Human Resource Management, and ASME-ITI) have suggested risk factors to attend to when determining the potential danger an individual may represent. Several prominent experts in campus violence and workplace threat assessment have also recommended key considerations salient when assessing risk and threat.

Note. From Brian Van Brunt (2012), "SIVRA 35," available at the National Behavioral Intervention Team Association website (www.nabita.org/resources/sivra-35/). Copyright 2012 by Brian Van Brunt.

Based on these risk factors, the SIVRA-35 places key research into the hands of those faculty and staff meeting as front-line decision makers to assign sanctions and treatment and make determinations about continued enrollment for the student who poses a risk.

SIVRA Administration

The utility of the SIVRA-35 depends first on the rapport developed between the assessor and the subject. The assessor should avoid rattling off SIVRA-35 questions in a formal and potentially off-putting manner. The best way to obtain accurate data is through a conversation with the individual based on mutual respect and a stated commitment to serving the best interest of the individual. This will decrease the individual's defensiveness (some degree of defensiveness is normal given the nature of the interview) and will lead to more genuine responses.

There is no set of risk factors or list of concerning behaviors that can predict a future violent event. The SIVRA-35 is a useful reference tool when conducting a structured interview during a violence risk assessment. Ideally, the assessment should take place after the assessor has reviewed incident reports, available documents related to conduct in the educational setting and in the immediate community, and any other information that has led to the initial concern. Any violence risk assessment involves static and dynamic risk factors, contextual and environmental elements, and mitigating factors. There is no current tool or computer model that can accurately predict future violent behavior, and no tool is ever a substitute for professional expertise. Therefore, the use of structured professional judgment in combination with documentation and consultation with trusted colleagues is the current best practice.

While the SIVRA-35 primarily assists those conducting violence risk assessments through narrative, structured questions, there is a quantitative, numeric scoring key to further assist staff in their decision making. A single administrator will either ask questions directly to the person being assessed or review relevant incident reports and other forms of data to determine a true or false answer for each item.

SIVRA-35 Items

1. There is a direct communicated threat to a person, place, or system.
2. The student has the plans, tools, weapons, schematics, and/or materials to carry out an attack on a potential target.
3. The student displays a preoccupation with the person or object he/she is targeting.
4. The student has an action plan and timeframe to complete an attack.
5. The student is fixated and focused on his target in his actions and threatening statements.

6. The student carries deep grudges and resentments. He can't seem to let things go and collects injustices based on perceptions of being hurt, frustrated with someone, or annoyed.
7. The target is described negatively in writing or artistic expression. There is a narrow focus on a particular person that has a level of preoccupation or fascination with the target. There is a pattern of this behavior, rather than a one-time act.
8. There has been leakage concerning a potential plan of attack.
9. The student has current suicidal thoughts, ideations, and/or a plan to die.
10. The student talks about being persecuted or being treated unjustly.
11. The student has engaged in "last acts" behaviors or discusses what he wants people to remember about his actions.
12. The student seems confused or has odd or troubling thoughts. The student may hear voices or see visions that command him/her to do things.
13. The student displays a hardened point of view or strident, argumentative opinion. This is beyond a person who is generally argumentative or negative.
14. The student has a lack of options and/or a sense of hopelessness and desperation.
15. The student is driven to a particular action to cause harm.
16. The student has had a recent breakup or failure of an intimate relationship. The student has become obsessed in stalking or fixated on another person romantically.
17. The student acts overly defensive, aggressive, or detached given the nature of this risk/threat assessment. Seeks to intimidate the assessor or displays an overly casual response given the seriousness of the interview.
18. The student displays little remorse for his actions, lacks understanding for the view for potential victims, and acts with a detachment or bravado during the interview.
19. The student has a weapon (or access to weapon), specialized training in weapon handling, interest in paramilitary organizations, or veteran status.
20. The student glorifies and revels in publicized violence such as school shootings, serial killers, or war or displays an unusual interest in sensational violence. The student uses weapons for emotional release and venerates destruction.
21. The student externalizes blame for personal behaviors and problems onto other people despite efforts to educate him/her about how others view these actions. The student takes immediate responsibility in a disingenuous manner.
22. The student intimidates or acts superior to others. The student displays intolerance to individual differences.

23. The student has a past history of excessively impulsive, erratic, or risk taking behavior.
24. The student has a past history of problems with authority. The student has a pattern of intense work conflicts with supervisors and other authorities (e.g., Resident Advisor, Conduct Officer, Professor or Dean).
25. The student handles frustration in an explosive manner or displays a low tolerance for becoming upset. This is beyond avoiding responsibility or calling mom/dad or a lawyer.
26. The student has difficulty connecting with other people. The student lacks the ability to form intimate relationships. The student lacks the ability to form trust.
27. The student has a history of drug or substance use that has been connected to inappropriate ideation or behavior. Substances of enhanced concern are methamphetamines or amphetamines, cocaine, or alcohol.
28. The student has mental health issues that require assessment and treatment.
29. The student has poor and/or limited access to mental health services and support.
30. Objectification of others (perhaps in social media or writings).
31. The student seems obsessed with another person, location, or behavior the individual has little control over.
32. The student has oppositional thoughts and/or behaviors.
33. The student has poor support and connection from faculty, administration, and staff. The student has an unsupportive family system and peers who exacerbate bad decisions and offer low-quality advice or caring. They experience evaporating social inhibitors.
34. The student experiences overwhelming, unmanageable stress from a significant change such as losing a job, a conduct hearing, failing a class, suspension, or family trauma. This stress is beyond what would normally be expected when receiving bad news.
35. The student has a drastic, unexplained behavior change.

The SIVRA-35 is scored online.[1]

---

[1] The National Behavioral Intervention Team Association website (www.nabita.org/resources/sivra-35/) provides references for each item, omitted here for space considerations.

Appendix D

ATAP "Risk Assessment Guideline Elements for Violence: Considerations for Assessing the Risk of Future Violent Behavior"

The Association of Threat Assessment Professionals (ATAP)

The Association of Threat Assessment Professionals (ATAP) disclaims liability for any personal injury, property, or other damages of any nature whatsoever, whether special, indirect, consequential, or compensatory, directly or indirectly resulting from the publication, use of, or reliance on this document. In issuing and making this document available, ATAP is not undertaking to render professional or other services for or on behalf of any person or entity. Nor is ATAP undertaking to perform any duty owed by any person or entity to someone else. Anyone using this document should rely on his or her own independent judgment or, as appropriate, seek the advice of a competent professional in determining the exercise of reasonable care in any given circumstance.

ATAP Risk Assessment Guideline Elements for Violence Committee

The Committee was established in October of 2002 by the Association of Threat Assessment Professionals (ATAP) in response to a perceived need for a multidisciplinary group to consider how future violence risk was being assessed in a wide variety of settings, both in the public and private sectors. As the preeminent organization for violence risk assessment and threat assessment professionals worldwide, ATAP has an important role to play in helping both the public and private sectors assess, manage, and understand situations involving potential violence risk whether from stalkers, school children, domestic abusers, coworkers, criminals, domestic and foreign extremists, or emotionally and mentally destabilized individuals.

This is the first time that ATAP has made the decision, as an organization, to become involved in providing considerations and guidelines for these types of threat assessment[1] and risk assessment undertakings. ATAP felt that publishing guidelines was a necessary step in moving this field of endeavor toward a common framework that could be used to provide a contextual and methodological understanding for the opinions that are formulated in this arena. Further, guidelines provide a means to evaluate the foundation and the robustness of these opinions.

We, ATAP and the Committee, do not consider this document to be the end of the discussion, but the beginning. It is our hope that through dialogue and use, this guideline will continue to evolve in order to improve opinions concerning the risk of future violence. This is essential, as these opinions are used to incarcerate and release people from custody, restrict freedom of movement and association, regulate pos-

---

[1] ATAP recognizes that the term "threat assessment" has been utilized to describe a variety of activities across a range of contexts (e.g., generalized assessment of terrorism risk, vulnerability assessment). For the purposes of this document, threat assessment is defined as the determination of the level of targeted violence risk posed by an individual or group toward a specific target.

session and use of property, and determine the use of limited resources to monitor and intervene in individuals' lives.[2]

Risk Assessment Guideline Elements for Violence: Considerations for Assessing the Risk of Future Violent Behavior

1.0 Title
2.0 Revision History
3.0 Committee Members
4.0 Scope
5.0 Summary
6.0 Purpose
7.0 Keywords
8.0 Terminology
9.0 Practice Advisory: Psychology
10.0 Practice Advisory: Law
11.0 Practice Advisory: Information Gathering
12.0 Bibliography
13.0 Appendix A: ATAP Model Violence Risk Assessment Process

1.0 Title

The title of this document is *Risk Assessment Guideline Elements for Violence: Considerations for Assessing the Risk of Future Violent Behavior.*

2.0 Revision History

Baseline Document; 9/4/2006

3.0 Committee Members

Chairman
James S. Cawood, CPP
President, Factor One

---

[2]ATAP recognizes that threat assessment activities are either performed by or involve a range of professionals from different backgrounds (e.g., mental health, law enforcement, security) who are obligated to meet different standards of practice appropriate to their respective professions. This document and all its parts are not intended to serve as an ethical standard or dismiss the applicability of other empirically supported factors or procedures appropriate to the situation at hand. The nature of the questions asked; time, setting, and situational factors; and applicable laws should be taken into consideration when performing risk assessments. As this document evolves, different scenarios and potential conflicts may arise and will be considered. These guidelines do not replace the need for judgment, thorough training, and consultation with colleagues when appropriate.

Members

Michael A. Crane, Esq.
Vice President-General Counsel IPC, International Corporation

Kate Killeen, Esq.
Deputy Executive Director, California District Attorneys Association

Glenn S. Lipson, PhD, ABPP
Diplomat in Forensic Psychology, American Board of
Professional Psychology

Kris Mohandie, PhD
Forensic Psychologist, Operational Consulting International, Inc

Michael Prodan
Sr. Special Agent/Criminal Profiler, South Carolina State
Law Enforcement Division

Jodi B. Rafkin, Esq.
Former Assistant U.S. Attorney, U.S. Attorney's Office

Gary S. Reynolds Senior
Vice-President-Director Financial and Electronic Crime
Investigations, Wells Fargo Bank

Mario J. Scalora, PhD
Asstant Professor of Clinical Psychology and
Law/Psychology Training Program, University of Nebraska,
Lincoln

Stephen W. Weston Esq. Lt. (Retired)
Office of Dignitary Protection, California Highway Patrol

William J. Zimmerman
Detective Protective Intelligence Division/Threat Assessment,
United States Capitol Police

4.0 Scope

The Association of Threat Assessment Professionals' Risk Assessment
Guideline Elements for Violence (RAGE-V) has applicability for both the
private and public sectors. The RAGE-V is an exploration and explanation of interrelated processes and activities that will assist in evaluating
the potential risk of future physical violence from a known individual,
including those inspired or motivated by group philosophy or beliefs.

5.0 Summary

The RAGE-V is an approach to assist individuals and organizations
to consider the factors and steps necessary to provide for thorough,
well-considered opinions concerning the potential risk of future physical violence from a known individual. It is based on a wide review of
relevant literature, as well as the practical processes developed and
implemented for this purpose by a wide range of professionals and organizations that make up the violence risk assessment community. The

applicability of these considerations, in any specific case, may depend on the situation, context, discipline of the individual assessor (e.g., education, licensing), and the particular circumstances and questions for the evaluation.

6.0 Purpose

At the present time, many assessments of future violence risk assessments are conducted in an eclectic manner, without an agreed upon approach or process, either on the part of the requestors of these assessments, or the assessors that provide them. This often leaves the individual being assessed and the venues that use these assessments without an adequate understanding of what elements might be considered, if not acted on, for arriving at valid assessment conclusions. It also means there are end users of these assessments that are at a loss about how to determine whether the underlying assessment methodology used in any individual assessment was based on a solid foundation that allows for that assessment to be trusted. Ideally, a solidly based and trusted assessment would be the basis for taking actions that would significantly affect the safety and liberty of individual citizens and society as a whole.

The purpose of this document is to provide well-grounded considerations and practical suggestions, based upon a cohesive, multidimensional understanding of appropriate violence risk assessment process elements and informational resources. It also provides a stepwise process to be considered during each assessment of potential violence risk. This document was designed to be used by all providers and end users of these assessments to provide a quick reference for suggesting essential considerations and resources that could be used in specific cases, or as a guideline for questioning assessors about their methodology and decision making in a specific scenario. This document has been developed by a multidisciplinary team of assessors and reviewed by a wide array of assessors, academics, and end users, and represents the currently perceived best practices for consideration in a wide range of assessment cases. It is an important step toward the development of practice standards for violence risk assessment.[3]

7.0 Keywords

Mitigation Strategies, Violence Risk Assessment

---

[3]While thorough and detailed assessments are desired, situations may arise which challenge the ability to obtain relevant information or address factors included within these practice advisories due to emergency/time constraints. As a result, the assessor is advised to practice within relevant professional standards and advise their client of the relevant limitations of the violence risk assessment conclusions presented.

8.0 Terminology

Approach-Behavior: Actions toward a target of interest that are escalating with a particular goal in mind.

Assessor: The person using this document to aid in the formation of an opinion of violence risk.

Commitments: In this context it refers to involuntary or less than voluntary hospitalizations for psychological problems. Hospitalizations occur when someone poses a danger to themselves or others.

Inevitability: The belief that no matter what actions one takes the course of events will not change.

Mitigation Strategies: Implementation of measures to lessen or eliminate the occurrence or impact of an incident of potential violence.

Process Variables: Examines the interplay between one's own beliefs and how that fuels or prevents actions and behaviors.

Protective Inhibitors: Beliefs, relationships, injuries, lack of resources, or abilities that can limit whether a person is likely to follow through with dangerous conduct.

Violence Risk Assessment: The process of identifying behaviors that may signal an individual's preparation to commit a violent act, assessing those behaviors in the context of that person's past history of behavior and other known incidents of violence that have demonstrated those behaviors, quantifying the level of risk from this behavioral information by using professional judgment and objective, appropriate tools to provide a balanced assessment, and presentation of that assessment to the requestor of the assessment, in such a way, as to qualify the opinion and its limitations appropriately.

9.0 Practice Advisory: Psychology

Behavioral information of interest could include:

Process Variables
- Approach behavior
- Evidence of escalation—threats, proximity seeking
- Fantasy rehearsal
- Evidence of deterioration—deteriorating mental state, psychosis
- Actively violent state of mind—suicidal or homicidal thoughts
- Command hallucinations, thought insertion/withdrawal, paranoia of imminent threat
- Diminishing inhibitions
- Diminishing or impaired coping
- Inability or limited view or ability to pursue other options
- Obsession
- Evaporating protective inhibitors
- Sense of inevitability (tunnel vision, foregone conclusion)

- Pre-attack or ritualistic preparatory actions (writing of suicide note, suicide video, religious rituals, purchase of camouflage clothing)
- Recent acquisition or preparation of weapons, escalation of practice with no sanctioned reason
- Subject's response to assessment and inquiries.

Risk Factors
- Would you tolerate the same behavior from a student without a disability?
- Have weapons-use connected to emotional release, fascination with destructive power
- Motivational factors (What is driving the individual?) delusion, fanatical beliefs, revenge, entitlement, grandiosity, need to force closure
- Drug use—methamphetamine, cocaine, alcohol, steroids
- Head trauma
- Criminal history, including history of violence, homicide, stalking, threats, assaultive behavior, violation of conditional release
- Prior voluntary or involuntary commitments
- Past suicide attempts, or suicide ideation, to include suicidal thoughts, statements, gestures, and attempts
- Adverse responses to authority and limit setting
- Reference groups, heroes, affiliations, and community attachments
- History of mental problems that compromise coping, or enhance appeal of violence—may include:
  Depression
  Paranoia
  Psychopathy
  Bipolar
  Personality disorders (narcissistic, paranoid, borderline, antisocial)
  Perceptions of injustice or insoluble problems.

Inhibitors/Stabilizers
Consideration of available inhibitors and the persons' access and utilization of them:

- Treatment availability, utilization, and past receptivity
- Family
- Other social support
- Spiritual or religious beliefs opposing violence
- Connectedness and healthy affectional bonds.

Triggers
Identification of potentially stabilizing or destabilizing triggers:

- Pending perceived negative job event
- Rejection and abandonment

- Increased psychosis
- Civil (family court, child custody, etc.) or criminal justice system event(s)
- Disruption of support system
- Financial problems.

Analysis Guidelines
Consideration of multiple behavioral and risk factors:

- Consideration of contextual factors
- Consideration of deterrent factors, mitigating factors, or inhibitors to risk, as well as risk factors
- Consideration of potential stressors as well as resiliency factors
- Access sufficient credible, first-hand collateral data sources
- Avoidance of over-reliance on single factors in most cases
- Factors considered must be scientifically relevant or those typically considered within the field based upon empirical and published literature
- Must assess the impact of gathering information and investigative/threat assessment process itself upon risk.

Objective Instruments and Tools
When appropriate, utilize objective instrument(s) or tool(s) appropriate for the context (e.g., psychopathy-related instruments [PCL-R, PCL-R SV; etc.]; HCR-20; Spousal Risk Assessment Guide [SARA]; Violence Risk Assessment Guide [VRAG]; Level of Service Inventory–Revised; Cawood/White Assessment Grid; Mosaic-DV; The Classification of Violence Risk [COVR]; and others).[4]

- Assessor must avoid sole reliance on checklist/instrument/tool
- Assessor must be trained and qualified on relevant instrument or tool
- Instrumentation utilized must be reliable and valid as well as appropriate for the issue at hand
- Assessor must be aware of the limitations of any instrumentation utilized
- Assessor must stay current with new developments and outdated versions.

---

[4]We are encouraging the use of Structured Professional Judgment (SPJ) which is aided by the use of tools and other appropriate practice parameters. Issues of reliability, validity for certain types of assessments or subjects, peer review acceptance, and training in the technique or method should be considered before relying on any protocol or tool. The listing of the above instruments and tools should not be considered an endorsement of said instruments or tools. The user can decide on whether they are appropriate. The above listed instruments and tools are known more widely in the mental health and law enforcement assessment communities. Being known does not mean that they are defensible in a court or other venue.

Additional Considerations

When conceptualizing risk level, assessor must recognize professional limitations pertinent to the threat assessment.

- Seek out relevant consultation or expertise when necessary
- Qualify assessment when necessary (e.g., availability of information, recognize assumptions, potential changes in relevant context, time limited nature of assessment)
- Be aware of the complex contextual, legal, ethical, and regulatory issues that impact the violence risk assessment process.

10.0 Practice Advisory: Law

The legal system often views psychological testimony with distrust and disbelief. There is the perception that either side to a legal case or controversy can, for enough money, find an "expert" who will say what they want to hear. One of the goals of this assessment guideline is to foster consensus and bolster credibility in the area of violence risk assessment. The laws governing what must be disclosed to different parties and what might be considered admissible are contextual, issue sensitive, and jurisdictional.

For civil testimony on the risk of future violent behavior to be admissible in court in the United States, taking into account the jurisdiction, the expert might have to comply with the standards set forth in *Daubert v. Merrell Dow Pharmaceuticals Inc*, 509 U.S. 579 (1993), and *Kumho Tire Co. v. Carmichael*, 526 U.S. 137 (1999). Criminal courts may have different standards, as do some state courts. The trial judge, when relying on Daubert, must be satisfied that the evidence is based on scientific knowledge, or is reliable, and ensure that the evidence will assist the trier of fact, or is relevant. The Daubert court decision provided four factors that could be used in this evaluation: 1) whether the theory has been tested or is testable; 2) whether the theory or study has been subject to peer review; 3) whether there is a known or potential error rate; and 4) whether the technique is generally accepted in the relevant field (Daubert, 509 U.S. at 594).

Each discipline or field of investigation imposes upon its members sets of different legal controls and expectations. For example, a law enforcement officer may have additional obligations pertaining to searching law enforcement databases not accessible to other individuals in the private sector. Mental health assessors may have duties to protect and warn in different jurisdictions. Psychologists, in particular, may have the burden of selecting appropriate measures relying upon testing and ethical standards. Warnings regarding protections against self-incrimination differ for different disciplines and, thus, the burden shifts accordingly based upon these expectations. This document cannot address practice and professional standards for all the disciplines involved in violence risk assessment or dangerousness appraisal. It does not take the place of any individual assessor's need to know what standards and procedures are in their area of expertise. Nonetheless, there is a shared foundation and approach that all professionals in this area can be held accountable to when performing an assessment and arriving at their opinions.

For civil cases in the United States, it is becoming standard, based on Rule 26 of the Federal Rules of Civil Procedure, for expert witnesses offering an opinion on the risk of future violent behavior to provide a written report prior to testifying. This report sets forth their opinions and the reasons for their conclusions, information relied upon, qualifications of the expert witness, and compensation being exchanged for the assessment and testimony. Any assessor offering an opinion on the risk of future violent behavior should have an appropriate basis for their opinion and documentation in a form suitable for its intended purpose, which may include the production of written reports.

Attorneys for all parties to the litigation should review that report carefully before the assessor/expert witness takes the stand. The assessor/expert witness should be questioned on the methodology they used. The assessor/expert witness's background and experience in the field of threat assessment should also be questioned. How many assessments have they done? Have they qualified as an expert in a court of law? If so, how many times? What materials have they reviewed and relied on in forming their opinion? Who have they spoken to, and for how long? Section 9.0 of this guideline provides a good checklist of issues to explore with an assessor/expert witness.

11.0 Practice Advisory: Information Gathering

In general, the more behavioral information available about the subject of an assessment, the greater the ability to provide an accurate assessment. The ability to gather information in any specific case, and at any particular stage of an assessment, will depend on the immediacy of the issues, and the civil rights and employment context of the person being assessed. Different assessors have different access to information and some of this information may be protected by law. The list below includes the types of information that have been found to be helpful in assessments; however, depending on the circumstances of each individual case, this information might not be available in a timely manner, could be protected from disclosure, or not legally attainable.

Obtain Information on Victim/Target/Reporting Subject
- Past history of reports
- Motivation for reports
- Possibility of unintentional or intentional misinformation.

Focus of Information on Victim/Target/Reporting Subject
- Is the subject/target of the threats a chronic victim? Or is the individual in a position or situation that typically receives threats or inappropriate contacts?
- Is the victim connected to a controversial situation or have they been in the media recently?
- Is the report being made out of fear, desperation, retaliation, safety or the want of attention?
- Is there a possibility that the information reported was skewed, misunderstood, or fabricated?

Information on the Subject of Assessment
- Current location
- Ability to access subject/victim
- Research behavior(s)
- Motivation: both positive and negative
- Past history of threatening or violent behavior, including stalking
- Criminal history: local, county, state, federal: person of interest-arrest, conviction; reporting party of incident, victim
- History of behavior in a jail or correctional institution, if applicable
- Probation or parole history, if applicable
- Civil court history: federal, state, local level
- Vehicle operation history
- Mental history (when available)
- Substance abuse
- Military history/training
- Support structure in area
- Weapons seeking, possession, recent acquisition, or recent modification
- Changes in behavior

Focus of Information on Subject
- Is the subject in a location or does the subject have the ability to approach or attack the victim or not? (e.g., in jail, indigent, incapacitated)
- Does the subject have immediate access to the victim? (e.g., family, coworker)
- Positive motivation of the subject to get to victim? (i.e., love, hate, wronged, personal issue)
- Negative motivation of the subject? (i.e., embarrassment, loss of employment, financial, incarceration)
- Does the subject have a history of violent or threatening behavior? Typically, this may be in a criminal history report, however, this trait may have never been reported and may have never resulted in a criminal arrest or prosecution. Interviews with neighbors, family members, or coworkers should be conducted. Other sources for this

information include restraining orders or divorce documents. Determine the provocation, circumstances, and extent of any reported past violence (e.g., involving weapons, type and extent of injury)

- Does the subject have a history of criminal actions? Specifically crimes that indicate the subject is non-compliant to the standard rules of society (e.g., trespass, disorderly conduct, fail to obey a lawful order)

Other Sources of Information for Past Violent Behavior

- *Premises history:* Law enforcement records of response to an address. Check all past addresses of a subject.
- *Contact history:* Check all jurisdictions where the subject has lived or worked for field interviews, listed as suspect, witness or victim.
- Obtain copies of police reports where the subject was involved as a suspect, witness, or victim. Good source of past conduct.
- Court records supporting a restraining order, divorce proceedings, civil case, or child custody.
- Interview neighbors of past addresses including apartment managers. Can be an excellent source for information on disturbances, police responses, and past boy or girlfriends.
- Does the subject's vehicle operating history record disclose a recent trend of violation?
- Does the subject have a history of mental health treatment or non-compliance with treatment/medication?
- Does the suspect display signs of some form of obvious mental illness? (e.g., delusions, hallucinations, grandiose ideations, paranoia, homicidal/suicidal thoughts)
- Does the subject have a history of substance abuse? Criminally documented, self-disclosed, or confirmed by witnesses.
- Does the subject have training in weapons tactical operation, or knowledge of the tactical or commercial use of explosives? This training is not limited to military service. The suspect could belong to a gun club, militia, or be self-taught.
- Is there any information indicating the subject may be seeking or preparing a weapon or destructive device?
- Is there evidence of "final act" behaviors (e.g., last will, destroying own property, giving property away, ritualistic acts)?
- Is there evidence of research, planning, or stalking-type behaviors? This type of evidence could include visits to libraries, use of the internet to research potential victims, diaries, equipment lists, "hit lists," target information files, etc.
- If safe and appropriate, take advantage of opportunities to establish communication with the subject to determine future intentions. Also make a thoughtful analysis into whether the situation would allow safely seeking additional sources of insight into the subject's future intentions, such as family members, friends, coworkers, neighbors or utilizing these additional sources to monitor the subject's future behavior.

Appendix E

Reality Therapy
WDEP Worksheet

WDEP stands for **W**ants and needs, **D**irection and what they are doing, an **E**valuation of his or her behavior, and **P**lanning and commitment to change. For more information about setting goals and making concrete plans, see Francis and Van Brunt (2010) and Glasser (1975, 2001).

The full worksheet is presented on the next page.

Reality Therapy WDEP Worksheet

WANTS: "What do I want?"
Write down the "wants and needs" that are in your world. Include what you need to do with school.

School: _____

DOING AND DIRECTION: "What is the direction your life is taking? What are you doing now to obtain your wants or fill your needs?"
Focus on what you are doing *now*, your current behavior, and the direction that is taking you.

A) _____
B) _____
C) _____

EVALUATION: "Does your present behavior have a reasonable chance of getting you what you want and need now, and will it take you in the direction you want to go?"

No | Yes

PLANS AND COMMITMENTS (GOALS): "What plans could you make now that would result in a more satisfying life?"
Identify specific ways to fulfill yor wants and needs (goals) by changing what you are doing now, and formulate a new plan.

A) _____
B) _____
C) _____

DID THE PLAN WORK?
No

DID THE PLAN WORK?
Yes

KEY

Goals: S = Simple; A = Attainable; M = Measurable; I = Immediate; C = Consistent; ConC = Controlled by client; ComC = Committed to by client; T = Timely.

Appendix F

An Existential Exercise

Use

This exercise works well with patients who are having difficulty with their place in the world. They may have some difficulty with viewing their future, be struggling with anxiety, be fearful of death, or be having trouble sorting out choices.

Method

The process is one that can be adapted in many different ways. I like to use a series of five index cards and ask patients to write a single word or quality they would use to describe themselves. These may be roles the patient plays (father, mother, son, daughter) or ways other people view the patient (shy, outgoing, smart, angry . . .).

The idea is to capture the core ways patients view themselves, the roles they take on, and the ideas/emotions they may employ to defend themselves against the true realities of the world (death, meaningless-ness, freedom, anxiety, lack of control). The first step of this exercise is to have patients clearly visualize the ways they see themselves as people existing in the world, whether this be through how they see themselves, how others see them, or how they would like to be seen.

The second part of the exercise asks patients to spend some time imagining themselves without these qualities. With patients who can handle taking this experience to the fullest, I ask them to reflect on one of the terms on a single index card and then rip up the card and throw it away. Patients are then asked to visualize themselves, to the fullest extent possible, without the comforting (or pathological) roles and qualities written on the destroyed card.

I often have patients do this over a series of days prior to their next session. After going through the five cards, they come back into session and we discuss how they felt imagining the qualities they hold so dear to be removed from their lives.

Discussion Afterward

The purpose of the experience is to help the patient confront the true realities of life . . . what it means to exist in a finite body, pursuing desires that will have no true lasting impact 100 years from now. This experience has helped empower patients to directly face their fears and anxieties that may be causing difficulties in making choices for the future or overcoming everyday anxiety situations. Patients peel away their daily, comforting masks (sometimes comforting, sometimes pathological, such as anxiety, fear, and sadness) to then take solace in the ultimate truths . . . that we are all alone, we must make choices and have little to say about how the fates move us around. We can survive any why by adapting with the right how.

I adapted this exercise from Yalom's (1980) text *Existential Psychotherapy*. The stoic and pre-Socratic philosophers also support this idea by suggesting that the path to ultimate peace is found through accepting that the universe is in constant change. (Or as Heraclitus famously said, no one ever steps into the same river twice.) We have very little impact on what life brings to us; our only choice lies in how we choose to live our lives. Like Sisyphus pushing his boulder up the hill for all eternity, we choose the manner in which we suffer and have no control over the tasks assigned to us.

REFERENCES

Albrecht, S. (2010). Threat assessment teams: Workplace and school violence prevention. *FBI Law Enforcement Bulletin, 21*, 15–21.

American Counseling Association. (2014). *ACA code of ethics*. Alexandria, VA: Author.

American Psychiatric Association. (2013). *Diagnostic and statistical manual of mental disorders* (5th ed.). Washington, DC: Author.

American Psychological Association. (2010). *Ethical principles of psychologists and code of conduct (2002, amended June 1, 2010)*. Retrieved from http://www.apa.org/ethics/code/index.aspx

American Society of Mechanical Engineers Innovative Technologies Institute. (2010). *A risk analysis standard for natural and man-made hazards to higher education institutions*. New York, NY: Author.

ASIS International and the Society for Human Resource Management. (2011). *Workplace violence prevention and intervention: American national standard*. Washington, DC: Author.

Associated Press. (2006, April 24). *Puyallup high school student arrested for alleged gun plot*. Retrieved from www.seattlepi.com

Association of Threat Assessment Professionals. (2006). *Risk Assessment Guideline Elements for Violence (RAGE-V): Considerations for assessing the risk of future violent behavior*. Sacramento, CA: Author.

Barbassa, J. (2011, April 7). Rio gunman kills 12 children. *The Associated Press*.

Barnes, T. (2011, April 7). Brazil shooting said to be first school massacre in nation's history. *Christian Science Monitor*.

Beck, J. (2008). Outpatient settings. In R. Simon & K. Tardiff (Eds.), *Violence assessment and management* (pp. 237–257). Washington, DC: American Psychiatric Press.

Besley, A. C. (2002). Foucault and the turn to narrative therapy. *British Journal of Guidance & Counseling, 30*(2), 125–143.

Blair, C. (2008). *Better test performance the Navy SEALs way.* Retrieved from http://studyprof.com/blog/2008/11/25/better-test-performance-the-navy-seals-way/

Bowden, C. (1999). Houston and Ramiro. *Esquire, 131*(2), p. 74.

Boysen, G. (2012). Teacher and student perceptions of microaggressions in college classrooms. *Journal of College Teaching, 60,* 122–129.

Breivik, A. B. (2011). *Complete manifesto "2083—A European declaration of independence."* Retrieved from http://publicintelligence.net/anders-behring-breiviks-complete-manifesto-2083-a-european-declaration-of-independence/

Butcher, J. N., Graham, J. R., Ben-Porath, Y. S., Tellegen, A., & Dahlstrom, W. G. (2001). *Manual for administration scoring and interpretation of the MMPI-2.* Minneapolis: University of Minnesota Press.

Byrnes, J. (2002). *Before conflict: Preventing aggressive behavior.* Lanham, MD: Scarecrow Education.

Calhoun, F., & Weston, S. (2009). *Threat assessment and management strategies: Identifying the howlers and hunters.* Boca Raton, FL: CRC Press.

Camus, A. (1989). *The stranger.* New York, NY: Vintage Press.

Carpenter, J. (Director). (1978). *Halloween* [Motion picture]. Los Angeles, CA: Compass International Pictures.

Choe, J. Y., Teplin, L. A., & Abram, K. M. (2008). Perpetration of violence, violent victimization, and severe mental illness: Balancing public health concerns. *Psychiatric Services, 59*(2), 153–164.

Chua-Eoan, H., & Monroe, S. (1997). Mississippi gothic. *Time, 150*(16), 54.

Close, H. (1998). *Metaphor in psychotherapy: Clinical applications of stories and allegories.* Atascadero, CA: Impact Publishers.

Cobb, C., & Avery, B. (1977). *The rape of a normal mind.* Markham, Ontario, Canada: Paper Jacks.

Coen, J. (Director), & Coen, E. (Director). (1998). *The big Lebowski* [Motion picture]. Los Angeles, CA: Polygram Filmed Entertainment.

Cooper, G. (2013, September 24). *Prosecutors: Who tipped off cops to New Braunfels teen's Facebook threat?* Retrieved from www.kens5.com/news/Prosecutors-search-for-Canadian-woman-who-tipped-police-off-about-teens-Facebook-Comment-224960832.html

Corey, G. (2001). *Theory and practice of counseling and psychotherapy* (6th ed.). Belmont, CA: Brooks/Cole Thompson Learning.

Cornwell, T. (1997). Pupil shoots headteacher. *Times Educational Supplement* (no. 4209), p. 20.

Couch, A. (2011, January 12). Arizona shooting suspect Jared Loughner: 5 of his strange ideas. *Christian Science Monitor.*

Craven, W. (Director). (1984). *A nightmare on Elm Street* [Motion picture]. New York, NY: New Line Cinema.

Cunningham, S. (Director). (1980). *Friday the 13th* [Motion picture]. Los Angeles, CA: Paramount Pictures.

Curry, V. (2003). Thurston High School: The effects of both distal and emotional proximity in an acute instance of school violence. *Journal of School Violence, 2*(3), 93–120.

Darabont, F. (2010). *The walking dead* [TV series]. New York, NY: American Movie Channel.

de Becker, G. (1997). *The gift of fear and other survival signals that protect us from violence.* New York, NY: Dell.

Deisinger, E., Randazzo, M., & Nolan, J. (2014). Threat assessment and management in higher education: Enhancing the standard of care in the academy. In J. R. Meloy & J. Hoffmann (Eds.), *The international handbook of threat assessment* (pp. 107–125). New York, NY: Oxford University Press.

Deisinger, G., Randazzo, M., O'Neill, D., & Savage, J. (2008). *The handbook for campus threat assessment and management teams.* Boston, MA: Applied Risk Management.

Dietz, P. E. (1986). Mass, serial, and sensational homicides. *Bulletin of the New York Academy of Medicine, 62,* 477–491.

Dobuzinskis, A. (2011, January 15). California student arrest may have averted disaster. *Reuters.* Retrieved from http://www.reuters.com/article/2011/01/15/us-student-arrest-california-idUS-TRE70E24F20110115

Doug, S. (2006, September 15). Gunman's writings presaged rampage. *The Washington Post.*

Douglas, K. S., Hart, S. D., Webster, C. D., & Belfrage, H. (2013). *HCR-20 V3 Assessing risk for violence user guide.* Burnaby, Canada: Mental Health, Law, and Policy Institute, Simon Fraser University.

Dyer, S. (2008, February 25). Shooting at Louisiana Technical College leaves threee students dead; motive unclear. *Community College Week, 20*(13), 4.

Eells, G., & Miller, H. (2011). Assessing and responding to disturbed and disturbing students: Understanding the role of administrative teams in institutions of higher education. *Journal of College Student Psychotherapy, 25*(1), 8–23.

Elliot, D. (2013). Colorado theater shooting victim–witnesses can attend James Holmes trial. *Huffington Post.* Retrieved from http://www.huffingtonpost.com/2013/08/28/colorado-theater-shooting_n_3832677.html

Ellis, A. (2007). *The practice of rational emotive behavior therapy.* New York, NY: W. W. Norton.

Engel, P. (1989). *Saved by the bell* [Television series]. New York, NY: NBC.

Epston, D. (1992). The case of the night watchman. In M. White & D. Epston (Eds.), *Experience, contradiction, narrative and imagination: Selected papers of David Epston and Michael White 1989–1991* (pp. 123–124). Adelaide, Australia: Dulwich Centre Publications.

Fein, R. A., & Vossekuil, B. (1998). *Protective intelligence and threat assessment investigations: A guide for state and local law enforcement officials* (NCJ 170612). Washington, DC: National Institute of Justice.

Fein, R., Vossekuil, B., & Holden, G. (1995). *Threat assessment: An approach to targeted violence: National Institute of Justice Research in action.* Washington, DC: National Institute of Justice.

Ford, A. (2011, May 3). UCA expels foreign exchange student after deadly Facebook rant. *University of Arkansas Examiner.*

Foucault, M. (1965). *Madness and civilization.* New York, NY: Random House.

Francis, P., & Van Brunt, B. (2010). Classroom management 102: Working with difficult students. *Magna Communications Online Training.* Retrieved from www.magnapubs.com

Frankl, V. (1965). *The doctor and the soul.* New York, NY: Alfred A. Knopf.

Gibbs, N., Grace, J., Gwynne, S. C., Harrington, M., Jackson, D. S., Shapiro, J., & Woodbury, R. (1999). On March 4, Eric Harris and Dylan Klebold sat for this class picture. On April 17, they both went to the prom. What they did next left their school in sorrow and disbelief [Cover story]. *Time, 153*(17), 20.

Gibbs, N., & Roche, T. (1999, December 20). The Columbine tapes. *Time Magazine.*

Glasser, A. (1975). *Reality therapy: A new approach to psychiatry.* New York, NY: Colophon Books.

Glasser, A. (2001). *Counseling with choice theory: The new reality therapy.* New York, NY: Colophon Books.

GlobalGrind Staff. (2012). "Die, all of you": T. J. Lane, alleged gunmen in high school shooting, writes chilling letter (details). *GlobalGrind.* Retrieved from http://globalgrind.com/2012/02/27/tj-lane-alleged-gunmen-chardon-high-school-shooting-letter-die-all-you-details/

Gregg, T., & Siegal, A. (2001). Brain structures and neurotransmitters regulating aggression in cats: Implications for human aggression. *Progress in Neuro-Psychopharmacology and Biological Psychiatry, 25,* 91–140.

Grossman, D. (1996). *On killing: The psychological cost of learning to kill in war and society.* Lebanon, IN: Little, Brown, and Company Back Bay Books.

Gurman, A., & Messer, S. (1995). *Essential psychotherapies: Theory and practice.* New York, NY: Guilford Press.

Hammer, J. (1998, June 8). "Kid is out of control." *Newsweek, 131*(23), 32.

Hart, S., & Logan, C. (2011). Formulation of violence risk used evidence-based assessment: The structured professional judgment approach. In P. Sturmey & M. McMurran (Eds.), *Forensic case formulation* (pp. 83–106). Chichester, England: Wiley-Blackwell.

Hart, S., Sturmey, P., Logan, C., & McMuran, M. (2011). Forensic case formulation. *International Journal of Forensic Mental Health, 10,* 118–126.

Headley, S. (1994). Classroom suicide. *Education Week, 13*(28), 4.

Hemingway, E. (1987). *The snows of Kilimanjaro and other stories.* New York, NY: Scribner.

Hempel, A., Meloy, J. R., & Richards, T. (1999). Offender and offense characteristics of a nonrandom sample of mass murderers. *Journal of the American Academy of Psychiatry and the Law, 27*, 213–225.

Hewitt, B., & Harmes, J. (1997). The avenger. *People, 48*(18), 116.

Hornblower, M., Faltermayer, C., Grace, J., Monroe, S., & Woodbury, R. (1998). The boy who loved bombs. *Time, 151*, 42–44.

Hughes, J. (Writer and Director). (1985). *The breakfast club* [Motion picture]. Los Angeles, CA: Universal Pictures.

Hull, C. (1952). *A behavior system.* New Haven, CT: Yale University Press.

Jerome, R., & Foster, J. (2002). Day of wrath. *People, 57*(4), 95.

Johnson, K., Kovaleski, S., Frosch, D., & Lipton, E. (2011, January 9). Suspect's odd behavior caused growing alarm. *New York Times.* Retrieved from http://www.nytimes.com/2011/01/10/us/10shooter.html?pagewanted=all&_r=0

Jones, T. (1998). Look back in sorrow. *Good Housekeeping, 227*(5), 118.

Keen, J. (2008, February 17). Student, shot in head, ran back for girlfriend. *USA Today.*

Kelley, K. (2006, September 30). Colorado: Gunman wrote of suicide. *The New York Times*, p. 13.

Kendig, M. (1990). *Alfred Korzybski: Collected writings, 1920–1950.* Englewood, NJ: Institute of General Semantics.

King, S. (2003). *The gunslinger.* New York, NY: Plume.

Kleinfield, N., Rivera, R., & Kovaleski, S. (2013, March 29). Newtown killer's obsession, in chilling detail. *New York Times.* Retrieved from http://www.nytimes.com/2013/03/29/nyregion/search-warrants-reveal-items-seized-at-adam-lanzas-home.html

Knoll, J. (2010). The "pseudocommando" mass murderer: Part I, the psychology of revenge and obliteration. *Journal of the American Academy of Psychiatry and the Law, 38*, 87–94.

Kopp, R. R. (1995). *Metaphor therapy.* New York, NY: Brunner/Mazel.

Langman, P. (2008). *Eric Harris diversion documents.* Retrieved from http://www.schoolshooters.info/eric-harris-diversion.pdf

Langman, P. (2009a). Rampage school shooters: A typology. *Journal of Aggression and Violent Behavior, 14*, 79–86.

Langman, P. (2009b). *Why kids kill: Inside the minds of school shooters.* Basingstoke, UK: Palgrave Macmillan.

Leavitt, M., Spellings, M., & Gonzales, A. (2007). *Report to the President on issues raised by the Virginia Tech tragedy.* Retrieved from https://www.ncjrs.gov/App/publications/abstract.aspx?ID=240621

Leone, H. (Director). (1967). *The good, the bad and the ugly* [Motion picture]. Produzioni Europee Association (PEA).

Li, F. (2012, March 15). Student brings knife to school in fear of being bullied. *WILX10*. Retrieved from http://www.wilx.com/news/headlines/Student_Brings_Knife_to_School_in_Fear_of_Being_Bullied_142727365.html

Lucas, G. (Director). (1977). *Star wars* [Motion picture]. Los Angeles, CA: 20th Century Fox.

MacCulloch, M., Snowden, P., Wood, P., & Mills, H. (1983). Sadistic fantasy, sadistic behavior and offending. *British Journal of Psychiatry, 143*, 20–29.

Martine, E. (2009, December 10). Jason Michael Hamilton's rifle jammed after 2 shots in Northern Virginia college shooting, say cops. *CBS/Associated Press*.

May, R. (1983). *The discovery of being.* New York, NY: W. W. Norton.

McEllistrem, J. (2004). Affective and predatory violence: A bimodal classification systems of human aggression and violence. *Journal of Aggression and Violent Behavior, 10*, 1–30.

Meloy, J. (1997). Predatory violence during mass murder. *Journal of Forensic Science, 42*, 326–329.

Meloy, J. (1998). *The psychopathic mind: Origins, dynamics, and treatment.* Northvale, NJ: Jason Aronson.

Meloy, J. R. (2000). *Violence risk and threat assessment: A practical guide for mental health and criminal justice professionals.* San Diego, CA: Specialized Training Services.

Meloy, J. R. (2001). Communicated threats and violence toward public and private targets: Discerning differences between those who stalk and attack. *Journal of Forensic Science, 46*, 1211–1213.

Meloy, J. R. (2006). The empirical basis and forensic application of affective and predatory violence. *Australian and New Zealand Journal of Psychiatry, 40*, 539–547.

Meloy, J. R. (2012). Predatory violence and psychopathy. In H. Hakkanen-Nyholm & J. Nyholm (Eds.), *Psychopathy and law* (pp. 159–175). London, England: Wiley.

Meloy, J. R., Hart, S., & Hoffmann, J. (2014). Threat assessment and management. In J. R. Meloy & J. Hoffmann (Eds.), *The international handbook of threat assessment* (pp. 3–17). New York, NY: Oxford University Press.

Meloy, J. R., & Hoffmann, J. (Eds.). (2014). *The international handbook of threat assessment.* New York, NY: Oxford University Press.

Meloy, J., Hoffmann, J., Guldimann, A., & James, D. (2011). The role of warning behaviors in threat assessment: An exploration and suggested typology. *Behavioral Sciences and the Law, 30*, 256–279.

Meloy, J. R., Hoffmann, J., Roshdi, K., Glaz-Ocik, J., & Guldimann, A. (2014). Warning behaviors and their configurations across various domains of targeted violence. In J. R. Meloy & J. Hoffmann (Eds.), *The international handbook of threat assessment* (pp. 39–53). New York, NY: Oxford University Press.

Meloy, J. R., & Mohandie, K. (2014). Assessing threats by direct interview of the violent true believer. In J. R. Meloy & J. Hoffmann (Eds.), *The international handbook of threat assessment* (pp. 388–398). New York, NY: Oxford University Press.

Meloy, J. R., & O'Toole, M. E. (2011). The concept of leakage in threat assessment. *Behavioral Sciences and the Law.* Advance online publication. doi: 10.1002/bsl.986

Miller, W. R., & Rollnick, S. (1991). *Motivational interviewing: Preparing people to change addictive behavior.* New York, NY: Guilford Press.

Mohandie, K. (2014). Threat assessment in schools. In J. R. Meloy & J. Hoffman (Eds.), *The international handbook of threat assessment* (pp. 126–147). New York, NY: Oxford University Press.

Mohandie, K., & Duffy, J. (1999, December). Understanding subjects with paranoid schizophrenia. *FBI Law Enforcement Bulletin, 68*(12), 8–17.

Mullen, P. E., Pathé, M., & Purcell, R. (2009) *Stalkers and their victims.* Cambridge, England: Cambridge University Press.

Nay, R. (2004). *Taking charge of anger.* New York, NY: Guilford Press.

Nydell, M. (1996). *Understanding Arabs: A guide for Westerners.* Yarmouth, ME: Intercultural Press.

Odgers, C. L., Moffitt, T. E., Tach, L. M., Sampson, A., Taylor, R. J., Matthews, C. L., & Caspi, A. (2009). The protective effects of neighborhood collective efficacy on British children growing up in deprivation: A developmental analysis. *Developmental Psychology, 45,* 942–957.

O'Neill, D., Fox, J., Depue, R., & Englander, E. (2008). *Campus violence prevention and response: Best practices for Massachusetts higher education.* Boston, MA: Applied Risk Management.

O'Toole, M. E. (2000). *The school shooter: A threat assessment perspective.* Quantico, VA: National Center for the Analysis of Violent Crime, Federal Bureau of Investigation.

O'Toole, M. E., & Bowman, A. (2011). *Dangerous instincts: How gut feelings betray.* New York, NY: Hudson Street Press.

O'Toole, M. E., & Smith, S. (2014). Fundamentals of threat assessment for beginners. In J. R. Meloy & J. Hoffmann (Eds.), *The international handbook of threat assessment* (pp. 272–282). New York, NY: Oxford University Press.

Owens, R. (2009, November 5). Fort Hood shooting. *ABCNews.* Retrieved from http://abcnews.go.com/Archives/video/nov-2009-fort-hood-shooting-14884777

Owens, R. (2010, December 15). Fla. school shooting hero's teary tale: "I'm no hero, folks." *ABCNews.* Retrieved from http://abcnews.go.com/US/florida-school-board-shooting-survivors-recount-pure-terror/story?id=12399935

Paul, G. L. (1967). Strategy of outcome research in psychotherapy. *Journal of Consulting Psychology, 31,* 109–118.

Perls, F. (1947). *Ego, hunger and aggression.* New York, NY: Vintage Press.

Perls, F. (1951). *Gestalt therapy.* New York, NY: Julian Press.

Perls, F. (1969). *Gestalt theory verbatim.* Lafayette, CA: Real People Press.

Plath, S. (2005). *The bell jar.* New York, NY: Harper Perennial Modern Classics. (Original work published 1971)

Pow, H. (2012). You don't even know ****ing terror yet ... *Daily Mail Online.* Retrieved from http://www.dailymail.co.uk/news/article-2235785/Jared-Cano-case-Cell-phone-video-shows-Florida-student-planned-blow-school-foiled-2011-attack.html

Prochaska, J., Norcross, J., & DiClemente, C. (1994). *Changing for good.* New York, NY: HarperCollins.

Raine, A., Meloy, J., Bihrie, S., Stoddard, J., LaCasse, L., Buchsbaum, M. (1998). Reduced prefrontal and increased subcortical brain functions assessed using positron emission tomography in affective and predatory murders. *Journal of Behavioral Science and the Law, 98,* 319–332.

Randazzo, M., & Plummer, E. (2009). *Implementing behavioral threat assessment on campus: A Virginia Tech demonstration project.* Blacksburg: Virginia Polytechnic Institute and State University.

Rogers, C. (1961). *On becoming a person.* New York, NY: Houghton Mifflin.

Rogers, C. (1980). *A way of being.* New York, NY: Houghton Mifflin.

Rooney, M. (2002). Student kills 3 U. of Arizona professors. *Chronicle of Higher Education, 49*(11), A12.

Runk, D. (2009, April 10). 2 killed in Henry Ford Community College shooting. *The Huffington Post.*

Sander, L. (2008). At Northern Illinois U., leaders grapple with a tragedy. *Chronicle of Higher Education, 54*(25), A26.

Sandoval, E., & Siemaszko, C. (2013, November 26). Inside Adam Lanza's lair. *NY Daily News.* Retrieved from http://www.nydailynews.com/news/national/newtown-shooter-planned-death-obsessed-columbine-article-1.1528626

Scalora, M., Simons, A., & Vansly, S. (2010, February). *Campus safety: Assessing and managing threats* (FBI Law Enforcement Bulletin). Washington, DC: Federal Bureau of Investigation.

Slater, D. (2009, January 24). Va. Tech suspect was fond of victim. *Richmond Times-Dispatch.*

Smith, K. (1994). *Clerks* [Motion picture]. Los Angeles, CA: Miramax Films.

Smith, S. (2007). From violent words to violent deeds? Assessing risk from threatening communications. *Dissertation Abstracts International, 68*(03), 1945B.

Smith, S., Woyach, R., & O'Toole, M. E. (2014). Threat triage: Recognizing the needle in the haystack. In J. R. Meloy & J. Hoffmann (Eds.), *The international handbook of threat assessment* (pp. 321–329). New York, NY: Oxford University Press.

Smith, T. (2010, February 17). Accused Alabama professor has history of violence. *All Things Considered (NPR).* Retrieved from http://www.npr.org/templates/story/story.php?storyId=123812172

Smolowe, J. (2010, May 24). A deadly romance: The lacrosse killing. *People, 73*(20), 60.

Sokolow, B., Lewis, S., Manzo, L., Schuster, S., Byrnes, J., & Van Brunt, B. (2011). *Book on BIT*. Malvern, PA: National Behavioral Intervention Team Association.

Speer, R. (2014, May 28). A selfie-era killer: Social media and Elliot Rodger. *The New York Post*. Retrieved from http://nypost. com/2014/05/28/a-selfie-era-killer-social-media-and-elliot-rodger/

Spinoza, B. (1901). *Ethics including the improvement of understanding*. New York, NY: Wiley.

Stringer, E. (1999). *Action research*. Thousand Oaks, CA: Sage.

Sue, D. (2010). *Microaggressions in everyday life: Race, gender, and sexual orientation*. Hoboken, NJ: Wiley.

Sue, D., Bucceri, J., Kin, A., Nadal, K., & Torino, G. (2007). Racial microaggressions and the Asian American experience. *Cultural Diversity and Ethnic Minority Psychology, 13*, 72–81.

Sue, D., Capodilupo, C., Torino, G., Bucceri, J., Holder, A., Nadal, K., & Esquilin, M. (2007). Racial microaggressions in everyday life: Implications for clinical practice. *American Psychologist, 62*, 271–286.

Sue, D., Lin, A., Torino, G., Capodilupo, C., & Rivera, D. (2009). Racial microaggressions and difficult dialogs on race in the classroom. *Cultural Diversity and Ethnic Minority Psychology, 15*, 183–190.

Sullivan, R. (1998). A boy's life. *Rolling Stone*, no. 795, 76.

Synder, Z. (1994). *Stargate* [Motion picture]. Los Angeles, CA: Canal+ Production.

Tarantino, Q. (Director). (1994). *Pulp fiction* [Motion picture]. Santa Monica, CA: Miramax Films.

Tarantino, Q. (Director). (2003). *Kill Bill* [Motion picture]. Santa Monica, CA: Miramax Films.

Teicher-Khadaroo, S. (2011, August 19). Columbine lessons may have prevented Tampa school shooting. *The Christian Science Monitor*.

Turner, J., & Gelles, M. (2003). *Threat assessment: A risk management approach*. New York, NY: Routledge.

U.S. Postal Service. (2011). *Threat assessment team guide*. Retrieved from http://www.nalc.org/depart/cau/pdf/manuals/2012/PUB%20 108.pdf

Van Brunt, B. (2007). *Thematic Apperception Test (TAT): Administration and interpretation*. Prescott, AZ: Borrego.

Van Brunt, B. (2012). *Ending campus violence: New approaches to prevention*. New York, NY: Routledge.

Van Brunt, B. (2014). *The New Orleans interviews: Threat assessment training*. Malvern, PA: National Behavioral Intervention Team Association.

Van der Meer, B., & Diekhuis, M. (2014). Collecting and assessing information for threat assessment. In J. R. Meloy & J. Hoffmann (Eds.), *The international handbook of threat assessment* (pp. 54–66). New York, NY: Oxford University Press.

Vann, D. (2008). Portrait of the school shooter as a young man. *Esquire, 150*(2), 114.

Vaughan, S. (1998). What makes children kill? *Harper's Bazaar*, no. 3442, 546.

Viding, E., & Firth, U. (2006). Genes for susceptibility to violence lurk in the brain. *Proceedings of the National Academy of Sciences. 103*, 6085–6086.

Virginia Tech Review Panel. (2007). *Mass shootings at Virginia Tech, April 16, 2007 report of the review panel presented to Timothy M. Kaine, Governor Commonwealth of Virginia.* Retrieved from http://cdm16064.contentdm.oclc.org/cdm/ref/collection/p266901coll4/id/904

Wachowski, A. (Writer and Director), & Wachowski, L. (Writer and Director). (1999). *The matrix* [Motion picture]. Los Angeles, CA: Warner Brothers.

Wallace, A. (2011, February 28). What made this university scientist snap? *Wired Magazine*. Retrieved from http://www.wired.com/2011/02/ff_bishop/

Wan, J. (2004). *Saw* [Motion picture]. Los Angeles, CA: Evolution Entertainment.

Warren, L., Mullen, P., & McEwan, T. (2014). Explicit threats of violence. In J. R. Meloy & J. Hoffmann (Eds.), *The international handbook of threat assessment* (pp. 18–38). New York, NY: Oxford University Press.

Weizel, R. (2013). *Newtown shooter report falls short, Connecticut panel says.* Retrieved from www.globalpost.com/dispatch/news/thomson-reuters/131220/newtown-shooter-report-falls-short-connecticut-panel-says

White, M. (1988–1989). The externalizing of the problem and the re-authoring of lives and relationships. *Dulwich Centre Newsletter*, pp. 5–28.

White, M., & Epston, D. (1990). *Narrative means to therapeutic ends.* New York, NY: W. W. Norton.

White, S. (2014). Workplace targeted violence: Threat assessment incorporating a structured professional judgment guide. In J. R. Meloy & J. Hoffmann (Eds.), *The international handbook of threat assessment* (pp. 83–106). New York, NY: Oxford University Press.

Woodford, M., Howell, M., Silverschanz, P., & Yu, L. (2012). "That's so gay!": Examining the covariates of hearing this expression among gay, lesbian and bisexual college students. *Journal of College Health, 60*, 429–434.

Yalom, I. (1980). *Existential psychotherapy.* New York, NY: Basic Books.

Zimmerman, J. L., & Beaudoin, M. (2002). Cats under the stars: A narrative story. *Child and Adolescent Mental Health, 7*, 31–40.

INDEX

Tables and exhibits are indicated by t and e following the page number.

(Continued)

(Continued)

Kelly (case study) *(Continued)*
  in maintenance and relapse
    prevention stage, 184
  in precontemplation stage, 181–182
  in preparation for action stage, 183
  resistance to change, 179
  self-efficacy support for, 181
Kinkel, Kipland ("Kip"), 90, 91
Klebold, Dylan, 96, 103, 126–127
Kopp, R. R., 158–159
Korzybski, Alfred, 195

L

Lane, T. J., 20, 91
Langman, Peter, 102–103, 104
Langman typology, 102–104
Lanza, Adam, 6, 99, 104, 126
Last resort warning behaviors, 105, 117
Last straw syndrome, 19
Law enforcement, techniques used in,
  7t, 90
Leakage, 8–9, 88, 89, 117
Legacy tokens, 87–88
Length, of assessment, 26
Listening
  active, 146–148
  empathetic, 36, 148
Little cricket bombs, 96
Logan, C., 124
Logistics, in case management plans, 136
Logotherapy, 193
Loughner, Jared Lee
  costuming by, 89
  disruptive behavior prior to
    shooting, 12–13
  financial stress of, 99
  objectification and depersonalization
    by, 90
  organization and planning by, 86
  quiet period of, 15
  social media posts by, 18, 86
Loukaitis, Barry, 128
Love, Yeardley, 6
Lucretius, 191

M

Maintenance stage of change, 184
Major depression. *See* Depression

Manic thoughts, 104–105
Manifestos, 15, 30, 87
Mapping process, 157–158
Matt (case study)
  activating events for, 168–169, 169t
  anger management for, 171
  background information, 166–167
  goal setting for, 172
  mental rehearsal for, 172
  normalizing behaviors, 170
  self-talk for, 172–173
  trigger events for, 167–168
May, Rollo, 193–195
Meaninglessness, in existentialism, 193
Meloy, J. R., 1, 2, 6, 9, 32, 88–89, 105,
  116–117
Memory impairments, 130
Menezes de Oliveira, Wellington, 107,
  125
Mental illness, 101–108
  anxiety, 104, 129, 194–195
  autism spectrum disorder, 12, 104
  bipolar disorder, 104–105
  delusional thoughts and paranoia,
    105, 130
  depression, 102, 104, 105–106
  irrational thoughts and, 106–108
  isolation from society and, 104
  Langman typology on, 102–104
  personality disorders, 104
  schizophrenia, 86, 101, 103, 130
  suicide and suicidal ideation, 24,
    105–106, 110
Mental rehearsal, 172
Metaphors, in narrative therapy,
  157–158, 159–162, 162e
Microaggressions, 37–38, 207
Microassaults, 37
Microinsults, 37
Microinvalidiations, 37, 38
Military, objectification and
  depersonalization techniques used
  in, 90
Miller, H., 32
Miller, W. R., 177, 181
Minnesota Multiphasic Personality
  Inventory, 26
Minorities. *See* Culture and diversity
Missed appointments, 27
Mohandie, K., viii, 32, 106

Powell, Anthony, 100
Precontemplation stage of change,
181–182
Predatory violence, 3
Preparation for action stage of change,
182–183
Pressure cooker bombs, 96
Prochaska, J., 181
Profit, as motivator of violence, 125
Proximity, as motivator of violence, 126
Pseudo-commandos, 89, 116
Psychological assessments, comparison
with threat and violence risk
assessments, 6, 7t
Psychopathic shooters, 103–104
Psychotic shooters, 103

R

Race. *See* Culture and diversity
Racing thinking, 131
Radio controlled (RC) cars, 96
RAGE-V (Risk Assessment Guideline Elements for Violence), 111–112, 219–230
Rampage shooters, 102–104
Ramsey, Evan, 103
Randazzo, M., 28, 118
Rapport, techniques for establishing,
31–32, 33e
Rational emotive behavior therapy,
168–169, 169t
Rationalizing behaviors, 16
RC (radio controlled) cars, 96
Reactive violence, 3
Reality therapy, 183, 231–232
Reasoning, lack of, 131
Referral sources, in assessment, 27–30
Rejection, as motive for violence, 100
Relapse prevention stage of change,
184
Release from pain, as motivator of
violence, 126
Repeat scenarios, 134, 135t
Report to the President on Issues Raised by the Virginia Tech Tragedy (Leavitt et al.), 104
Resident Evil (video game), 95
Residential life history, in assessment, 29
Resistance, in therapy, 179
Revolvers, 94–95

Rifles, 95
Risk analysis, defined, 2
Risk Assessment Guideline Elements for Violence (RAGE-V), 111–112, 219–230
Risk assessments. *See* Violence risk
assessments
Risk factors for violence, 109–120
in *Dangerous Instincts*, 118–119
determining presence and
relevance of, 123–124
in FBI four-pronged approach,
113–115
in *Handbook for Campus Threat Assessment and Management Teams*, 117–118
Meloy warning behaviors, 116–117
in *Risk Assessment Guideline Elements for Violence*, 111–112, 219–230
SIVRA-35, 110, 124, 215–218
by Turner and Gelles, 112–113
in U.S. Postal Service Threat
Assessment Team Guide, 110–111
Risk formulations, 124–134
destabilizers and, 130–131
diachronic nature of, 132–133
disinhibitors and, 127–130
fertility of, 133–134
individualization of, 132
motivators and, 125–127
as narratives, 132
overview, 124–125
testability of, 133
Risk resolution, recommendations for, 2
Rodger, Elliot, 30
Rogers, Brandon, 6
Rogers, Carl, 34, 140, 144, 147, 148, 149, 165
"The Role of Warning Behaviors in Threat Assessment" (Meloy et al.), 116–117
Rollnick, Stephen, 177, 181
Rose-Mar College of Beauty shooting
(1966), 126
Roshdi, K., 105

S

Saari, Matti Juhani, 18, 90
St. Pius X High School shooting (1975), 129